£8 95
26 A5
T

Unbridled
Power?

Unbridled Power?

An interpretation of New Zealand's constitution and government

Geoffrey Palmer

Oxford University Press

Wellington Melbourne Oxford

Oxford University Press
222–36 Willis Street, Wellington

Oxford London Glasgow
New York Toronto Melbourne Wellington
Kuala Lumpur Singapore Jakarta Hong Kong Tokyo
Nairobi Dar es Salaam Cape Town
Delhi Bombay Calcutta Madras Karachi

ISBN 0 19 558046 X

Photoset in times roman by Whitcoulls Ltd, Christchurch
Cover design, Lindsay Missen
Cover illustration, Tom Scott

Contents

Preface

1 Government New Zealand style 1
Key components 2
Separation of powers 4
The process for making decisions 5
Checks and balances 10
Conclusion 15

2 The queen and the governor-general 17
Monarchy or republic? 17
The governor-general 18

3 Cabinet, caucus and the prime minister 22
Cabinet 22
Caucus 25
How powerful is the prime minister? 27
Conclusion 31

4 The state services and quango land 32
Departments 32
Quangos 36

5 Parliament 40
The member of parliament 40
What parliament does 45
The speaker 63
Privilege 64

6 Select committees and legislation 67
Bills and negotiations 67
Select committees 69
Improvements 73

7 The fastest law in the west   77

Too much law   79
Drafting   82
Presentation   87
Some examples of how New Zealand legislates   89
Conclusion   94

8 More fast law – regulations   95

Regulations in New Zealand   98
Emergency regulations   103
Parliamentary scrutiny of regulations overseas   105
Conclusion   108

9 What the courts can do   109

The courts and the constitution   110
Administrative law   114
Regulations and by-laws   118
Government reversal of court decisions   120
Conclusion on the courts   122
The ombudsmen   123

10 A written constitution and/or a bill of rights?   126

A written constitution   126
A bill of rights?   130
Can parliament be trusted?   136

11 A second house of parliament?   141

The idea of a second chamber   141
The New Zealand experience   143

12 Electoral law   147

Referenda   148
How the electoral system works   150
Possible changes   153
Conclusion   156

13 Access to official information   158

Secrecy in New Zealand   158
Demands for open government   162
A New Zealand solution   164

14 Recommendations   167

Bibliography   175

Tables

1 Estimated workload of members of parliament   44

2 Parliamentary time spent on categories of business according to space in *New Zealand Parliamentary Debates*   47

3 Parliamentary time spent on categories of legislation according to space in *New Zealand Parliamentary Debates*   68

4 Changes made to bills by select committees as reported back to the house in 1977   73

5 Changes made to bills by the Committee of the Whole House in 1977   73

6 Numbers of statutes and regulations   81

7 Printed pages of statutes and regulations   81

8 Parliament's last week of sittings in 1978   92

9 Voting figures for eligible voters, 1969–75   151

10 1966 election: votes cast compared with seats gained in parliament   152

11 1969 election: votes cast compared with seats gained in parliament   152

12 1972 election: votes cast compared with seats gained in parliament   152

13 1975 election: votes cast compared with seats gained in parliament   152

14 1978 election: votes cast compared with seats gained in parliament   153

Figures

1 Government's financial decision-making structure   48

2 Regulations published annually since 1936   96

Preface

People today seem disillusioned with the way their governments make decisions on their behalf. In New Zealand the time has arrived for a review of the rules about how we are governed. The press for change is in the direction of finding ways to protect people from government. In the years since Mr R. D. Muldoon became prime minister, interest in the way New Zealand is governed has quickened. It may not be too much to say the permanent contribution of the first Muldoon administration to the history of New Zealand has been to demonstrate the need for constitutional change. I have discovered also, while teaching constitutional law, that young New Zealanders know little of how they are governed. And what they do know, they accept uncritically. I have not tried to write a constitutional treatise but rather to explain how the system works and how it should be changed. I aim to question and provoke as well as to inform.

A number of people have helped me with the project. The Internal Research Committee at the Victoria University of Wellington provided assistance which made the task possible. My research assistant, Michael Burrowes, proved to be an indefatigable researcher and he spent many hours in the bowels of various libraries around Wellington. Mr Gordon Christie, member of parliament for Napier shared with me the mountain of paper with which members of parliament are deluged. Dr R. M. Alley of the Political Science Department at Victoria University of Wellington was good enough to read the manuscript in draft and give me many valuable comments. One of the joys of teaching law at Victoria comes from the array of public lawyers on the faculty who have stimulating but widely differing views – I am grateful to them all, but I must single out Professor K. J. Keith, who read and commented on the whole of the manuscript, and Ms Deborah Shelton. There were other people located in other parts of Wellington who helped me, but prudence suggests that they should go un-named. My secretary, Mrs Helen Bark, cheerfully typed and re-typed the manuscript.

This book aims to give an overview of government in New Zealand. To do so in simple terms is by no means easy and perhaps my greatest debt is owed to scholars who have worked in specialized aspects of the themes dealt with and on whose work I have relied to paint the big picture. Those sources appear in full in the select bibliography at the end of the book.

Geoffrey Palmer
10 December 1978

1
Government New Zealand style

Many nations have a document called a constitution which lays down the framework of government. New Zealand has no constitution in that sense. We have:
- a few general principles, some of them rather vague
- some laws about government passed by parliament
- some political and judicial institutions
- some judicial decisions

These are the features which make up our constitutional arrangements – the ground rules for government. Many of the rules cannot be enforced in any court. The rules do not stand still but develop over time. The relationship between the different organs of government is uncertain.

Certain features of our government can be explained only by reference to history, much of it British, as the central components of our system were inherited. However, to a substantial extent New Zealand has been in charge of its own rules for government since 1857. Any notion that New Zealand was tied, in a constitutional sense, to the apron strings of mother Britain ended in 1947, when the Statute of Westminster Adoption Act passed through the New Zealand parliament. The time for relating our rules for the conduct of government to those of the British has passed. The machinery under which the New Zealand democracy works, or does not work, must now be evaluated against New Zealand conditions.

The open texture of our constitutional arrangements means that there are few formal restraints upon the power of government. Whether the existing restraints upon the use and abuse of governmental power are sufficient in New Zealand is one theme of this book. The other centres on what measures should be taken where the need for change is established. Constitutional changes should not be embarked upon lightly as they concern the framework of rules within which our whole community must function. No rules are more fundamental than these; none of greater importance. And experience in many countries suggests that it is easier to get constitutional issues wrong than it is to get them right.

Key components

The component parts of the New Zealand system comprise:
- the queen, represented in New Zealand by the governor-general
- the House of Representatives (parliament)
- the executive – the cabinet ministers and the public service, and a host of government corporations and tribunals set up to deal with particular issues
- the judiciary

The relationship between these units is complex. They all have different functions, and their responsibilities frequently overlap. The division between formal legal powers and the actual exercise of political power adds to the confusion. For example, bills passed by parliament cannot become law unless they have received the royal assent. That situation seems to indicate that the governor-general could refuse to sign a bill passed by parliament. But neither the queen nor the governor-general would dare do such a thing. Both must act on the advice of ministers. That instruction cannot be found in the law anywhere, but if it were not followed there would be a constitutional crisis.

The most important functions of the governor-general are:
- to act as ceremonial and diplomatic head of state and titular commander-in-chief of the armed forces
- to send messages to parliament and assent to bills passed there
- to appoint ministers
- to call parliament together, dissolve or adjourn it, all in accordance with advice received from the ministers of the government
- to chair meetings of the executive council (which consists of government ministers and the governor-general) which passes a type of law called orders-in-council or regulations

The functions of the New Zealand parliament are:
- to raise the money by which the business of government may be conducted and to approve expenditure
- to pass statutes, the most important of our laws
- to provide a place for the airing of grievances
- to act as a check upon the manner in which government is actually carried on
- to serve as a forum for party political contest

The executive branch of government, which includes cabinet ministers, the public service and a large number of other bodies connected to the government to a varying degree, conducts the government. The executive decides upon the policies to be pursued, collects the taxes, pays the social welfare benefits and performs the countless numbers of tasks which citizens demand of modern government.

The judicial branch of government is the courts. The judicial branch provides authoritative interpretations of the laws where disputes arise.

2

Its function is to provide fair, impartially administered justice according to law.

Parliament, the executive and the judiciary constitute the three principal branches of our government. But not all government is central government. We have in New Zealand an extensive system of local government by way of city· councils, county councils, regional authorities, harbour boards, hospital boards and the like which all exercise important powers set out in statutes passed by parliament. This book concerns central government and cannot deal with the problems of local government in any detail. But an important goal to be achieved is the devolution of greater powers to regional government in New Zealand. The regions should be given a capacity to tax. That would promote responsible government in the regions and give local people the ability to decide their own destiny in their own way to a greater degree than at present.

At the base of New Zealand's constitutional arrangements lies the New Zealand Constitution Act 1852, a statute passed by the United Kingdom parliament. Since 1947 the New Zealand parliament has had the power to amend that law and it has done so. For example, the original act provided for an upper house in the form of the Legislative Council, a body which was abolished by a New Zealand statute in 1950. The most important provision in the act states: 'The General Assembly shall have full power to make laws having effect in, or in respect of, New Zealand or any part thereof and laws having effect outside New Zealand.' The act says that the General Assembly consists of the governor-general and House of Representatives. There are a few other provisions left in the 1852 act, but for the most part it has been swept away. As a general indication of the structure of government in New Zealand the New Zealand Constitution Act 1852 gives little clue. And what it does say is seriously misleading – to read the statute, for instance, it might be thought that the governor-general exercises real power, but this is not so.

The deficiencies of the New Zealand Constitution Act bring us face to face with one of the primary difficulties of the New Zealand constitution. It is not written down in any one place and much of it is not written down at all. For example, cabinet is a vital part of the New Zealand government but there is no legally authoritative statement of its functions and powers. Such problems make it hard to define the limits of power placed on the various components of the New Zealand government. It is a state of affairs not without its advantages, the main one being flexibility: the way government is conducted can change to meet changing conditions.

The various components of the New Zealand government are constituted in a number of different statutes. The courts are established under several acts of parliament. Many government departments are established by statute although there is no real need for this, as the government has legal power to set up departments of state without statute if it wishes. The public service, in terms of its recruitment and functioning is governed by statute to a large extent. That vital hall-mark of any democracy – the free election – is governed by statute too. Some aspects of parliament are governed by the Legislature Act. All these statutes can, of course, be repealed or amended by parliament at any time.

Separation of powers

A concentration of power in one group or one person always presents dangers. Where power is divided between several groups such dangers will be reduced. A short example will illustrate the point. A ruler with absolute power may do all of the following things: a) pass a law which makes shop-lifting an offence punishable by death; b) direct the police force to apprehend only shop-lifters; c) adjudicate on all cases of shop-lifting to decide who is guilty of it; d) execute the offenders. Such a ruler would be carrying out three functions – legislative, executive and judicial. Our system has three separate branches of government which correspond in a very rough and ready way to the legislative, executive and judicial. If any one of them carried out all three tasks as in the example above we would live under an autocracy. The functions of New Zealand's three main branches of government are not identical in fact with the functions which the names of the branches would indicate. The powers have overlapped and been amalgamated; and a complete separation of powers in the pure sense would be impractical Nonetheless, the theory of 'the separation of powers' provides a useful touchstone against which to find the location of powers in the New Zealand government and judge the propriety of the arrangement.

Many advantages flow from dividing up power between different sections of government. The famous English legal writer William Blackstone wrote in 1765: 'In all tyrannical governments, the supreme magistracy, or the right both of *making* and *enforcing* the laws is vested in one and the same man, or one and the same body of men; and wherever these two powers are united together, there can be no public liberty.' (*Commentaries on the Laws of England*, p.142) If we think about that statement in connection with the 1978 controversy about the prosecution of some freezing workers under the industrial relations laws, we can see what Blackstone was driving at. In 1976 the executive branch of government secured the passage through parliament of a law to make certain conduct by freezing workers a criminal offence. The executive branch then supported the taking of prosecutions by one of its officers against freezing workers at Ocean Beach. It was the same branch that later applied for an adjournment of the cases and, when it was refused, offered (as prosecutor) no evidence in support of the

4

prosecution. Finally the executive decided to change the law to remove criminal penalties from the legislation and amending legislation was passed. It is true that different people within the executive made some of the decisions, but all those decisions were taken within the executive branch. A certain mixing of the executive, legislative and even judicial powers can be detected in that set of events. Such events are possible because in New Zealand the government in office effectively controls both the legislative and executive branches. Where the powers are divided, one part of the government can act as a check on the other part of the government.

Some systems of government exhibit a great deal more in the way of separation of powers than our own. Australia and the United States offer the most ready examples. The Australian constitution formally allocates the legislative, executive and judicial powers of the Australian Commonwealth to the parliament, the queen and her ministers, and the High Court of Australia respectively. In the United States the president as chief executive, the Congress as legislator, and the Supreme Court as the most important repository of the judicial power all perform very different functions and each acts as a check upon the excesses of the others.

Able and ambitious people will be attracted to positions in the various branches of government. They will all want to do their jobs well, to the limits of the power which resides in the office. Tensions will arise. Those tensions will be healthy because they cause the behaviour of one branch of government to be modified by the attitudes of the others. Power will be spread around and shared. So the chance to be free from concentrations of arbitrarily exercised power is increased.

We cannot have, in any practical way, either complete separation or complete fusion of powers. Some co-ordination of the various policies and administration in government as a whole is necessary; it would be impossible with complete separation of powers. Complete fusion, on the other hand, would tend to make control of the government by the people impossible. The trick is to get sufficient co-ordination but not so much as becomes oppressive and unresponsive to the wishes of the public. Governmental power can be rendered less oppressive by dividing it up between various branches. And government can be made responsive by subjecting it to popular control in the form of elections.

The process for making decisions

So far the rules under which we are governed have been introduced. We turn now to the way in which decisions are made under those rules.

First, it is worth remarking on one of the enduring characteristics of New Zealand governments – their strength. New Zealanders have seen government as responsible for ensuring that everyone has, as John Roberts has put it, 'a modest home on a separate plot of land, a protected job in both senses of limited competition and assured employment, free education for children and a mild boom to make it possible for the restless to achieve spatial if not social mobility'. (In *Thirteen Facets*, p.67) In some other countries, notably the United States, people tend to regard government as a necessary evil which should use and be invested with powers to the most limited extent possible.

New Zealand, almost since its beginning, has never followed that view. To the New Zealander, the government is his friend. It does things for him which he wants done. Most governments in most countries look after things like education, law and order, taxation, the army, navy and air force. The New Zealand government does much more as do countries which have developed a welfare state. It provides free hospital treatment when a person is sick, monetary benefits when his income stops, finance with which to buy a house, or it may even provide the house itself. The government owns and operates the railways, the airlines, the electricity generating capacity, all the television and most of the radio stations, all the universities, most of the coal mines, much of the forestry, a fair number of hotels, an international shipping line, an extensive inter-island ferry service, and a number of farms. Government sells insurance, writes wills, administers deceased estates, conducts several large banking businesses and runs the biggest contracting business in New Zealand. To many people around the world such a state of affairs would indicate a condition of 'galloping socialism'. But it is an accepted state of affairs in New Zealand and occasions little serious political debate.

With the demands which have been made upon government in New Zealand it is hardly surprising that we are a highly regulated and much governed society. The time has come to ask whether we have not gone too far and created a juggernaut which is out of control. When all sorts of people want government to do all sorts of things it becomes imperative to have a set of ground rules for making decisions which are fair to everyone and provide for justice in the broadest sense. A British minister, Richard Crossman, once wrote: 'The modern state, with its huge units of organization is inherently totalitarian, and its natural tendency is towards despotism. These tendencies can only be held in check if we are determined to build constitutional safeguards of freedom and personal responsibility.' (*Socialism and the New Despotism*, p.24)

The central democratic element in our government is the election of members of parliament. Elections must be held at least every three years and they may be held more frequently if the government so decides. The country is divided into electorates, each represented by a member of parliament. There are at present ninety-two members of parliament. Political parties select candidates to run in the elections, and one party or another usually commands a majority in the House of Representatives, although coalition government is not impossible. The government is formed from the members of the majority party in parliament; the leader of the majority party becomes prime minister. In the National Party the leader selects those of his colleagues who are to hold ministerial office. In the Labour Party, caucus elects the cabinet ministers by secret ballot, then the prime minister allocates the tasks.

The cabinet is selected from the majority party in parliament. So it is ensured that parliament will not pass legislation or approve measures which are unacceptable to the cabinet. In the New Zealand system the executive controls virtually everything that parliament does; not what is said but what is decided there. There are qualifications to the rule. Sometimes on matters of conscience, such as abortion or capital punishment, members of parliament vote according to their own views and not according to party policy. And the members of the government caucus can and sometimes do stop the cabinet from pursuing a certain course. In theory the members of parliament could combine to turn a government out by passing a motion of no confidence in it or by denying it funds to continue. Under the domination of a two party system where party discipline is exceedingly strict, as it has been in New Zealand since 1935, this possibility is remote and theoretical. And that fact has robbed parliament of far too much power and a great amount of its prestige. Parliament has never governed, but the capacity it possessed to unhorse the government now seems to have been lost. The capacity could be revived with the presence of several parties in the House of Representatives, one holding the balance of power.

Only ministers sit in cabinet. Ministers advise the governor-general on how the queen's government should be conducted and that advice is always taken. Ministers are usually given charge of particular departments of state. Almost forty such departments exist, each with different functions. A minister may be in charge of more than one department as there are only about twenty ministers. The minister is political head of the department. There is also an administrative head, a permanent public servant, who is responsible for the work and administration of the department.

How does the machinery of government decide which policies to adopt? In other words, how does government make decisions? The mechanisms tend to be extremely complex and the pattern of decision-making differs markedly from one kind of decision to another depending upon the field in which the decision falls, the importance of the issue and the interests at stake. In simplified form the process works as follows.

Political parties perform important functions in our method of government. Members of a political party tend to agree on their broad approach to public affairs. At conferences they discuss what policies to adopt. At election time they present to the public manifestos containing, often quite specifically, the measures they will adopt if they are elected to office. Many ideas which end up in the law or as part of government policy come from political parties. These tend to be the most important proposals in terms of scope; in terms of numbers, more proposals emanate from the public service. Public servants, who are responsible for administering the various statutes and schemes which make up the programmes of New Zealand government can see the defects which arise in their administration and are in a strong position to suggest changes. Pressure groups, such as the Manufacturers Federation, Federated Farmers, the insurance companies or the Federation of Labour urge changes which will help their members and oppose those against their interests.

Whenever a policy is proposed it will be subject to scrutiny by the officials of government. The constitutional role of the public servants is to advise the minister in charge of their department and to carry out his orders. But in fact public servants enjoy a dual function of both initiating policy developments themselves and advising government on other policy ideas. Public servants tend to control much of the detail of policies, subject to the supervision of cabinet ministers. Officials have the influence of information at their disposal.

Whether a policy proposal comes from a member of the public, a pressure group, a party manifesto or elsewhere, the minister concerned is a key figure in any decision to adopt or reject initiatives. The minister receives a report from his department on the idea. That report indicates weaknesses in the proposal, poses alternatives and comments on practicability.

Once a week while parliament is in session all members of parliament of each party meet to discuss tactics and policy in confidence. This meeting is called 'caucus'. Caucus committees sometimes are set up to deal with particular matters and to help a minister who refers a policy proposal to it for discussion. After that the proposal may go to a committee of cabinet. Cabinet committees sometimes initiate policy too.

The apex of the decision-making system is cabinet itself. Cabinet meets on Mondays, fifty times a year. It will consider more than 1,500 cabinet papers in a year and make forty decisions at a typical meeting. Cabinet papers will be presented by ministers or will have been prepared by cabinet committees. Few major items of government policy are settled without the approval of cabinet or a cabinet committee. All proposals involving government expenditure are examined by Treasury before being decided on by cabinet. Treasury opposes many proposals which are put up.

All proposals go to cabinet via ministers. Cabinet submissions are usually written by public servants in the name of their minister. After cabinet has decided upon a proposal it may be discussed in the government caucus. Sometimes the views of caucus will be sought first.

8

Occasionally the back-bench members of parliament revolt against the policy of their ministers. It does not happen often because cabinet ministers usually make up between a third and a half of the numbers in the caucus and they are the most experienced members. When revolts do occur the public seldom learns of it because caucus proceedings, like cabinet, are secret.

If a proposal requires legislation for its implementation a bill is drafted by parliamentary counsel, legally trained specialists who draft laws on behalf of the government. No bill can be drafted unless the Cabinet Legislation Committee has so ordered. The committee and cabinet will approve the bill when it has been drafted. Usually a group of officials works with the parliamentary counsel in production of the bill, providing detailed instructions on policy and ironing out problems. Then the bill is usually sent to the government caucus before being introduced into the House of Representatives by the minister responsible for it.

When legislation is introduced into the House of Representatives it is read a first time. That debate is usually quite short and consists of opposition members questioning the minister about the bill. The opposition do not see the bill until it is introduced although usually it will have been widely discussed by ministers, public servants and government members of parliament.

If the bill is an important one it may be referred to a select committee of the House of Representatives. This committee consists of both government and opposition members of parliament, with the government members enjoying a majority. A select committee considering legislation or some aspect of policy often holds hearings at which members of the public and interested organizations can present their views on the subject; sometimes submissions are heard in public and can be reported on by the news media. The minister in charge of the bill is usually a member of the select committee which considers the bill, and the committee does not make recommendations which are at odds with government policy. But the select committee procedure is most beneficial. It enables changes to be made as a result of views expressed by the public. And changes often are made, although these are more likely to concern detail than fundamental principle.

When the bill is reported back to parliament there is further discussion about what was done by the select committee. Later the main parliamentary debate on the bill is held – the second reading debate. That is a wide-ranging debate on the policy and its principles. Where the bill is a matter of contention between the political parties the debate may be long drawn out and even bitter. Some time after the second reading, the House of Representatives turns itself into a Committee of the Whole House and considers the bill clause by clause. At this stage amendments are considered. Usually amendments are sponsored by the government and no amendments can be made unless the government agrees, because the government holds a majority. After the committee stages, the bill is read a third time. The third reading debate is usually quite short, although it may go on for some hours on a hotly contested issue. After being read three times in the House of Representatives, the bill is sent to the governor-general to receive the royal assent. When that has occurred the bill is a statute.

Discussing the machinery of government in New Zealand, J. F. Robertson, the permanent head of the Ministry of Defence wrote in 1978:

All we do know is that it is a highly complex organizational structure related intimately to the unique social requirements of the process of Government in New Zealand. It is certainly not exportable – I am not sure that anybody outside New Zealand would want ours anyway. Like machinery in the physical sense, it needs maintenance to sustain it; it often breaks down, it sometimes runs slow when it should run fast, and there is always someone tinkering with it. It consists of Cabinet, Cabinet Committees, Caucus, Caucus Committees, Parliamentary Select Committees (including the Public Expenditure Committee), Departments and some statutory bodies or committees. All interact in a constantly moving pattern of relationships.

(*New Zealand Journal of Public Administration*, vol.40, no.1, p.33)

Two points arising out of the above analysis should be stressed. Firstly, the bulk of the important decisions are not made in or by parliament; parliament is a body which rubber-stamps decisions made in the interlocking pattern of committees described. (That is not to say members of parliament do not take any part in making the decisions, as they are members of some of the committees.) Secondly, secrecy forms a notable feature of the process. All *deliberations* of cabinet, cabinet committees, caucus, caucus committees and parliamentary select committees are secret. The advice which a department gives the minister is confidential. The cloak of secrecy covers everything of any importance in the decision-making structure. Only parliament itself is open and parliament rarely decides anything on its own.

Checks and balances

The foregoing describes how power works – now we must consider whether the restraints upon its exercise are sufficient. The issue is simple: are there sufficient checks upon the power of the government in New Zealand? My conclusion is that although the power of executive government in New Zealand is not entirely unbridled, it is extensive enough to cause concern. We need to examine how the power of government might be matched with effective, continuing restraints.

Law

The first and most important check upon executive power in New Zealand comes from the law. The government must act in accordance

10

with the law. In a fundamental manner the judicial branch of our government does control actions of the executive. Proof of the proposition goes back to a celebrated English case decided by Lord Chief Justice Camden in 1765. In *Entick* v. *Carrington* messengers of the king, under a warrant issued by the secretary of state, entered the plaintiff's premises and searched and seized papers. The plaintiff brought an action for trespass and breaking and entering. He succeeded and was awarded £300 in damages. Many ingenious arguments were advanced to justify the seizure under the warrant but none of them was accepted. It was said that similar general warrants had commonly been issued by the secretary of state since the time of the revolutionary settlement in 1688. The legality of such warrants had not been challenged hitherto. Then the crown sought to liken the warrant to a search for stolen goods; but the court was quick to point out that none of the precautions surrounding search warrants for stolen goods existed with the type of warrant before the court. Then it was argued that the issuance and execution of such warrants was necessary for the ends of government. But Lord Camden said that the common law of England did not understand the reasoning about state necessity. Neither could the warrant be justified on any argument of utility. He came to the conclusion that unless the warrant could be shown to be legal either by a statutory provision or by a rule of the common law, then the action must succeed. 'If it is the law it will be found in our books. If it is not to be found there, it is not the law.' (*Entick* v. *Carrington*, p.437)

That case and its subsequent reception by our constitutional history has established that government must act according to law in everything that it does. The proposition is fundamental. As Professor A.V. Dicey put it in his book, *The Law of the Constitution:* 'A man may with us be punished for a breach of the law, but he can be punished for nothing else'. (p.202) No doubt it is a salutary thought that public authority must point to some specific rule authorizing any action taken which affects a person's rights. But it must be observed that the concern of the court is not with the content of the rules but with their existence. To meet the test in *Entick* v. *Carrington* it is only necessary that a statutory provision or common law rule which justifies the action taken should be shown to exist. It is not the central concern of the court that the provision may be arbitrary, unfair or oppressive. Under our constitutional arrangements the court cannot strike down an enacted rule however bad. There must be rules, but the quality and content of the rules, at least of those made by the legislature, are determined by the political process.

It should not be thought that *Entick* v. *Carrington* is today a dead letter. Mr Justice Woodhouse relied upon it in a judgment delivered in the New Zealand Court of Appeal in 1977. In that case a Mr Payn was driving a car at 2 a.m. which collided with a properly parked vehicle. Hearing the crash the owners came out. Mr Payn and the owners exchanged names and addresses. When the owners suggested a traffic officer be called, Mr Payn left abruptly and walked home to his house nearby. Traffic officers were told that Mr Payn smelt of liquor. They went to his house and knocked on the door. Mr Payn told the officers he had drunk some alcohol before driving and that he had drunk beer fast since coming home. The officers invited Mr Payn to take a breath test, he refused and asked the officers to leave his property. They did, but returned later after receiving instructions. Mr Payn again refused to take a breath test and refused to accompany the officers for the purposes of taking a blood sample. They thereupon arrested Mr Payn. He was convicted of failing to accompany the officers and of driving with an excess of alcohol in his blood. (He was also convicted of careless driving but made no complaint about that.) The Court of Appeal decided that the traffic officers could only exercise their statutory powers to request and conduct a breath test if they were on private property with the leave and licence of the occupier. A traffic officer has no right to enter private property forcibly, the court said. So the officers could not lawfully arrest Mr Payn in the circumstances they did. Mr Justice Woodhouse said:

In a matter of this quality, involving as it does claims made on behalf of officials that they are entitled to encroach upon fundamental civil liberties and the peaceful enjoyment of private property, I think it is of the greatest importance that all concerned should know exactly where they stand. As long ago as 1765 that is a principle that was expressed with great emphasis in the famous case of *Entick* v. *Carrington* . . .

(Transport Ministry v. Payn, p.50)

The officers had no specific rule of law upon which they could rely to authorize what they did. So what they had done was not legal and the convictions were quashed. The point about *Entick* v. *Carrington* today is whether the protection it offers is sufficient. A determined government can always change the rules of law to justify the sort of action taken by the officers in Payn's case. Indeed, the legislature in New Zealand has been most generous in its granting of powers to officials to enter private property.

Public opinion

In a democracy public opinion can provide a substantial check upon the use of power. Public opinion can be expressed in many ways. The most important barometer of public opinion is the election of parliament every three years. While the elections are for members of parliament in individual electorates, the government can properly be said to be on trial. If people do not like the performance of government they can change it by voting for candidates opposing the government. That will deprive the government of a majority in the House of Representatives with the result that it will cease to hold office.

There has been a tendency in New Zealand to reserve judgment upon a government until the end of its three-year term. That means public opinion, expressed in voting, works in response to the total rather than individual decisions of a government. Obviously opinion will be formed on the general impact of many individual decisions, but the style of New Zealand government resists widespread public involvement in each decision as it is made. Sometimes the strength of opinion forces a continuing response, as with the Vietnam war, the Manapouri scheme and the abortion issue. But such cases are exceptional. It would be better, it would be more democratic, and would lead to decisions of higher quality, in my view, if there was greater opportunity for public participation in all important decisions on a continuing basis. The authoritarian nature of decision-making in New Zealand may have worked well for a number of colonists, but it cannot function fairly in a pluralist society with people of different races and creeds, all of whom have different aspirations and outlooks.

A key vehicle for public opinion acting as a check upon government is the news media. The ways in which news is reported, editorial opinion is expressed, television and radio current affairs programmes are handled affect the capacity to probe and question the decisions of government. The knowledge that such scrutiny will occur acts as a constraint upon the making of the decisions themselves. How potent a force the media can be in alerting public opinion to the actions of government depends on many factors. It is fair to say that while the media in New Zealand functions as a fair and accurate reporter of events, the capacity to probe and question is less highly developed. And the amount of probing which the media can do is shaped by how much the public is interested in the fruits of that sort of journalism. If people do not buy newspapers which undertake that task or do not watch the television programmes which do it then less investigation will be done.

The capacity of the mass media to spotlight government decisions is handicapped by the secrecy of the decision-making process. The public service in New Zealand, unlike its equivalent in Canberra, is less likely to leak information to the media; confidential government documents do not often find their way into the newspapers in New Zealand. The law of defamation poses another restraint upon the media. The liability for false facts which lower someone's reputation is strict under our law and it is easy to make mistakes. But more important than these factors may be the commercial constraints upon the media which flow from the disposition of people who own and control newspapers and the bureaucratic constraints upon those who act as 'gatekeepers' for the electronic media.

Certainly it cannot be asserted in New Zealand that the activities of the press and the electronic media have reached the stage where they can be regarded as the fourth estate of government, with a vital role in checking the power exerted by government. Such a claim is often made for the press in the United States, and the history of that country is not short of examples to support such a claim.

Parliament

Parliament provides the focal point for public opinion. Discussions in parliament can bring issues to public attention and help to crystallize opinion on them. The opposition in parliament can and does attack decisions of the government, suggest alternative policies and question ministers on their performance. The knowledge that ministers must face up to a barrage of questions, criticisms and political attacks will always be kept in mind when those ministers are making decisions. Ministers are experienced politicians first, and administrators and policy-makers second. They want to avoid making a rod for their own backs. Experienced politicians know a good deal about public opinion. They receive a lot of letters from the public. They know what sort of issues will cause trouble; they know about the importance of timing decisions; they know how to present decisions in the best possible light. The political debate in parliament upon the decisions of government, despite its weaknesses, represents an important restraint upon government while parliament is in session.

Ombudsmen

Connected to parliament, and acting as a check on the power of government, are the ombudsmen. New Zealand borrowed the idea of an ombudsman from Scandinavia in 1962. Since then the institution has proved a considerable success and there are now three ombudsmen. They are able to investigate, either on complaints made to them by members of the public or on their own initiative, any administrative decision, recommendation, act or omission of government departments, related organizations and local authorities.

The investigation must focus on how the decision affects any individual. The ombudsmen can look at government files and can make recommendations for the alteration of decisions. If no appropriate action is taken the ombudsmen can report to the prime minister and to parliament. Every year a long report is made to parliament in which instances of decisions investigated are given. In the year ended 31 March 1978 more than 2,000 complaints were made to the ombudsmen. The introduction of the ombudsmen has had a healthy effect on decision-making in the New Zealand government. The check on government brought to bear by the ombudsmen is the check of independent scrutiny and the publicity of government decisions which affect individuals.

Auditor-general

In the field of the financial expenditures of government, parliament exerts an influence through the Public Expenditure Committee. Parliament's watch-dog is the auditor-general. He subjects departmental expenditure to audit and reports upon maladministration in financial matters. The auditor-general is an important check against financial corruption and inefficiency in government. Mercifully, documented cases of financial corruption have been exceedingly rare in government. Corruption is an every day part of government administration in many countries and we can be grateful that we are essentially free from it in New Zealand.

Pressure groups

New Zealand abounds with organizations which are formed to promote various kinds of activity. There are trade organizations such as the Employers Federation, the Manufacturers Federation, the Retailers Federation and Federated Farmers. There are professional organizations such as the New Zealand Law Society, the Medical Association of New Zealand, the Post-Primary Teachers Association, and the New Zealand Educational Institute. There are organizations such as the Federation of Labour and the Combined State Services Organization which represent thousands of workers. Recreation organizations such as the New Zealand Rugby Football Union and the New Zealand Deerstalkers Association represent particular points of view. The network of these pressure groups influences government at every turn by making representations to ministers, to members of parliament, to public servants, to parliamentary select committees, to caucus committees and even cabinet committees on occasion.

It has been said that a politician is a person kept upright by pressure on all sides, or suggested that there is something sinister about the influence of pressure groups. But in a democracy it is inevitable that people with similar interests will organize themselves to protect those interests. Often new interests will not be well represented among the chorus of entreaties sung to government. But if the interest to be promoted strikes a chord in the community, the organization will follow. The tactics of pressure groups vary from issue to issue and from organization to organization. Some will offer campaign contributions to political parties. Those with big memberships will threaten to suggest that members vote a certain way. Others will threaten to conduct a campaign through the media against certain government decisions. Perhaps the most effective weapon of the pressure group is to provide the government with information about how a decision will affect people and to make rational arguments based on that information as to why any policy should or should not be adopted. Despite the confidential nature of the decision-making process, most arguments in favour of a policy need to withstand the scrutiny of the public gaze in the end.

Conclusion

The main checks on the power of government to take decisions in New Zealand are:

- government must act in accordance with the law as it exists at the time the decision is made and some decisions can be reviewed in the courts
- government must take into account public opinion
- government must undergo parliament's inspection of the policy
- government actions must undergo scrutiny from the ombudsmen and auditor-general
- government must consider the views expressed by various pressure groups

I do not believe that those constraints upon decision-making in the New Zealand government are sufficient to ensure careful, measured decisions, as later chapters will demonstrate. There is widespread disenchantment with the way the political process works in New Zealand. People no longer believe what political parties say. Political fighting also encourages over-simplification of issues, distortion and lies. The manner in which public decisions are made in our system does not encourage citizens to believe that broad justice is achieved. In between the tri-ennial *blitzkriegs* upon their sensibilities citizens have too little opportunity to participate in the way decisions are made on their behalf. There is a distrust in our system of government that stems from people's lack of faith in the process by which decisions are reached.

My concern is not with the content of any particular decision but with the ground rules of our society. When we talk of a 'constitution' what we mean is the framework of rules within which our society arrives at decisions. The improvement of those rules can lead to widespread improvement in the quality of decisions and in the attitude with which people regard them. In New Zealand the direction of change should be towards the provision of more checks and balances against the exercise of power by government.

2

The queen and the governor-general

Monarchy or republic?

That we have a Queen of New Zealand means that our constitution is in the form of a monarchy. The authority of the crown remains important from both a legal and a political point of view. Almost all the powers of the monarch are exercised in fact by the queen's New Zealand ministers. Her ministers inherit a tradition of strong government. And the fact that it is the queen's government which they conduct confers legitimacy upon them.

It is an important feature of our government that ministries may come and go but the monarchy goes on for ever. That means any particular ministry is not the embodiment of the state, but merely its agent. The advantage in the arrangement becomes obvious if our situation is compared with that in the United States. There the president is both the chief executive and the head of state for ceremonial and diplomatic purposes. On occasions, under such an arrangement, it becomes easy to confuse criticism of the policies of a president with lack of loyalty on the part of the critic for his country. During the Vietnam war the inability to distinguish the two caused considerable difficulty. In New Zealand such problems do not arise so easily. Here it is much more difficult to say that criticism of the policies of the ministry amounts to disloyal and unpatriotic conduct. That is not to say that politicians in New Zealand do not attempt to attach those labels, only that it remains much more difficult to do so than in the United States.

Some may argue that reform of New Zealand's constitution should start with the monarchy. But any attempt to do away with the monarchy would be fraught with political dangers as a republic would be unacceptable to a majority of the population in New Zealand in 1979. The monarch is the source of the authority for cabinet; removal would require a new set of rules for the appointment of ministers. Worse still, a new set of rules for choosing the head of state would have to be devised and at this point in our history the office would almost certainly have to be an elective one. Thus the office would be the subject of political contests between the parties.

If the head of state were to be an elected official it would be necessary to define the powers and duties of the office. If the head of state were to exercise real power once more that would constitute a break with the manner in which our system of government has been evolving. It would be possible to use the new office to check the executive. For example, it may be possible to provide the new head of state with power to veto legislation which could be overridden only by a two-thirds vote in parliament. But there are better means of providing checks and balances than by reconstituting the office of governor-general. And if the head of state were to have no power, it is hard to see why any reconstitution should be tried.

The monarchy itself cannot be said to be the source of any existing discontent concerning the functioning of government in New Zealand. Along with the monarchy come a number of functions of solid practical use. The idea of 'Her Majesty's Loyal Opposition', from whose ranks the alternative government will come, connects with the monarchy. The queen, as the fountainhead of justice, links the monarchy with the rule of law, an idea which lies at the very heart of our democracy and one which establishes a set of protections for liberty. In the continuity of that tradition lies an important contribution of the monarchy.

Some of the functions of the monarchy in New Zealand are surrounded by mystery and symbolism, but the institution is no less valuable for that. The monarchy has a ceremonial function. It enjoys important responsibilities in diplomacy and foreign relations, mainly of a formal nature these days. The monarch is titular head of the armed services. The monarchy stands for government in accordance with principles, principles which transcend the political prejudices of the temporary custodians of the machinery of state. Although it would be much simpler for New Zealand to change from a monarchy to a republic than it would be for the federation of Australian states to do so, it is less likely to happen in the foreseeable future. We cannot do without a head of state and it is hard to see how we can do better than the queen represented by a governor-general.

The governor-general

What has been suggested above is that the governor-general is a ceremonial figurehead, a puppet who dances to strings pulled by the cabinet ministers. The law requires that he carry out many important functions of government such as affixing the royal assent to bills passed by parliament, but in doing such tasks the governor-general exercises no independent judgment. He must follow the advice of the queen's ministers. In 1867 the British writer, W. Bagehot, wrote that the monarch had three rights: 'the right to be consulted, the right to encourage, the right to warn'. (*The English Constitution,* p.111) It has sometimes been said that a New Zealand governor-general enjoys the same three rights.

The evidence we have suggests that the New Zealand practice does not approach the solemnity reserved for Queen Victoria in 1867. Sir John Marshall, one of the longest serving ministers in the history of New Zealand, summed up the position in 1977 as follows:

Today even the Governor-General's right to be consulted, to encourage and to warn are not exercised in any formal or regular way. The Prime Minister does not report regularly to the Governor-General as the British Prime Minister reports to the Queen. In 20 years as a Minister, I seldom attended at Government House for consultation, even less for encouragement and never for warning. Even when I was Prime Minister, the consultations with the Governor-General were infrequent, although our relationship, socially and on state occasions, was cordial. . . . In my experience the Governor-General has always acted on the advice of his Ministers. (*Parliamentarian,* vol. 58, p.13)

Certain exceptional situations could arise, however, in which the part played by the governor-general would be much greater than that of an automaton marching to ministerial orders. The extent to which the governor-general enjoys residual powers to act on his own view is a controversial area among constitutional experts, a controversy inflamed by the Australian Governor-General Sir John Kerr's dismissal of the ministry of Mr E.G. Whitlam in 1975. (Mercifully the particular set of events which happened in Australia could not arise in New Zealand, because we have only one house in the legislature and because of other features of the Australian scene not found in New Zealand.) A number of situations do exist, however, where the powers of the governor-general could become a matter of critical importance in New Zealand.

If, in a general election, the two main political parties were tied or if neither held a clear majority, the balance of power being held by a third party, a decision would have to be made about who would form a government. The governor-general must invite someone to form a government. Let us imagine that Party A has forty members of parliament, Party B has forty members of parliament and Party C has twelve. Prior to the election Party A was the government. After the election does the leader of Party A have the first chance to form a government for which he will need the support of Party C? The leader of Party A would still be prime minister after the election and he may advise the governor-general to invite him to try to form a government. Is the governor-general bound to accept that advice or should he first consult the leaders of Parties B and C to see where their preferences lie? Party C would be in a strong position to secure concessions from both major parties and may well decide to support the party which offers the most by way of ministerial office and the implementation of its desired policies.

To put another twist on the situation, let us imagine that the prime minister in office says no government can be formed and advises the governor-general that another general election should be held immediately. Is the governor-general obliged to take that advice or can he require the house to meet and see whether a government can be formed? A less likely possibility arises where a ministry supported by a political party defeated at the polls refuses to resign from office and refuses to advise the governor-general to call parliament together. Another variation, calling for the exercise of personal discretion by the governor-general, would be where the political party with the majority in the house had no leader and no mechanism for deciding upon a leader.

The key issue in all these situations is whether the governor-general can:

- act without advice on his own initiative
- act after receiving advice but not following the advice tendered
- refuse to act after receiving advice to act

It seems clear that a governor-general in New Zealand should never act against the advice of his ministers who have the support of a majority in the House of Representatives. If the governor-general acted otherwise he would be guilty of forfeiting the political neutrality of the crown by taking sides. Nonetheless, exceptional situations could arise where the governor-general would have to make important decisions on his own initiative.

In New Zealand we have no written rules for dealing with any of the above cases. Some people have suggested we should settle the rules in some authoritative written form so that the uncertainty about what may happen in a crisis is removed. An Australian prime minister, Dr H.V. Evatt wrote: 'If Parliamentary government is to endure, it is essential that the terrain of this constitutional no man's land should be finally explored.' (*The King and his Dominion Governors*, p.120) One of the reasons for uncertainty is the fact that the position of governor-general himself is not secure. The queen would probably remove a governor-general and replace him with another if advised to do so by her New Zealand ministers. Whether it is practicable and useful to spell out what should be done by a governor-general in exceptional situations is arguable. Part of the problem arises from trying to interpret the meaning of the events which have occurred. Writing down the rules will not remove that aspect of the uncertainty; it is impossible to provide for every contingency. Experience in other countries shows that effort made at spelling it all out can be defeated by politicians determined to subvert the constitution. If it was all written down in a constitutional document perhaps the courts could review the exercise of the power, although it is not really the type of question suitable for resolution by a court.

The situations in which a governor-general in New Zealand could be called upon to exercise an independent judgment are few. It has never happened in modern times, and it may never happen. But if it did occur it would be necessary that the governor-general be seen to be the neutral representative of the monarch in New Zealand. In 1977 Sir Keith Holyoake, a former respected prime minister of New Zealand, was appointed governor-general. A few months before taking office, he had been a minister without portfolio in the Muldoon government. He was a figure whose long political career was closely identified with the National Party. Appointing such a man to the office of governor-general without broad political support suggests that the office is not politically neutral. Writing of Sir Keith's appointment, Professor W.H. Oliver stated:

Unlike those of his predecessors of aristocratic origins or status, he has no degree of distance at all from the New Zealand political scene. His record is, overwhelmingly, one of political partisanship. . . . As recently as the 1975 election, his performance on television (the National Party's election eve programme) was characterised by extreme and indeed bitter partisanship. Between the election and his resignation he has not been much in the public eye. Still, he was during that period a Cabinet Minister, and so shares the collective responsibility for very recent policies and practices – everything from the Moyle affair to random checks on overstayers. His partisanship is not buried deep in the past; it is a matter of very recent record.

(*New Zealand Comment,* vol. 1, no. 1, p.3)

In fact Sir Keith might act impartially, but it would be hard to dispel the appearance of partisanship. And appearance is important in convincing citizens of the integrity of their political institutions. The ultimate referee, when the chips are down, should not belong to one of the teams playing the game. In highly exceptional circumstances the queen's representative can act as protector of the constitution. The capacity to play that role will not be much improved by trying to write down what the governor-general should do. But we should strive to keep the office free from political controversy and appoint people who enjoy broad support throughout the community.

Except in the exceptional situations discussed, the governor-general should act on the advice of his ministers. In fact he invariably does so. But the 1917 Letters Patent and Royal Instructions from which the governor-general derives many of his powers suggest otherwise. The instructions provide that he may reject the advice of his ministers 'if he shall see sufficient cause to dissent' from the opinion of his ministers. The power has never been exercised and should be removed. Indeed the Letters Patent and Royal Instructions are, in the words of D.L. Stevens, the most recent scholar on the question, 'in dire need of revision'. For similar reasons a provision in the Constitution Act which suggests that the governor-general, in his own discretion, may refuse to assent to bills passed by parliament should be altered.

3

Cabinet, caucus and the prime minister

Cabinet

Cabinet is the power house of New Zealand government. Most important decisions made by government are made by cabinet or cabinet committees; others are made by individual ministers. An incredible amount of decision-making power is concentrated in the New Zealand cabinet. Many problems are pushed up through our governmental system for resolution by cabinet. Subject to the restraints mentioned in chapter 1, the New Zealand cabinet:

- acts as final decision-maker on all important matters of policy
- approves the content of all regulations, which are laws made under the authority of statutes
- decides the content of statutes to be passed by parliament
- makes the decisions on government spending
- co-ordinates the administration and gives orders to the public service on how to carry out administration
- acts in ways designed to further its own political survival

In 1970, B.E. Talboys, then an experienced minister and later deputy prime minister, characterized cabinet in the following way:

In New Zealand all the major decisions are made by Cabinet whether or not they involve more than one department. In fact, it is Cabinet which governs. It is Cabinet which determines the financial authorities granted to Ministers and unless a Minister has this authority he cannot spend, regardless of what the relevant Act may say. The sanction is not that of the law, of course; it is that of his Cabinet colleagues.

(*New Zealand Journal of Public Administration*, vol. 33, p.3)

Although committees of cabinet form an important feature of cabinet's work, no hard and fast rules exist concerning the committees. Committees come and go according to the issues of the day, but some are more or less permanent fixtures. Some of the important committees, such as Works and State Services, enjoy power to make final decisions on questions which come before them, although the full cabinet could reverse a committee decision. Cabinet committees cannot be considered separately from cabinet itself – they are all part of the same decision-making complex. At various times in recent New Zealand history there have been as many as thirty committees, or as few as ten. Some committees, such as Civil Defence, hardly ever meet. Others, like the committees dealing with economic questions and government expenditure, meet regularly.

The cabinet committees that existed in 1978 were:
- Economic
- Expenditure, to scrutinize proposals for government spending of money
- Family Affairs, to examine measures to promote family life
- Legislation and Parliamentary Questions, the most important function of which is to arrange and settle the content of the government's legislative programme
- Honours and Appointments, to consider people for the hundreds of positions to which government can make appointments and to consider people for the award of honours and titles
- Works, to consider and review annual programmes of government works
- Transport, to consider policies and expenditures in the transport field
- Regional Development, to review questions relating to local government and assistance to regions
- Civil Defence
- Communications, concerned with broadcasting and related policies
- Science
- State Services, to keep the machinery of government under review
- Social Affairs
- Defence
- Terrorism

In 1970, Mr Talboys, in the same article quoted earlier, wrote that he was a member of fifteen cabinet committees and this 'means spending 10 to 12 hours each week at meetings of Cabinet or its committees and many more hours preparing for such meetings'. (p.1) Cabinet committee meetings, unlike full cabinet, are often attended by officials who discuss issues with ministers and tender their advice.

For the formal meetings of cabinet on Mondays, cabinet papers are prepared by departments under the supervision of the minister. A standard format is laid down for cabinet papers, although it allows for a fair amount of flexibility. When a proposal involves expenditure, a Treasury report on the proposal is circulated to every member of cabinet. The department in charge of proposals has the right of reply. The views of other departments on the proposal will also be available. The documentation so prepared is designed to give ministers a set of views to weigh in reaching the cabinet decision on the subject.

The business of cabinet is carried out under the supervision of the secretary to cabinet, a high-ranking permanent public servant who heads the unit which services cabinet. The cabinet office arranges the agenda and prepares the minutes recording decisions. While these functions are under the formal control of the prime minister, in reality the cabinet office functions with a great deal of independence. To a large extent the agenda arranges itself depending upon what papers have been prepared for cabinet consideration.

The concept of ministerial responsibility is often said to be a great protection against the abuse of power by ministers. Ministerial responsibility may mean that ministers are responsive to public opinion because the government can be voted out of office at elections. Or it may mean that ministers are accountable to parliament for their actions and those of their officials. The second meaning has attracted most discussion.

It is a custom of government that ministers share collective responsibility for the policies of the government. The principle cannot be directly enforced in any court but rests on usage. It is said that there must be unity in cabinet once decisions have been taken; this amounts to little more than the loose notion that the members of cabinet should stand or fall together. They cannot evade responsibility for government policy.

Another aspect of the concept of ministerial responsibility concerns individual ministers. A minister must answer questions in parliament concerning the activities of those departments for which he is responsible. It is sometimes said that the minister must resign when he or one of his officers has blundered. That has not happened in New Zealand since 1934 and where circumstances might indicate resignation a minister can shelter behind the collective responsibility of cabinet mentioned above.

Neither collective responsibility nor individual responsibility seems to amount to much in New Zealand. It seems to have become accepted that ministers in New Zealand can disagree with one another. For example, in 1978 the minister responsible for the Department of Internal Affairs said he was in favour of some form of revenue sharing for local authorities; the minister of finance and prime minister said that he was not. Both made their positions clear in public. No doubt there is a great deal more disagreement in cabinet than ever becomes public, but on occasions when it is convenient, the disagreement can be made public. In recent years in New Zealand, ministers have never managed to find an issue of principle upon which they disagree with their colleagues and which is of such importance to them that they feel compelled to resign.

The concept of ministerial responsibility is not, however, totally bankrupt. It does have some important practical consequences for our government. The government is legally liable for acts of the public servants under the minister's control and can be sued in respect of them. The minister can be asked questions in parliament about the actions of his department. The minister must answer in parliament for things which may have gone wrong; the minister and no-one else is responsible to parliament in that way. He is supposed to take steps to see that his department functions efficiently and to ensure that he is consulted on all matters of importance. The permanent head of the department is answerable to the minister. There needs to be continuing consultation between the minister and his departmental officers on a day to day basis.

Cabinet government poses an affront to the idea of separation of powers; cabinet combines a number of legislative, executive and even adjudicative functions. Cabinet commands great resources. In the thirty-six departments coming under the State Services Act there were more than 78,000 employees in 1978. Most of those people could be called upon by the appropriate minister to carry out orders which he wanted carried out. The minister would not do it directly, he would tell the permanent head what he wanted done. As long as it was not contrary to law, outside the range of the department's activities, or contrary to a cabinet decision, the permanent head would have to carry out the orders.

Many public servants are people of great skill and expertise; in some spheres of activity the government has at its command a virtual monopoly on the talent available in New Zealand. And the orderly activities of the public service generate a great deal of information, much of which is information available only to the government. That information is another weapon in the armoury of executive power. The capacity of those wishing to scrutinize or oppose government is directly affected by the amount of information available to them from government. No group of managers or directors in New Zealand can bring to bear the range of resources and the width of powers available to cabinet.

Caucus

The role of caucus is one of the minor mysteries of New Zealand government. Some say it exerts real power, others that it is a rubber-stamp for cabinet. The truth lies in between. Both major political parties conduct regular weekly meetings of their members of parliament. In the case of the Labour Party several party officials also attend. Caucus meets in secret and provides the opportunity for ironing out differences which may exist between members of the parliamentary party. An opposition caucus mainly debates strategy and tactics in parliament and related questions. Both parties have governing bodies which include people outside parliament as well as members of parliament. So party caucuses are in no sense sovereign decision-makers for the party. The procedures of both caucuses are informal. The party leaders decide the agenda and chair the discussions; individual members can ask to have items produced on the agenda.

For the governing party perhaps the most important role of caucus is as a sounding board for the condition of public opinion on questions of the day. Sometimes ministers even speak as if caucus had the final say on important controversial questions which are the responsibility of the executive. It is probably true that the more controversial an issue the more caucus will be concerned with it. And on some issues caucus may decide that the policies of the ministry are unacceptable and must be changed. The best short description of caucus I have seen comes from former National Party speaker, Alfred Allen. He wrote in 1971:

> . . . at caucus meetings, where all are regarded as equal, and some prove themselves a little more equal than others, Members are extremely outspoken and the utterances and actions of individual Members come under very close scrutiny. A word picture of a Member is often so vividly painted that it enables him to see himself clearly as others see him.
>
> While Cabinet Ministers form the executive Government, they are always ready and willing to bring all matters of major importance before caucus before becoming irrevocably committed to any course of action. While it is unusual, I have on occasions seen the strongly presented recommendation of a Minister turned down in no uncertain manner and on other occasions a Cabinet decision reversed or abandoned.
>
> At our caucus meetings every Member is encouraged to express his views for or against any and every proposal before caucus, and very often a decision is deferred to enable those against to marshal support and fully prepare their case.
>
> (*Parliamentarian*, vol. 52, p.37)

Caucus committees play an important part in determining the attitude of caucus. Ministers sometimes refer government bills to a caucus committee before introducing them to parliament, although there is no fixed practice about it. But caucus is consulted on almost all legislation before it is introduced into the house. Departmental officials are often involved in supplying information to government caucus committees. Caucus continues to have an influence on legislation when the bill is before a select committee and the political implications of suggested changes are discussed. Although the influence of caucus has grown in recent years, particularly in the National Party, the main thrust of its activities seems to be directed at promoting the political health of the party. Sometimes that will provide a useful check upon executive action; in other instances it may encourage excesses in policy.

Caucus cannot be counted as a systematic auditor of government policy. Caucus and caucus committees help in the formulation of government policy, but the areas of concentration shift depending on political circumstances at the time. In the context of the present discussion, however, some conclusions can be reached about caucus. Caucus provides:
• a check on both cabinet and individual ministers

- a barometer of political opinion available to the ministry on controversial issues
- a forum for determining political strategy and tactics

Caucus deliberations are secret and it is hard to see how they could be made more open and still function effectively. Caucus does carry out some useful functions in filtering policies before the government becomes committed to them, but the emphasis on party advantage, which necessarily dominates all activities in caucus, ensures that caucus cannot be relied upon as a major source of protection for the public against the actions and decisions of the executive.

How powerful is the prime minister?

The charge has sometimes been made, in the United Kingdom and in New Zealand, that government by cabinet is in eclipse. What we have now, it is said, amounts to a presidential system with the prime minister as president. R.H.S. Crossman described in 1963 a phenomenon he called 'prime ministerial government'. Lord George-Brown's statement about why he resigned from Mr Harold Wilson's cabinet in 1968 echoes the same theme:

I resigned on a matter of fundamental principle, because it seemed to me that the Prime Minister was not only introducing a 'presidential' system into the running of government that is wholly alien to the British constitutional system . . . but was so operating it that decisions were being taken over the heads and without the knowledge of ministers, and far too often outsiders in his entourage seemed to be almost the only effective 'Cabinet'.

(in V. Herman and A.J. Alt, *Cabinet Studies – A Reader*, p.103)

Few contest that a prime minister has great power and authority, but many hold the view that such has been the situation for years. Certainly it seems clear, in both Britain and New Zealand, that the prime minister is a good deal more than the first among equals; how much more, it is not easy to determine, especially in New Zealand.

Much of the prime minister's power will always depend upon personality and temperament. Some people like team-work; some find the delegation of decisions uncongenial and want to have a hand in as many as possible. Legend in Wellington and Professor Keith Sinclair's biography suggest that Walter Nash was the latter sort of prime minister. No doubt the political success of a prime minister contributes to the degree of power he can exercise; a prime minister who, as party leader, wins elections consistently will hold more sway with colleagues than one who has been dogged by electoral failures.

The prime minister's right to appoint other ministers can also be regarded as a source of strength. In a National government the prime minister selects the ministers and allocates the portfolios. With Labour, caucus elects the members of cabinet but the prime minister allocates the portfolios. Even with National, however, there are constraints upon a prime minister's freedom: it is felt that candidates for cabinet must have had experience in the House of Representatives. In 1975 Prime Minister Muldoon had only twenty-eight members of parliament with parliamentary experience from which to select a cabinet of twenty people and provide a speaker, chairman of committees and two whips. No doubt in a much larger parliament than New Zealand's the power of appointment by the prime minister would amount to a more significant source of power. But when it is appreciated that cabinet selection is limited by a number of factors such as representation of geographical areas, age and experience, the power of appointment cannot be counted as highly significant in the circumstances of New Zealand in the seventies.

The right to dismiss a minister might be regarded as a potentially greater source of prime ministerial power except for the fact that it is a power which seems hardly ever to be exercised in modern New Zealand politics. Ministers do retire from time to time by not offering themselves for re-election, but ministers are not dismissed from office as they sometimes are in the United Kingdom and Australia. It could theoretically happen, and for that reason must be considered as part of the prime minister's inventory of power. The idea of team solidarity seems to be stressed in New Zealand's cabinet. When Mr Marshall and Mr Rowling both became prime ministers mid-way through parliamentary terms there were ministerial reshuffles and new faces appeared in cabinet but these changes cannot be regarded in the same light as dismissals. Late in 1978 Mr Muldoon dropped one minister when forming his new cabinet.

Indeed not only do prime ministers tend not to dismiss ministers (at least openly) in New Zealand, ministers do not resign either. Not infrequently in the United Kingdom a minister who is in disagreement with his colleagues on matters considered by the minister to be of great importance will resign. Resignation disassociates the minister with policies of which he disapproves. Such resignations have not occurred in New Zealand since the second world war and the practice must be regarded for the moment as a dead letter. The size of the house and lack of further political opportunity in New Zealand after resignation seem to militate against it. Resignation does not necessarily mean political extermination in the United Kingdom, whereas it probably would in New Zealand.

The prime minister can advise the governor-general to dissolve the House of Representatives at any time and hold a general election, but such a step has not been taken in New Zealand since 1951. It might be expected in New Zealand that the prime minister would discuss such a step with at least some of his colleagues, if not the whole cabinet. Because elections must be held every three years in New Zealand the threat of holding an early election cannot be counted of great significance in the catalogue of prime ministerial power.

The prime minister is the chairman of cabinet. His opinion will carry great weight on all issues, whereas individual ministers will tend to be regarded at their most authoritative in dealing with matters inside their own portfolios. As Sir Keith Holyoake once put it: 'the Prime Minister must maintain a fatherly oversight over the progress of his Cabinet colleagues, particularly in their work of implementing policy.' (in *Readings in New Zealand Government*, p.73) There is no formal voting in cabinet. And although the prime minister is responsible for summing up cabinet discussion, he is not able to get away with stating his own view for long if his colleagues disagree with him.

The public regard the prime minister as the chief spokesman of the government on all important issues. He holds the major press conferences, and what he says gains great attention in the media. He is not restricted in what he says, as his colleagues usually are, to matters within the particular portfolios he holds. So to some extent a prime minister is the government's trouble-shooter: when a problem gets hot the prime minister may well intervene in the handling of it.

To the above sources of power must be added two which are linked with the administration of Mr R.D. Muldoon. First, it must be observed that from 1975 to 1979 Mr Muldoon held the portfolio of minister of finance. The minister of finance is an important person in any government because all questions of expenditure involve him. He is minister in charge of the Treasury, which is the most powerful department of state. Treasury is powerful because it subjects all spending proposals of other departments to scrutiny and often says 'No'. Any proposal to cabinet accompanied by an adverse report from the Treasury is bound to be closely scrutinized, even if it is eventually approved. Many expenditures which do not go to cabinet must receive the approval of the minister of finance. Control over the public purse belongs to the minister of finance and his treasury officials and that power constitutes an important counterweight to the proposals of those ministers who wish to spend money. Economic policy lies at the heart of government policy in New Zealand. So the minister of finance who presides over this financial machinery is a pivotal figure in government; when he is also the prime minister the concentration of power in one individual is overwhelming.

Second, to the impressive panoply of power outlined so far, Mr Muldoon added an innovation of his own. The prime minister has responsibility for co-ordinating the policies of government, making sure that one minister is not doing something incompatible with the actions of another, ironing out clashes of responsibility and that sort of thing. In this task successive New Zealand prime ministers have been helped by officials in the Ministry of Foreign Affairs, who constituted the Prime

Minister's Department. Mr Muldoon moved the unit away from Foreign Affairs and added some functions. The department comprises the following sections:

- the prime minister's personal ministerial office
- a press office to act as publicity co-ordinator for the ministry as well as the prime minister
- the cabinet office to service cabinet and its committees
- the External Intelligence Bureau, which centralizes intelligence functions previously carried on by the Departments of Defence and Foreign Affairs
- an advisory group of about eight people to provide the prime minister with an extra source of advice

The novel features of the new department stem from the re-vamped press office and the policy advisory group, popularly known as the 'Think Tank'. Some people felt that even if the development of the policy advisory group was not an attempt to cut down the power of Treasury, it certainly was intended to give the prime minister an effective overview and greater control of all crucially important policy.

Members of the new group were not recruited exclusively from the public service. Three came from the private sector on contract. Whatever views are held concerning the propriety of the new arrangement, it undoubtedly provides a useful source of advice on policy to the prime minister – advice which could be at odds with that received from the ordinary departments of state. The group is able to analyse and probe all proposals and it should help achieve greater co-ordination between government policies. There is nothing sinister about a minister having a group of special advisers to whom he can listen. But if the prime minister has such a high powered team and no other ministers do, more power tends to accrue to the prime minister. The group will obviously become an important focus for negotiations of the type which go on between officials prior to any cabinet paper being sent up. So the prime minister's new department is an important source of power. When the prime minister has such an advisory group and also holds the finance portfolio, the concentration of power in one man's hands seems too great. The dual responsibilities also raise the question of priorities in use of the prime minister's time.

Added to all of the above must be the fact that the prime minister is always minister in charge of the Security Intelligence Service. In that capacity he is empowered by statute to issue warrants allowing that service to tap telephones and to issue interception warrants in relation to any communication not otherwise lawfully obtainable. The service is empowered to investigate terrorism, subversion and espionage, concepts which are but vaguely defined. Those are awe-inspiring powers in a free society; the formal checks upon their exercise are minimal.

Conclusion

Hardly any of the powers of cabinet, caucus or the prime minister rest upon any legal foundation. The present system has evolved, as is a custom of our government. There is nothing to stop it evolving further. The powers at present concentrated in cabinet and the prime minister could well be curbed: either some power should be removed from the cabinet area, or countervailing powers should be located elsewhere. As we shall see later, the legislative function of parliament has been damaged to a great extent by domination from cabinet reinforced by rigid party discipline. If parliament were able to stand up to cabinet rather than act subserviently, it would function as a more effective check on the executive branch of government.

The powers of the executive and legislative branches of government could be separated entirely, to enable each branch to act as a restraint upon the other. At present cabinet ministers must also be members of parliament; if members of cabinet were not members of parliament, cabinet domination of both caucus and parliament would be more difficult. Such a situation would certainly mean that parliament could exert more influence upon the conduct of government than it has ever done. Cabinet ministers would continue to conduct the government and preside over the public service. The money for government would be voted by parliament and statutes would continue to be passed there. The executive branch of government could propose measures, but parliament would have the dispositive power. One disadvantage with such a system, which is the basis of the United States government, is that ministers are not answerable to parliament for their conduct of government.

A related proposal comes from Nigel Roberts of the University of Canterbury. After studying what occurs in Norway and Denmark he suggests that it should be permissible to choose ministers from among non-parliamentarians. Such ministers would have the right to speak in parliament but not to vote. The suggestion has the advantage of increasing the availability of talent for the demanding and important post of cabinet minister. Furthermore, it would enable the blurred line between executive and legislative functions to be made more clear than it now is. From a legal point of view such a constitutional alteration could easily be made in New Zealand.

These proposals for change deserve serious consideration. An increased separation of powers between the executive and the legislative arms of government would go a great distance towards reducing the domination of the executive which characterizes New Zealand government. But change may be accompanied by other consequences which would cancel out the advantages. Cabinet government as we know it could be destroyed, not merely moderated. Uncertainty and delay in making decisions could develop. More curbs upon executive power are needed rather than a new type of executive.

4

The state services and quango land

Departments

New Zealand, in the words of a 1962 royal commisssion on the state services, 'has been so well served for so long by loyal, incorruptible, and politically neutral State servants that it may be inclined to assume that this is part of the natural order of things'. (paragraph 20) That situation undoubtedly still holds although the public service has altered its shape a good deal since 1962, partly as a result of recommendations of the royal commission.

In 1978 the departments of the New Zealand government could be grouped under five headings – economic development, law and order, welfare, government, provision of services.

Economic development

Ministry of Agriculture and Fisheries – promotion and encouragement of agriculture, pastoral, horticultural and fishing industries

Ministry of Energy Resources – promotion and co-ordination of production, supply, distribution and use of energy in all its forms. Includes electricity generation and coal mining

Forest Service – management of large forests

Department of Lands and Survey – management of crown land, parks and reserves, mapping and survey work

Railways Department – provision of rail, road and inter-island sea services

Rural Banking and Finance Corporation – granting of loans for farming

Department of Scientific and Industrial Research – scientific research for economic development and environmental control

Department of Tourist and Publicity – promotion of travel to New Zealand, travel agent and tourist operator

Department of Trade and Industry – development of industry and commerce and encouragement of exports

Ministry of Transport – information and advice for development of transport policy, road safety, marine safety, aircraft safety, meteorological service

Ministry of Works and Development – design and construction of public works

Law and order

Crown Law Office – legal advice to the government

Department of Justice – administration of facilities for the courts, penal policy and prisons, law reform, registration systems for land, births, deaths, elections, companies, etc.

Police Department – police functions

Welfare

Department of Education – provision of suitable education facilities and administration of education generally

Health Department – public health functions

Housing Corporation – provision of finance for private house purchases and management of state rental housing

Department of Labour – industrial relations, employment service, promotion of industrial safety

Department of Maori Affairs – assistance to Maoris and Pacific Island Polynesians

Department of Social Welfare – payment of social security benefits, provision of social welfare services

Government

Audit Department – auditing of financial transactions of government, local authorities and statutory corporations

Customs Department – collection of indirect taxation

Ministry of Defence – administration of defence forces

Ministry of Foreign Affairs – administration of foreign policy and external relations

Government Printing Office – printer and stationer to government

Inland Revenue Department – collection of taxes

Internal Affairs Department – administration relating to local government, cultural and recreational services and wildlife and other miscellaneous functions

Legislative Department – parliamentary services

Prime Minister's Department – servicing of cabinet and its committees, and advice to prime minister on policy matters, publicity functions; external intelligence functions

Department of Statistics – collection and publication of statistics

Treasury – accountants to government, advice on expenditure, advice on economic policy

Valuation Department – valuation of real estate
State Services Commission – reviews of machinery of government and of the efficiency and economy of each department, personnel authority for public service, training and management consultant services

Provision of services
Government Life Insurance Office – sale of life insurance
Post Office – operation of post and telecommunication systems
Public Trust Office – trustee, executor and administrator of estates
State Insurance Office – sale of all classes of fire, accident and marine insurance

Each department has a permanent head. He is appointed, in the case of those departments which come under the State Services Act, by a special committee which deals with higher appointments. There is little opportunity for political interference by ministers in the process, and the permanent head continues in his post even when there is a change in government. The permanent head is 'responsible to the Minister for the time being in charge of that Department for the efficient and economical administration thereof'. (State Services Act 1962, s.25) No appointment to the public service, including those at the top levels can be made from outside the service unless the person appointed 'has clearly more merit' than any officer from within the service who is qualified and available for the position. Promotion within the public service is on a clearly defined system of merit; dissatisfied applicants have the right of appeal to an impartial tribunal.

Steps should be taken to open up positions in the public service to outsiders who would serve there for a temporary period. The public service would benefit, especially at the higher levels from regular infusions of new ideas and talent. The permanent career service concept must be nourished and maintained, but greater flexibility in allowing people to move in and out of the service should be devised.

The manner in which those departments under the State Services Act work is carefully controlled by the State Services Commission which is responsible for:
- reviewing the machinery of government and the allocation of functions between departments
- reviewing the efficiency and economy of each department
- providing suitable office accommodation
- approving and reviewing staff establishments
- laying down staff training programmes
- providing management consultation services
- acting as the central personnel authority

In short, the New Zealand public service is politically neutral, loyal to whatever government is in power at any time. It is a system which has a great many strengths and should not be lightly interfered with. Nonetheless, some changes can be contemplated.

Some departments carry out trading functions such as selling insurance, do construction work, provide transport services and the like. There are more than 21,000 employees in the Railways and over 38,000 in the Post Office. It does not make much sense that the minister in charge of those departments should be held responsible and accountable for every little slip of every employee. Yet theoretically all those people are the minister's people carrying out the minister's instructions.

With enterprises the size of some of those outlined above, ministerial responsibility as a way of ensuring that the organizations are really accountable to the public does not work. The notion that it is possible for the minister to control everything that occurs is impractical; many of the important administrative tasks must be delegated to subordinates remote from the minister. As an Australian critic has remarked: 'Emphasis lies on control from above. The minister's will is the theoretical basis of all action; Cabinet minutes are the ultimate source of authority'. (*Royal Commission on Australian Government Administration*, Appendix, vol. 1, p.28) Yet many of the departments spend much of their effort dealing with members of the public, something which has a lower priority than serving the minister.

It is time to get rid of the system whereby the minister is, in theory, accountable for everything and in practice accountable for very little. We should move towards a system whereby the officials are publicly answerable for the responsibilities delegated to them by cabinet. A new system of public accountability should be introduced. A parliamentary select committee on government administration should have the power to summon before it public servants and the relevant ministers. It should examine in detail the aims and objectives of each department in turn, assess the degree to which they are being accomplished and make recommendations for change. The committee should emphasize the need for departments to be responsible to the needs of the public and should attempt to clarify the goals which the public servants are to pursue. And criteria need to be developed by which departmental performance is to be judged. In short, departments should be given greater control over the use of resources allocated to them to carry out administrative tasks, but they should be accountable directly to parliament for their administrative performance. That way the minister's own responsibility will be narrower, but it will be realistic then to expect him to be genuinely accountable for it.

I am suggesting a system of accountable management in the public service. Accountable management 'means holding individuals and units responsible for performance measured as objectively as possible. Its achievement depends upon identifying or establishing accountable units within government departments – units where outputs can be measured against costs or other criteria, and where individuals can be held personally responsible for their performance.' (*Report of the Committee on the Civil Service*, Cmnd 3638) That involves an increase in the managerial independence of public servants from ministers, with a corresponding increase in the public accountability of public servants for their own actions.

Quangos

We have in New Zealand a multitude of organizations established by government which are not departments. In Britain they have been dubbed 'quangos', short for quasi-autonomous national governmental organization. Quangos come in a bewildering variety of shapes and sizes. There are:

- statutory corporations established to carry out tasks – for example, Accident Compensation Commission, the Tourist Hotel Corporation, the Bank of New Zealand
- commercial companies in which the government owns all the shares – for example, Air New Zealand, the Petroleum Corporation of New Zealand Ltd
- tribunals set up by statute and empowered to decide questions more or less in the same fashion as a court – for example, the Accident Compensation Appeal Authority, the Planning Tribunals, the Indecent Publications Tribunal
- committees established to advise government – for example, the Torts and General Law Reform Committee, the Medical Services Advisory Committee, the Tobacco Research Advisory Committee
- incorporated societies – for example, the Rehabilitation League N.Z. (Inc.)

The reasons why quangos are established vary even more than their form of legal organization. They are set up:

- to avoid political control and having a minister responsible for the organization
- to avoid departmental procedures and controls which are exerted within the state services
- to relieve ministers of responsibility for detailed or specialized tasks
- to carry out fairly regulatory functions involving adjudication
- the desire to bring outside people into the management of the activity
- to allow for representation of special interests in the administration of some activity

In 1978 the cabinet office prepared a manual covering the boards, committees, tribunals, councils and related bodies which fall under forty-three ministerial portfolios. The list was intended to include all appointments which carry ministerial approval or recommendation. On my count there were 1,268 quangos with something over 5,000 people involved. Surely these figures are remarkable. Most appointees are paid or receive expenses. The quango system provides ministers with a set of patronage appointments. Most of the jobs are never advertised. Who said New Zealand does not have a spoils system?

Serious doubts exist about the public accountability of quangos in New Zealand. Those in the form of statutory corporations or companies are more or less free from direct ministerial supervision of their day to day operations. Quangos can be freer of Treasury control of their expenditure than a department; sometimes they have greater flexibility than the state services in fixing pay scales. Quangos can appoint and promote staff without the appeals which occur in the state services. Their real independence from government varies a great deal: almost always ministers appoint the key people, or at least some of them; but often the statutes establishing these bodies provide that government policy must be followed. For example, the Accident Compensation Act 1972 setting up the Accident Compensation Commission provides:

In the exercise of its functions and powers, the Commission shall give effect to the policy of the Government in relation to those functions and powers as communicated to it from time to time in writing by the Minister. (s.20)

A similar provision appears in the Broadcasting Act. Although many of the statutes provide that the directions should be tabled in parliament, others do not. It is obvious that a ministerial word in the appropriate ear will often achieve the desired result without a directive.

Several hundred quangos are no more than advisory committees of various types. For example, there is an Advisory Council for the Community Welfare of Disabled Persons, and there is a Tobacco Research Advisory Committee, whose purposes may well be incompatible with another quango, the Advisory Committee on Smoking and Health. Some quangos, however, have decision-making powers and it is thought that these should be run by specially qualified persons – for example, the Queen Elizabeth Arts Council of New Zealand or the Trustees of the National Library. And there are others where community participation is thought desirable – for example, the thirty-two Housing Corporation Allocation Committees which function in various parts of New Zealand to determine the allocation of state rental houses. Other organizations with considerable power, such as the National Roads Board and the Higher Salaries Commission and Licensing Control Commission, appear to have been established to take decision-making out of the hands of ministers and the political process as a deliberate choice.

There are other quangos which conduct substantial commercial operations – the Bank of New Zealand, the Tourist Hotel Corporation of New Zealand and the Totalisator Agency Board, the biggest gambling concern in the country. Air New Zealand Limited, which operates large internal and overseas airlines, is an ordinary company registered in the companies office, but the government owns all the shares.

The agricultural producer boards form another sort of government agency; they are established by statute, but are dominated by people elected by the producers. The relationship of the producer boards to government is complicated. The aim has been to promote and co-ordinate marketing and to stabilize farm prices. Organizations such as the New Zealand Dairy Board enjoy great powers granted by statute – for example, the Dairy Board has a monopoly on the acquisition and marketing of dairy produce for export. But the board is also bound to follow ministerial directives, which do not need to be made public.

Another government agency which functions under statute is the University Grants Committee. It advises government on all requirements for university education and acts as a buffer between government and the universities. The idea is that universities should be free from the prospect of ministerial interference; ministers, in turn, are free from being worried by the universities for money, buildings and expanded programmes. All the needs are investigated, co-ordinated and put to government by the Grants Committee.

Tribunals perform functions similar in many respects to those of the courts. They adjudicate in particular cases according to standards laid down by statute. For many activities some form of licence or registration is necessary – for example, to be a real estate agent, to export fish, to sell petrol, to run a road freight business or operate a taxi, to sell secondhand cars for a living, to open shops on Saturday, to sell alcoholic liquor and to be a chiropodist. There is even statutory provision for the registration of music teachers. A whole host of boards and authorities look after the registration of people for various purposes. Someone has to examine the evidence and decide whether an applicant meets the requirements for a licence or registration. The opportunity to provide for a hearing before some impartial decision-maker is required to make such licensing fair. There are almost a hundred quangos (other than courts) performing some kind of adjudicative function in New Zealand.

Some quangos perform important functions and they cannot be dispensed with. Others, such as the Co-operative Dairy Companies Income Tax Appeal Authority, have never met. Quangos have multiplied at a remarkable rate since 1945 and according to no ascertainable principle. In 1978, after the National government had abolished forty, there were still seventy-one more than there had been in 1975. They should be reviewed by a parliamentary select committee on government administration. The aim should be to eliminate as many as possible and to ensure that those which remain are properly accountable to the public through parliament and work in a way which serves the public interest. The following questions should be kept in mind in any such review:

• why can an ordinary department not do the particular job?

- in the case of tribunals, why can't the adjudication be carried out in the ordinary courts?
- in what ways is the quango accountable to parliament and the public?
- to what extent is the quango accountable to the minister?
- to what extent does the quango have clearly defined and coherent functions?
- to what extent does the quango overlap with other government bodies?
- in the case of each advisory body, does the record show that it has actually contributed anything of value?

If these questions are rigorously pursued by a parliamentary committee many quangos could be killed off, others re-organized and limits placed upon the creation of new ones. It is time to halt the growth of quangos in New Zealand.

5
Parliament

The functions of parliament are:
- to raise the money by which the business of government may be conducted and approve the expenditure of money
- to consider and pass bills into law
- to provide a place for the airing of grievances
- to act as a check on the manner in which government is actually carried on
- to serve as a forum for party political contest

The passage of laws through parliament gives those laws legitimacy because it is there they are approved by the elected representatives of the people. But legislation has become more and more a function of the executive branch of government. Parliament has the capacity to curb the executive, although it does not do that job adequately at present.

The New Zealand parliament today revolves around party contest. Much time is spent in party political attack and defence: the opposition attacks the party in government and the government members defend it. We have a combative, adversary style of politics in which neither side gives any quarter, and much effort is wasted in perpetual party conflict and constant electioneering. Given the importance of political parties in our system it would be idle to suggest that political confrontation can be removed from parliament. But one might suggest that its importance could be reduced considerably by promoting other functions at present neglected. Much of the so-called political 'debate' is sterile and acrimonious; it encourages posturing and the peddling of distorted half-truths.

The member of parliament
The duties of members of parliament comprise a range of unrelated functions. In 1946 Sir Arnold Nordmeyer wrote:

Parliament is essentially a representative body, a cross-section of national life. Fortunately it does not consist of experts: it is composed of ordinary people –

men and women who, as they are wise, will give heed to what experts have to say, remembering always that the experts are at least sometimes wrong.

(*New Zealand Journal of Public Administration*, vol. 8, p. 3)

One duty of members of parliament is to help their constituents with a wide variety of problems. Many of the complaints they hear are genuine; a proportion come from cranks. Usually the members of parliament act as a sort of clearing house for complaints. Many members of parliament conduct regularly weekly sessions where they are available to people who want to see them in their electorates; experienced members have told me that ten hours a week of diligent work will allow the inquiries of constituents to be dealt with thoroughly. The advent of the ombudsmen does not appear to have caused any change in the number of complaints against the bureaucracy and requests for help received by members of parliament. But the presence of the ombudsmen does give members a useful avenue of referral for the grievances of their constituents.

The member of parliament is regarded within his community as a sort of community leader. He is invited to many official functions within his electorate and asked to officiate at many different ceremonies – the opening of buildings and bridges, conventions and celebrations of various sorts. Indeed, usually a member of parliament will have so many invitations that if all were accepted any ordinary family life would be impossible. He also functions as a political organizer in the community. The number of people active in politics in New Zealand on a continuing basis is not such that the tasks of political organization can be delegated to others. Often the member of parliament and family will be engaged in organizing political meetings, fund raising, attending political meetings and speaking at them. The party faithful require care and feeding. Power struggles within political parties occur frequently so the member of parliament must remain attentive to those within his electorate and region. Without a secure home base the political future of the member will not be rosy. In addition the member of parliament needs to keep in close touch with the local authorities in his area. He is often expected to act as their emissary when he is in Wellington. Local industries may make similar demands.

In Wellington the member of parliament inhabits a different world. Parliament sits long hours, often into the early hours of the morning. Parliament is a self-contained community; the members of parliament are part of it, but they are not all of it. There are the messengers, the officials of the Legislative Department, the people who run Bellamy's, the members of the two research units, the team of lawyers from parliamentary counsel's office, the members of the parliamentary press gallery, the Hansard reporters, the secretaries and the librarians. Most of them are allowed to eat in Bellamy's, a well-provisioned catering service at parliament. They share long working hours when the session

41

is on. Many of them are often together at official receptions and cocktail parties.

The world of parliament in Wellington is a strained and artificial one. Tension arises from political and personal conflict, and alcohol is often used to reduce it. Combined with the ceaseless travelling for many members, these factors make it hard for members of parliament to function as normal human beings and to sustain personal relationships. The toll upon their health and family life is also substantial.

While parliament is in session the member is required to attend from Tuesday to Friday inclusive. The house sits from 2.30 p.m. to 5.30 p.m. and from 7.30 p.m. to 10.30 p.m. on Tuesday, Wednesday, Thursday and from 9 a.m. to 1 p.m. on Friday. The member of parliament must be available between all those times in order to vote in divisions. Because the New Zealand parliament is small members' attendance is much more rigorously enforced than in other parliaments. Special leave is required for periods of absence. Most members from out of Wellington live in quite uncomfortable boarding houses near parliament while the session is on; they take all their meals at parliament itself. The meals at Bellamy's are of a high standard and cheaper than in a commercial restaurant – members are charged $1.50 for a three-course dinner.

Both National and Labour have substantial research units housed in parliament buildings. The members of the units are appointed by the party leaders and paid for from public funds. Between 1976 and 1978 each research unit had a director, six research officers, two clerical assistants and one typist. Social Credit had one full-time research officer in 1978. These research units dig up information requested by members. They prepare background papers on particular topics and speech notes. They help with the drafting of questions and notices of motion. They monitor the debates in parliament and prepare material for rebuttal. They provide information to press officers for inclusion in press statements. They keep in touch with people outside parliament sympathetic to the political party they serve, to secure comment and information on topics which come up in parliament. They draft papers and act as a secretariat to caucus committees. The central concern of the research units, however, is the quick production of information, in a simple form, for use in parliamentary debate.

The great information resource available to members of parliament is the General Assembly Library. That library has a collection of 400,000 volumes, including every book published in New Zealand, and it contains a number of unique features. It has an up to date newspaper index dating from 1924 and using 600 index headings. An index of articles, under subject headings, appearing in a multitude of periodicals under subject headings is kept. The library operates a reference service so that a trained librarian will help any member secure information on any topic. Where members have indicated a special interest, the library makes arrangements to feed them material on the subject on a continuing basis. The General Assembly Library now has a computer terminal which can provide instant access to a wide range of statistical material. These resources to provide information to members of parliament are not nearly as extensive as those available even in Australia, but it might also be observed that a fair number of members do not use the facilities extensively.

At parliament buildings other facilities are available to members of parliament. A full travel service is available. Members of parliament travel a lot and not just between their electorates and Wellington and they are all entitled to free, unlimited air travel on Air New Zealand within New Zealand and to free rail travel. They also enjoy certain concessions on overseas travel after service in more than one parliament. The number of free overseas trips available to members of parliament is considerable; most of them relate to conferences and other meetings to which members are sent as official delegates. There is considerable discussion in the caucuses, and sometimes votes, about which members should go on a trip. Members of parliament also enjoy unlimited free telephone calls all over New Zealand and free use of the telegraph and postal facilities.

The Legislative Department is headed by the clerk of the House of Representatives and his staff. These people are the professional advisers to parliament on parliamentary procedure. They provide members with guidance on procedure when requested and advise them on the presentation of petitions; they keep the journals of the house, and they provide staff to service select committees. Often the latter task entails digesting the submissions and sometimes drafting the final report. The clerk's office is responsible to the speaker for some of its functions, but the minister in charge of the Legislative Department is the prime minister. In many ways it would be better if the Legislative Department were seen to be the servant of the legislature direct and not in any way beholden to the government. An expansion of facilities to service select committees would add to the independence of parliament in relation to the executive.

During the hours the house is not in session the member of parliament has plenty to be occupied with. On Thursday mornings caucus meetings are held. On Wednesday mornings select committees are in session; sometimes they sit at other times as well. The member needs to prepare for select committee meetings – reading the bill under consideration, or reading submissions to which witnesses are going to speak. Often the member of parliament is a member of several select committees. In June 1978, ten members were on four committees and fifteen were on three. On occasions the committees will be sitting at the same time, in which case the member needs to go between one and the other. A depleted opposition always suffers from this problem.

In between the constant round of meetings and sittings in the chamber, members of parliament need to read the hundreds of bills introduced in parliament each year and the hundreds of papers tabled, look at all the regulations issued, keep up to date with the news, and prepare speeches for delivery both inside and outside the House of Representatives. Members are forced to cut corners. They cannot do everything.

In 1976 Mr Michael Minogue wrote in the *New Zealand Law Journal* about the conditions in which members of parliament are expected to carry out their functions:

. . . I prefer to tell you bluntly that in important matters neither the citizen nor the member of parliament himself is well informed; to tell you also that the idea of a representative democracy in which Parliament is supreme is becoming an increasingly dangerous popular illusion . . . The plain fact of the matter is that the Member of Parliament is a victim of procedures that afford him scant time and opportunity to inform himself. For example, the MP can go to a Committee deliberation to find himself presented at short notice with departmental recommendations which he has never seen or heard of before. (pp.485,486)

There is a paradox here. The member of parliament has both too much information to absorb properly and too little of the right type. Mr Minogue believes freedom of information will help, but it could only help if the business of parliament were conducted in a more leisurely fashion so that there was more time available to consider the important questions which are discussed there.

All the foregoing illustrates that the work load of the members of parliament is very heavy indeed. Table 1 shows the estimated number of working hours of the ordinary back-bench member when parliament is in session.

Table 1   Estimated workload of members of parliament

Duties	Hours per week
Attending to needs of constituents	10
In the debating chamber or available for divisions (some other work such as correspondence or reading can also be attended to during this time)	22
Attending meetings of select committees, caucus, caucus committees	8
Attending official functions of various types both in Wellington and in electorate	5
Preparing speeches and reading material for select committees and parliament	10
Total	55

The hours shown in Table 1 exclude travelling time which, in the case of some members, can be extensive. The times listed above would be a minimum; no doubt many members spend a great deal more time on their duties than fifty hours a week. One of the features of the job is that it can absorb all the time a person has to give it – but it is also possible to coast and disguise the fact rather well, especially if the member is experienced. If a member is on the front bench in opposition his work load will be greater than indicated above. Many speeches outside the house have to be given. Strategy meetings have to be attended. If the member is also a cabinet minister then the demands on his time increase dramatically; it is inevitable that cabinet ministers neglect some of the ordinary tasks of a member of parliament in order to provide time for ministerial duties.

These conflicting roles all raise the issue of the true function of a member of parliament. Should he be regarded as a representative of the people, speaking for them in parliament, thereby moderating the action of the government? Should he be regarded as someone who has a serious part to play in the legislative process, scrutinizing legislation to show up anomalies and to contribute policy ideas? Should he be thought of as the local trouble shooter who helps people when they are in trouble? Or should he simply be content to secure sufficient political skills by becoming an apprenticed member of the executive? Most members of parliament aspire to be in cabinet. Nothing so destroys the independence of the New Zealand House of Representatives as that expectation. Perhaps the member of parliament should be regarded as a servant and leader of the political party to which he is affiliated so that he can contribute to it ideas for policy, keep the party faithful happy and working to see that the party is elected to government? Or is the member of parliament the watchdog for the people on the actions of the executive? The member of parliament in New Zealand does something of all the functions set out above, but excels at none of them. Because the member's energies are dissipated among many activities we are in danger of losing any adequate definition of his function. It should be observed, however, that the balance of time and effort spent by individual members on the various aspects of their work varies greatly according to their own interests and talents.

In my own view the area of greatest need is in the field of legislation. The passing of laws is parliament's function. That is the task upon which members of parliament should concentrate, coupled with probing, questioning and checking the executive. Less emphasis needs to be placed on their other roles and more on those two.

What parliament does

Procedure

What happens each day in the House of Representatives is determined by the printed order paper which comes out every day parliament is in session. The daily order of business is governed by the rules under which parliament operates which are called standing orders. These rules deal with all aspects of parliamentary procedure and cover 115 pages. They are supplemented by a printed series of speakers' rulings. The order of business is dealt with by the standing orders and is the same for each day. The leader of the House of Representatives (and until 1979 this has always been the prime minister) determines in what position the various bills appear. Orders of the day must be disposed of in the order they appear and they are subject to considerable change day by day. Standing orders provide that government orders of the day have precedence over others in certain circumstances. In substance, apart from recurring items such as question time, the leader of the house effectively determines the agenda of the house. The opposition, however, determines the bills to debate at length and those it will allow to pass unchallenged. On the estimates debates, which deal with government expenditure, the opposition decides which items to debate. And the opposition can always decide to contest some items of business and offer no resistance to others.

The order of business in the house during 1976-8 was:
- private business – motions relating to the passage of private bills
- presentation of petitions – petitions are presented to the house without debate. (A petition is a request by a member or members of the public asking for appropriate action to be taken.)
- presentation of papers – many different reports and documents must be presented to parliament each year
- giving notices of motion – this provides an opportunity for an individual member to raise any matter for possible future debate
- unopposed motions for returns – where a member wants documents tabled in the house
- questions for oral answer – where members put questions to ministers and, in certain circumstances, other members
- consideration of ministerial replies to questions – every two weeks there is an opportunity for debate on ministerial replies to questions
- leave to introduce bills – opportunity for the introduction of private members' bills and local bills (government bills may be introduced at any time)
- reports of select committees – when reports of select committees are tabled
- consideration of papers – an opportunity to debate papers presented to the house. (It is not availed of frequently.)
- orders of the day and notices of motion in the order in which they appear on the order paper. (The bulk of these comprise the various stages of legislation.)
- In exceptional circumstances, an adjournment debate on a 'definite matter of urgent public importance'. (Where that occurs it is done after question time.)

The order of business does not give a complete indication of the types of business which come before parliament in full session. The work can be divided up as follows:

- dealing with legislation at various stages
- debates on government policy and other matters not connected directly with legislation (this includes the budget debate which, although formally about the appropriation bill, is considered an opportunity for discussion of economic policy generally, and imprest supply debates)
- discussion of government estimates of expenditure
- questions and answers and relevant discussion
- notices of motion and their discussion
- reports of select committees on matters other than legislation
- private members' bills

Table 2 gives some impression of the relative amount of time spent by parliament on each of the functions above. The number of pages devoted to each category in the *New Zealand Parliamentary Debates* has been counted for three two-year periods, at intervals of ten years. By these means not only does a picture emerge of the priorities of parliamentary business, but also of how those priorities have changed over the last twenty years. Such a method of analysis gives no insight into the work of parliament outside the chamber, but it does give a guide to the pattern of work in the chamber. Although the final figures for 1978 were not available at the time of writing there was in that year a reduction in the amount of time spent on legislation, but a corresponding increase in time devoted to private members' bills.

Table 2   Parliamentary time spent on categories of business according to space in *New Zealand Parliamentary Debates*

Business	Percentage of space		
	1976-7	1966-7	1956-7
Legislation	44.6	34.0	27.1
General government policy	19.1	24.2	41.4
Expenditure	6.8	11.7	9.3
Questions and answers*	19.6	15.9	10.0
Reports of select committees**	0.8	3.4	4.0
Private members' bills	1.9	2.9	4.4
Notices of motion	4.1	6.1	2.4
Miscellaneous	3.1	1.8	1.4

*excludes those dealt with by written reply
**excludes those dealing with legislation

Parliament and money

Lack of financial resources is a major constraint on the policies of any government. And since spending by central government in New Zealand ‚amounted in 1976 to 40 per cent of gross national product, financial management is of crucial importance. Cabinet is the chief financial manager of government, and the two most important sources of power are the cabinet committees on the economy and expenditure. The key figure is the minister of finance, the major link between Treasury (the first in importance among the departments of state) and cabinet. Treasury is in charge of vetting all applications for public expenditure. It reports to cabinet on new proposals and an adverse Treasury report can spell death for new proposals. The Treasury has general overall responsibility for public finance and advice on economic and fiscal policy. The Treasury is in charge of compiling the government accounts. In recent years a systematic but complex process of assessing new policies has been instituted, spearheaded by the cabinet committee on expenditure. The easiest way to understand the structure of government's financial decision-making is to examine Figure 1.

Figure 1   Government's financial decision-making structure

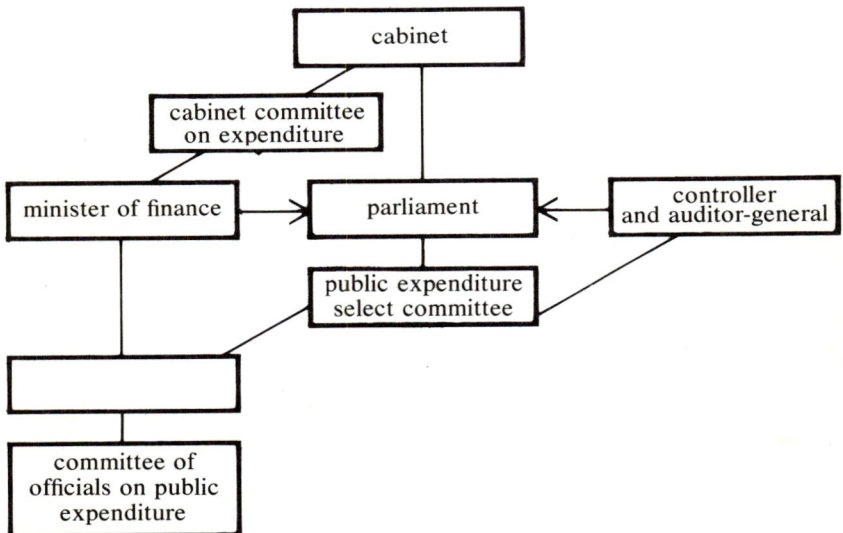

Two important tasks are carried out in the structure set out above: first, the decision on how much money government should spend and what it should be spent on; second, an examination to see that the money was spent on those things for which its expenditure was approved. In the year ended 31 March 1979 total government expenditure was estimated to be $7,751 million, which gives some idea of the magnitude of the appropriation function.

Many items of government expenditure are governed by the Public Finance Act 1977. The fundamental provision states: 'No expenditure of public money shall be made except pursuant to an appropriation Act of Parliament.' (s.53) Around that fact all the control systems function. The main appropriation in each year is included in the appropriation bill which accompanies the budget, which is the government's principal annual statement of economic policy. When government requires money in anticipation of the budget, an imprest supply bill is introduced.

The government is also obliged to set out its demand for money in detailed estimates which break down expenditure department by department. Those estimates are the subject of sixteen days' scrutiny in parliament, with the opposition having the power to decide which items to delve into and which to pass over. The Public Finance Act 1977 also makes provision for the expenditure of money 'in excess of or without the appropriation of Parliament' (s.55) subject to a limit of 2.5 per cent of the amount appropriated for the year where state servants have had an increase in pay or by 1.5 per cent otherwise. In 1974–5 and 1975–6 parliamentary appropriations were overspent by 5 per cent and 5.7 per cent. During the first three months of a financial year, money can be expended in anticipation of parliament making an appropriation. The provision is important because it means that parliament must be called together before the end of June in each year or the money will run out. Without supply, government cannot continue. That fact is potentially the biggest check of all on executive action.

When the Treasury has prepared the public accounts they must be forwarded to the Audit Office for audit. The controller and auditor-general has most important functions in checking executive action. Basically his office determines, by financial auditing methods, whether the money was spent in the manner authorized by parliament. The Audit Office audits:

- all public money and public stores
- all money and stores of a local authority
- many public bodies which are not government departments – it can be made auditor of statutory corporations and government owned companies

The Audit Office has extended powers to review the procedures of those government agencies it audits to see that resources 'have been applied effectively and efficiently in a manner that is consistent with the applicable policy of the government, agency, or local authority . . .'. (*Public Finance Act 1977,* s.25) The Audit Office cannot be the subject of orders from the minister of finance or any other minister; it reports to parliament. It is independent in a true sense. It is subject only to statute, and the relevant statute gives the Audit Office very wide powers.

In his annual report to parliament the auditor-general reviews faults he has found in government accounting. He analyses cases of over-expenditure, such as the Auckland International Airport Terminal, or the 'low standard of financial management and reporting in many areas of the education system'. (*Report,* 1978, p.13) He points out what went wrong, who was to blame and how such trouble can be avoided in the future. The publication of these reports exercises a salutary effect on those departments and local authorities whose financial control procedures are erratic.

In addition, the auditor-general now investigates the adequacy of general financial systems within government. In 1978 the *Report of the Controller and Auditor-General on Financial Management and Control in Administrative Government Departments* disclosed a serious situation. The findings are so important, the summary of conclusions will be set out in full:

2.1　Financial management in administrative departments is mediocre and lacks positive leadership. The focus of attention has been confined for too long to the narrow purpose of keeping expenditure within estimates. Although many departments are large and complex institutions with significant semi-commercial activities, the potential for effective management of resources has not been recognised.

2.2　There is a serious shortage of competent accountants able to provide a proper financial management service. Because of the absence of an obvious career structure, failure to recognise the appropriate status of accountants within departments, and the high percentage of retirements over the next few years, the problem could soon become critical.

2.3　Estimating procedures and approval systems are too rigid and complex. These are creating disincentives to good management and leading to unnecessary expenditure.

2.4　The centralised Government accounting system is not meeting the requirements of many departments.

2.5　Accountability to Parliament is inadequate. The Estimates and departmental reports do not contain sufficient information on the objectives and functions of departmental programmes, achievement of goals, or the full costs involved.

2.6　The functions of the inspection and regulatory agencies have not been sufficiently rationalised and modernised in their approach to place the activities of Government under an efficient and effective system of review.

2.7　The absence of direction from control agencies and the general failure to appreciate the proper role of senior departmental financial officers have been the primary causes of the problems identified.

2.8　The most significant change required is the establishment of the position of Chief Accountant of Government and the appointment to that post of a person of outstanding ability. Only if there is positive leadership in financial management can an effective and continuing programme of professional development of financial staff be established to provide management with the advice it so badly needs for the efficient use of resources.

2.9   Management should be more accountable for the use of resources entrusted to them. Wider systems of decentralised budgetary control should be introduced. Accounting systems and reports must be improved.

2.10   More flexibility is required to enable departments to plan their activities and gain better value for money. The Government balance date should be changed to 30 June with retention of the present budget cycle. (p.7)

It was heartening to see that in December 1978 the prime minister announced the formation of a Treasury task-force to spearhead financial management reforms in government. The move followed the report referred to above. The prime minister stated that it was imperative to see that the government followed the best management practices to 'give people value for the taxes they pay'. (*Evening Post,* 2 December 1978, p.8)

Complementing the watchdog role of the auditor-general is parliament's Public Expenditure Committee, one of parliament's more effective select committees. In the view of many observers, however, it could be much more effective if it had available more expert assistance independent of government. Its functions are to:
- examine departmental estimates and report what economies may be effected
- examine public accounts and the accounts of other undertakings in receipt of money appropriated by parliament
- carry out special examinations of administration
- investigate particular aspects of government spending, usually by sub-committees

Prior to the estimates of expenditure being debated in parliament they are scrutinized by the Public Expenditure Committee. Departmental officials attend and can be asked to elucidate the estimates. Information so obtained can be used later in the house during debate. Close investigation by the Public Expenditure Committee can be a searching experience for government officials. Indeed Mr R.D. Muldoon, who was once chairman of the committee, is reported as saying 'the chief weapon that the committee had was to make the various departmental people apprehensive about an investigation.' (quoted by McRobie in *Political Science,* vol. 26, p.41) Much depends upon effective chairmanship of this committee for it to have real impact.

The reports of the auditor-general provide a fruitful list of subjects for special investigation by the committee. Over the years sub-committees of the main committee (sometimes chaired by opposition members in a precedent which should be expanded) have conducted investigations into a host of subjects. Some of the most recent include:
- pillaging of cargo
- hospital board budgeting
- expenditure on fisheries patrol vessel *Ngati Moki*

- expenditure on 'The Governor' television programme by TV1 which was budgeted at a target of $365,850 in August 1976, but actually cost $705,000 by the time it was finished in May 1977
- use of vehicles by government departments

The reports are thorough. They are much enhanced by the work of well qualified advisory officers on the staff of the clerk of the House of Representatives, who service the committee. The recommendations of the Public Expenditure Committee are often heeded by the government. Government action is encouraged by the committee's practice of reporting each year on what progress has been made in implementing recommendations made in previous years. It is unfortunate, however, that the house rarely takes the opportunity to reinforce this by debating Public Expenditure Committee reports.

In 1977 the Public Expenditure Committee reported upon whether the public should be allowed access to meetings of the committee. The proposal was that the public and representatives of the press should be allowed to attend committee hearings at which the use of public money was under examination. The committee took the general view that the proposal should not be followed because it 'would not be in the public interest'. That view follows a paternalistic tradition of public availability of information in New Zealand. The argument which carried weight with the committee was that 'unhindered publication of information which, at the material time, could be incomplete, inaccurate or, to a third party under certain circumstances, misleading' was undesirable. (*Interim Report*, p.3) I do not find this reasoning convincing. Information and publicity are fundamental to effective parliamentary scrutiny. And if members of parliament are doing some of their best work on the committee, that fact should be brought to the attention of the public. It is argued that officials would be less candid if hearings were in public. Officials should be candid about the public's business and if the minister were also present during questioning they should have no fear in being frank. The fact that the equivalent committee in the United Kingdom parliament decided to open its proceedings on an experimental basis should be a lesson to New Zealand.

While the Public Expenditure Committee has had some success, it has not ensured, as the auditor-general's report set out above confirms, that parliamentary scrutiny of government expenditure is adequate.

The weaknesses of the New Zealand Public Expenditure Committee, as discussed by Ms Adrienne von Tunzelmann, are:

- a practice of approving the estimates too quickly without comment and not reporting to the house on them; in particular, examination of the supplementary estimates is cursory
- insufficient efforts by members to seek information across the whole range of government administration
- lack of parliamentary debate on the committee's work

- sometimes only sketchy information is supplied by the government as to why recommendations were not implemented
- the fact that the committee sits in private
- lack of time to carry out its work
- the lack of expert advisers independent of the government sector
- inability to scrutinize long-term planning proposals of the government
- the committee is prohibited from examining matters of government policy

Efforts should be made to remedy all the weaknesses catalogued above in order to make the Public Expenditure Committee a much more potent check on the decisions to spend public money by the executive arm of government.

Notices of motion

Notices of motion have become something of a farce in the New Zealand parliament. The parliamentary press gallery seems to have decided, wisely, that they are best not reported. Some examples are set out from the House of Representatives order paper of 30 August 1978.

Mr Lange to move, That this House deplores the delay of the Attorney-General in entering a stay of proceedings in respect of the Bastion Point prosecutions so that about one-quarter of the defendants are now convicted and three-quarters can never be because of the Attorney-General's action; demands that he take immediate steps to have the convictions already entered vacated so that justice will not be seen to depend on the accident of one's order on a Court list; requires an explanation from him as to how convictions were entered in the Magistrate's Court at Auckland against a number of defendants after his stay of proceedings had been announced; and deplores his past and present clumsy political interventions in the judicial process. (p.1347)

Mr Malcolm to move, That this House notes that the Leader of the Opposition held a meeting in Eden last night attended by 600-odd people, many of whom bused in from adjoining electorates, compared with close to 1000 local people the Prime Minister attracted last time he spoke in the area, and notes that the meeting was stormy, which is to be expected in an astute electorate such as Eden which has no faith in the credibility of either the Labour Party or its present leader, and that this House respectfully suggests that the Leader of the Opposition would be well advised to concede Eden to National and direct his efforts towards protecting his own marginal seat of Tasman where he is under great threat from the dynamic Ruth Richardson. (p.1349)

Mr Kirk to move, That this House notes in this morning's edition of the New Zealand Herald that the member for East Coast Bays received a rubbishing from the Auckland Hospital Board which said that statements in a newsletter put out by the member were inaccurate; that the member did not know at what stage of development the North Shore Hospital was; and that the member's claim that a children's hospital was being designed and built was also incorrect; and that this House asks, if the Minister of Health is so abysmally ignorant about hospital developments in his own electorate, what hope is there for the rational development of our health system with the current Minister? (p.1353)

Mr Falloon to move, That this House notes with some gentle cynicism the fact that the member for Rangitikei who came into the House determined to raise the standard of debate and reduce the level of interjection and rowdiness which he claims existed before his entry, managed to make 12 rowdy interjections in the first 3 minutes of a speech of the Minister of Education during the education estimates. (p.1356)

Opinions will differ upon the efficacy of these attacks. The first is a criticism of a ministerial action, perfectly appropriate but perhaps better made by other means. The second is an effort at party political embarrassment. The third draws attention to criticism made of a minister and attempts to use it to embarrass him. The last is a similar attempt in relation to the leader of the Social Credit Party. In sum, notices of motion are attempts at political point scoring; they have attracted some criticism even within parliament. On 27 October 1977 the acting speaker Mr J.R. Harrison complained about the increased numbers of notices of motion. In *New Zealand Parliamentary Debates* he is quoted as saying:

. . . it appears to me that some of the notices of motion are repetitious, if not tedious; some border on the frivolous; some appear to be more interested in the person of a member than the policy of a party; and some contain accusations that make it difficult for me to decide whether or not to accept the motions on the ground of whether they can be authenticated, but I suppose I must accept them as posing material for debate. I invite members to reconsider their attitudes to notices of motion. I am quite happy to vet them as far as I can – which is to a very limited extent – and to accept them, but I doubt very much whether they really achieve anything to the benefit of parliament as a whole. (vol. 415, p.3984)

The procedure should be reconsidered. It could be abolished with little loss. In the United Kingdom notices of motion are set down on the order paper without being read out, an improvement on the New Zealand practice.

Petitions

The right to petition parliament for redress of grievances is acknowledged as a fundamental principle of our constitution. It is a right which goes as far back as parliament itself. Petitions on a wide variety of topics are presented to parliament. There were 33 petitions presented in 1978, 41 presented in 1977 and 35 in 1976. Some petitions call for an alteration in the general law; others ask for some reconsideration of an administrative decision. Everyone has the right to present a petition and it is the function of parliament to consider the petition and make recommendations to government about what should be done.

Petitions must comply with the standing orders of the House. They must be couched in temperate and respectful language. They normally will be presented to parliament by the member from whose electorate the petitioner comes. They are then referred by the clerk of the House to a select committee. Petitions can be debated in the House only if the select committees to which they were referred say that they have no recommendation to make. That is rare as the committee has a range of recommendations open to it. Petitions can be referred to the government for inquiry, consideration, favourable consideration, most favourable consideration or any other purpose.

There are a number of limitations upon petitions. If legal proceedings could be taken, the house will not receive the petition. If the matter is one which could be the subject of complaint to the ombudsmen, it will not be considered. Neither will one on the same subject matter of an earlier petition unless new evidence is available. Petitions not dealt with during the life of a parliament lapse. That was the fate of nineteen petitions in 1978.

Notwithstanding these limitations, petitions have not infrequently borne fruit in New Zealand. They are an important safety valve in the political process – a last resort when there is no other hope of action. The petition against raising the level of Lake Manapouri is perhaps the most dramatic example in recent years. Each year the government is obliged to table in the house a report of what action it has taken on petitions referred to it. Quite explicit statements are made about what the government has and has not done. The 1977 report shows the sort of topics that petitions deal with:

- opposition to nuclear power stations and nuclear powered ships
- opposition to further alienation of Maori land
- asking that a decision to defer provision of a free-calling telephone service in South Auckland be reconsidered
- asking for an investigation of the problem of excess noise
- asking that 'God Defend New Zealand' be adopted as the national anthem
- asking that Sunday trading be allowed
- asking for a review of immigration policy
- asking that Wellington airport not be extended into Evans Bay
- asking that restrictions on the employment of relief teachers be withdrawn
- asking for regulations to protect spawning grounds and fishing grounds in the Firth of Thames and Hauraki Gulf
- asking for alterations in the plans of the Christchurch urban motorway
- asking for a full public inquiry into the financing and importation of illicit drugs
- asking that the Health Department be empowered to register and de-register doctors
- asking for repeal of the law prohibiting fortune telling
- concerning the termination of rail services
- concerning hospital extensions
- asking for change in the law so adopted people could have access to their original birth registrations
- concerning the law relating to abortion

On a number of these petitions government was able to report action or development which went some distance towards meeting the goal of the petitioners. Just three examples from the *Report on Parliamentary Petitions* for 1977 are given:

Petition No.   *Name*
28/1976   G H Latta and 7,750 others

Subject of Petition
Praying that 'God Defend New Zealand' be adopted as the National Anthem.

Nature of Order of the House Referring Petition to the Government
Referred to the Government for favourable consideration.

Decision of the Government
After consultation with Her Majesty The Queen, the Government placed on record by formal notice in the Gazette its decision that the two songs 'God Save the Queen' and 'God Defend New Zealand' have equal status as national anthems. 'God Save the Queen' would be more specially appropriate when loyalty to the crown is to be stressed and 'God Defend New Zealand' whenever the national identity of New Zealand is to be stressed.

Petition No.   *Name*
34/1976   I D Williamson and 73 others

Subject of Petition
Praying for the retention of the regulations protecting the spawning grounds and inshore fishing grounds in the Firth of Thames and the Hauraki Gulf.

Nature of Order of the House Referring Petition to the Government
Referred to the Government for most favourable consideration.

Decision of the Government
The Fisheries (General) Regulations 1950, Amendments No 25 and No 26 made on 27 June and 29 August 1977 respectively met the prayer of the petition.

Petition No.   *Name*
35/1976   R Ross and 740 others

Subject of Petition
Praying that the restrictions on the employment of relief teachers be withdrawn.

Nature of Order of the House Referring Petition to the Government
Referred to the Government for consideration.

Decision of the Government
Restrictions on the employment of relief teachers were withdrawn and the relief scheme re-introduced with minor modifications with effect from the second term of 1977.

The petition procedure has strengths but it could be improved. In 1978 the Repeal organization presented a petition to parliament containing 321,119 signatures. It was reported to be the third largest petition ever presented to parliament. It was considered by a select committee which was not open to the news media. It was not debated in the House. Hearings should be open and more opportunity for debate on petitions should be permitted. The report of the government on what action it has taken should be published.

Questions

Parliamentary questions offer members an important opportunity to question and probe the ministers of the crown concerning the administration of their departments. Much information is elicited by parliamentary questions each year and a good deal of it is information which would not otherwise become available to the public. Over 2,000 questions are asked in a usual year of parliamentary sittings.

Questions may be put to a minister relating to public affairs with which he is officially connected. Notice in writing must be given of questions; they are printed on the order paper. Replies must be concise and confined to the subject matter of the question. When the answer has been given, members have the opportunity to ask supplementary questions. Each day the house sits, forty minutes are devoted to the asking and answering of questions. Questions can also be dealt with in writing without being asked in the house and if questions are not reached they are dealt with in writing and printed in the records of parliamentary debates.

Questions are asked in parliament on many different topics for many different purposes. Some examples of the most common techniques will be given. First come the Dorothy Dix questions – questions asked of a minister by one of his political allies – to allow the minister to show himself and the government in a good light. The member knows the answer before he asks the question, but some of parliament's listening audience may not. An example is Mr Lambert's question of 17 August 1978:

Mr Lambert (Western Hutt) to the Minister of Social Welfare: Is it correct that the new national superannuation rates will be so much better than the old pension scheme under Labour that the loss of pensioner concessions will be made up in a fortnight?
Hon. H.J. Walker (Minister of Social Welfare): The net rates of national superannuation from 31 August 1978 will be higher than the rates of age benefit had that benefit been retained, to the extent of the $14.02 a week for married couples and $7.39 a week for single persons. The combined value of the telephone and television licence concessions is $1.65 a week, or $85.80 a year.
(*New Zealand Parliamentary Debates,* vol. 420, p.2736)

The reverse of the above type of question occurs when a member who has a shrewd idea of the answer to his question seeks to embarrass the government with it. Sir Basil Arthur's question to the postmaster-general on 11 August 1978 is such a question:

Hon. Sir Basil Arthur (Timaru) to the Postmaster-General: Can he confirm that, while there was no waiting list for telephones in Timaru as at 30 November 1975, as at 31 May 1978 the telephone waiting list in Timaru had climbed to 97, and can he advise the people of Timaru at what stage he intends to start putting into effect National's 1975 manifesto promise to reduce telephone waiting lists?

Hon. P.I. Wilkinson (Postmaster-General): As at 31 May last, as the member states, 97 applicants were awaiting telephone service in the Timaru district, as opposed to the city – 73 fewer than at 30 November 1975, when 170 applicants were on the district waiting list. The nil waiting list mentioned so eagerly by the member for Timaru for 30 November 1975 was for Timaru City only. National has implemented its 1975 manifesto promise. The national waiting list has been reduced from a peak of 30,288 at 31 May 1977 to 22,629 at 30 June 1978. At the end of this year the list is expected to be less than 20,000 – the lowest in more than 5 years, including the 3-year period of the last Labour Government.

(New Zealand Parliamentary Debates, vol. 419, p.2567)

Sir Basil Arthur's question contains another element which is a frequent feature of parliamentary questions. Members ask questions which relate specifically to their own electorates and elicit information of local interest. Sometimes such questions may even have the effect of committing the government publicly. Take the following question asked on 23 August 1978:

Marilyn Waring (Raglan) on behalf of Mr Wellington (Manurewa) to the Minister of Education: When will the Weymouth High School open?

Hon. E.W. Gandar (Minister of Education): The proposed opening date for the new Weymouth secondary school is February, 1982.

(New Zealand Parliamentary Debates, vol. 420, p.2836)

Sometimes members will ask a series of questions designed to build up a body of information on a particular topic or policy which can be used later in other debates or in some other way. Constituents or pressure groups may be interested in having information on a topic.

To intervene on another member's question by means of a supplementary question is a technique often used, with varying results. The following lengthy extract quoted from the *New Zealand Parliamentary Debates* of 4 November 1976 illustrates some of the problems which can arise in the questions procedure:

Mr H. N. AUSTIN (Hobson) asked the Minister of Education, Is it correct that the Whangarei Girls High School was forced to run fund-raising activities to extricate itself from a difficult financial situation, and, if so, why was this action necessary?

Hon. G. F. GAIR (Minister of Housing): I reply on behalf of the Minister of Education. It is not correct that the Whangarei Girls High School was forced to run fund-raising activities to extricate itself from a difficult financial situation.

Mr H. N. Austin: Was this fund-raising activity instigated by the high school board?

Hon. G. F. GAIR: It was not. I have an interesting letter from—

Hon. Dr A. M. Finlay: Just by coincidence.

Hon. G. F. GAIR: In reply to the honourable member's interjection, I believe in equipping myself with a well-prepared answer when I am asked to answer a question in the House. I took the trouble of discussing this matter with the Minister of Education who entrusted me with the task of replying. I have a copy of a letter from Mr K. G. Scudder, who is the chairman of the Whangarei High Schools Board, and there are several parts of this letter which would be of interest. The letter is addressed to Mr Gandar and dated 18 October, and reads: 'I was amazed and more than a little disconcerted by the reported comments of Mr Jonathan Hunt in the House on 14 October 1976. I therefore feel obliged in fairness to one of my schools to write and correct any misconceptions that may have arisen. I can assure you and your department that Mr Hunt must have received his information from some source other than either the High Schools Board or the principal of Whangarei Girls High School. If as was reported Mr Hunt claimed that a raffle of a car was run by the school to extricate itself from a difficult financial situation he was quite incorrect. The girls' high school has operated within its general purposes allocation and was at no stage in the red. The car raffle was a normal fund-raising activity carried out by the school's parent-teacher association to provide extra library books and other equipment for the school. The idea originated from the parent-teacher association and was not instigated by the board. It was however approved by the board after certain conditions and legal points had been written into the proposals. The fact that the raffle was a success did mean that the girls' high school was in a better position financially than the three other schools under my board's control at the end of the financial year. It must be remembered, and I hope it was pointed out to Mr Hunt, that the problems secondary schools have had with the general purposes grant and budgeting during 1973, 1974, and 1975 were in the main caused by the interminable delay in settling the grant and informing secondary school boards, for which Mr Hunt and Mr Amos, and their Administration must take full responsibility.'

Mr SPEAKER: Order! Although the letter is, I feel, relevant to the question, it is of such length I feel that unless it is coming towards the end we must not let it proceed. Is it almost finished?

Hon. G. F. GAIR: I have two very short sentences to read, which, I believe, will put this whole thing in perspective—'Since you have been Minister'—that is, since Mr Gandar had been the Minister of Education—'we have had an increase in the grant, and we do know what we are getting. Naturally, we would like more, but we can and will be able to budget and operate far more efficiently than we have been able to for nearly 3 years.'

Mr Hunt: Is the Minister aware that the information I was given was given to me by the secretary of the Post-Primary Teachers Association? [Interruption]. Perhaps I could start again?

Mr SPEAKER: Order!

Hon. W. L. Young: I think it would be better if you stopped.

Mr SPEAKER: Order! I will not have members interjecting while I am on my feet. In view of the continuous interjection from many quarters it is quite reasonable that the member should be allowed to repeat his question.

Mr Hunt: Is the Minister aware that I was given the information that I used in good faith by—

Mr Talbot: Now we are getting it.

Mr Hunt: Keep quiet, small change, or you will get spent. I will start again. Is the Minister aware that I was given the information that I used in good faith by the secretary of the Post-Primary Teachers Association that morning; secondly, that that information had been given to the secretary by the principal of that school, and the president of the Post-Primary Teachers Association branch; thirdly, is the Minister aware that notwithstanding the comments of the chairman of the board, that this money was needed for library books and essential scientific equipment to enable university entrance students to sit their university entrance examination in the practical requirements phase; and finally, is the Minister aware that this question is obviously planted?

Mr Birch: A point of order, Mr Speaker. It is quite out of order to ask a series of supplementary questions in the way in which the member endeavoured to ask them, and I believe that the member should be asked to withdraw them.

Hon. M. Rata: Taking into account the Minister's extremely long and controversial reply, which the member for New Lynn had not had access to until it was read by the Minister, and as it contained comment which the House had no access to, clearly the member was entitled at least to ask the questions that he asked as a result of the answer. In view of the time accorded the Minister, it is right that the member for New Lynn should be accorded the same extended time that the Minister had.

Hon. G. F. GAIR: Speaking to the point of order, I personally have no objection to the series of questions, although I believe the member for Franklin was perfectly correct in raising the point of order. However, in reply to the new point raised by the member for Northern Maori, the comment in my answer to the supplementary question asked by the member for Hobson was not my comment; it was the comment of the chairman of the board of governors of the Whangarei high schools.

Mr Hunt: Yes, and who's he? A rank Tory, I'll be bound.

Hon. G. F. GAIR: I did not hear the member.

Mr Hunt: A member of the National Party, I'll be bound.

Hon. G. F. GAIR: The member is allowing his partisanship to get the better of his judgment. It is quite obvious that he has been used, and allowed himself to be misused, by the secretary of the local PPTA.

Mr Hunt: No, the secretary in Wellington—one of your negotiating people.

Hon. G. F. GAIR: When the member makes an allegation in the House, he must be prepared to listen to the facts in the answer.

Mr Hunt: Obviously the member for Franklin did have a point when he raised the point of order, and I quite freely acknowledge that I did ask my question with a series of supplementary questions. I am perfectly prepared to rephrase the question and put it in the form of one question, if that would suit the convenience of the House.

Hon. E. S. F. Holland: I wish to refer to two rulings. The first is Speaker's ruling 116/3: 'A member may not ask several supplementary questions in the form of one.' That is precisely what the honourable member was doing. The other is Speaker's ruling 115/6, which states: 'It is irregular to preface a supplementary question with the words ''Is the Minister aware'' and then proceed with a massive statement of fact.' Which is also precisely what the member was doing. I suggest that he was offending both Speakers' rulings.

Mr SPEAKER: I have no doubt, as is in fairness admitted by the member for New Lynn, that the point is properly raised, and that the question is defective in two regards—first, it was a series of about six questions wrapped into one, and secondly it started with 'Is the Minister aware' which was followed by a string of what were intended to be questions but which became a speech. It does not matter whether the Minister says yes or no; the effect has been achieved by the misuse of the question system. I did not intervene because I thought the quotation in the answer of the Minister had been of too great length, and although it may well have been germane to an earlier statement which I do not remember, it was of such a nature that I thought it was fair that I should not be too rapid in rushing in when the member for New Lynn transgressed. I think the best procedure at this stage is for us to proceed with the next question.

Mr Hunt: I wonder if I could rephrase my supplementary question because it was the first one from this side of the House. I shall rephrase it in a short, concise way.

Mr SPEAKER: Very well.

Mr Hunt: As the information was given to me by the president and secretary of the New Zealand Post-Primary Teachers Association, would the Minister be prepared to accept from them a letter of explanation and then give me the facts he has there?

Hon. G. F. GAIR: I should be very pleased to convey the member's request to the Minister of Education. I am sure he would welcome any explanation that the president and the secretary of the PPTA might have to offer for the way in which the member has been misled. I believe the House is entitled to know certain of the facts. The financial position of the Whangarei Girls High School as at 31 January—

Mr Hunt: Oh, this isn't fair.

Mr SPEAKER: Order! As we have already had a lengthy quotation that has covered the same ground, I think this has gone far enough. I shall allow two more supplementary questions.

Mr Kirk: As the Minister supplied Mr Skudder's name and read his letter to square off a political argument, is Mr Skudder a member of the National Party?

Hon. G. F. GAIR: I have no idea. I know him to be the chairman of the Whangarei High Schools Board.

Mr Moyle: Would the Minister like our help?

Hon. G. F. GAIR: Mr Speaker, you apparently did not want to allow me to answer the first part of the question asked by the member for New Lynn. It was a long one, but he did raise several questions that stand unanswered. I was going to give only the bare figures.

Mr SPEAKER: Order! We are wasting a lot of time on this, and unless we get on with it—and there have been interruptions from members on both sides—I shall move on to the next question.

Mr Wellington: Could the Minister say why the member for New Lynn did not check the veracity of the information he was given with the board of governors, which has the final responsibility in these matters?

Hon. G. F. GAIR: I cannot account for the failure of the member for New Lynn to do what one would have expected him to do in the circumstances. All I can say is that the facts are available and they are quite indisputable.

Mr Prebble: A point of order, Mr Speaker. The member for Manurewa asked the Minister why another member did not do something. The Minister is certainly not responsible for the actions of other members, and he has been asked for an opinion. It was not a proper question at all.

Hon. David Thomson: The Minister may be asked about matters other than those connected with his portfolio. As I recall the appropriate Standing Order, he may be asked about matters of general public interest. Standing Order 75 states: 'Questions may be put to a Minister relating to public affairs with which he is officially connected, to proceedings in the House, or to any matter of administration for which he is responsible.' That certainly covers the question.

Mr SPEAKER: Standing Order 75 is the relevant Standing Order. However, there is not much profit in asking a Minister why another member did not do a, b, or c, so I do not think we will pursue the matter.

Mr Marshall: Could the Minister confirm that the question of financial difficulties for secondary schools has been a matter of widespread comment in recent weeks, and that as recently as 2 days ago there was a report in the *Evening Post*—

Mr SPEAKER: Order! This is not relevant to the question, which deals with a specific school. Now it seems we are to have a quotation from a newspaper, or a supplementary question ostensibly seeking elucidation of something that is far away from the original question, which related to Whangarei Girls High School.

Mr Marshall: Could I rephrase my question?

Mr SPEAKER: As long as it relates to the original question.

Mr Marshall: Could the Minister confirm that the question of financial difficulties in secondary schools, to which the original question related, is by now a matter of considerable concern throughout the country?

Hon. G. F. GAIR: I believe there is an element of misunderstanding, partly generated by the Labour Opposition, but the facts tend to disprove the allegation made by the honourable member. The general expenses grant in the last Labour Budget for the Whangarei Girls High School was $16,990 for the 1975–76 year. This covered miscellaneous running costs, class materials, school prizes, minor equipment repairs, heat, light, and power.

Mr Isbey: A point of order, Mr Speaker. The Minister is reading that letter again, and not replying to the question.

Hon. G. F. GAIR: Speaking to the point of order, Mr Speaker, I have here a series of figures written on a piece of paper showing the state of the general expenses account at this school over a period of years.

Mr Isbey: Would the Minister table it?

Hon. G. F. GAIR: I should be pleased to table it. When the point of order is disposed of, I am sure I will be invited to complete my answer to the honourable member for Wanganui.

Hon. Dr A. M. Finlay: Speaking to the point of order, Mr Speaker, I draw your attention to the original question, which asked, whether the school was required to run fund-raising activities for a particular purpose, and, if so why the action was necessary. Both questions are simple and they have both been simply answered. I find it difficult to determine how any further elucidation can be given by this lengthy process.

Mr SPEAKER: The point is properly raised. It is one that could be raised in respect of nearly every ostensibly elucidatory question ever asked in this House or in the House of Commons, where I have heard the same procedure. The position is that we started off with a question about Whangarei Girls High School. After some manoeuvring, and spending far too much time, we now have a question about school administration over New Zealand as a whole. The Minister can answer briefly if he wishes.

Hon. G. F. GAIR: The allegation in the honourable member's question was not correct, particularly in the case of the Whangarei Girls High School. In 1975–76 $16,990 was allocated for this purpose. This year it was $19,253, an increase of $2,263, or 13.3 percent. I would also make the point that in 1975 the first payment was not made to the high school until May; this year the first payment was made in February.

Question transferred to Supplementary Order Paper. (vol. 407, pp. 3633–6)

The Speaker

The lengthy extract just quoted serves to illustrate a number of points. It shows the procedural twists and tangles that parliament can so easily fall into. It demonstrates the point-scoring nature of so much that is done there. It illustrates the party political nature of so much of the contest. And it shows how easily questions of personality can be interpolated into the proceedings. Above all, however, it demonstrates the key role of the speaker in controlling the proceedings of the house. The way in which the speaker discharges his responsibilities is an important influence in setting the standard of debate in regard to both its propriety and its relevance to the matter being discussed. The speaker is responsible for keeping order. When the speaker stands up, any member speaking must be silent and resume his seat. He is responsible for ensuring that the standing orders governing debate are observed. He is empowered to direct a member to discontinue his speech if that member 'persists in irrelevance or tedious repetition'. (Standing order 204). He can order members whose conduct is 'grossly disorderly to withdraw immediately from the House during the remainder of that day's sitting'. (Standing order 205) The speaker is also able to name and suspend a member who flouts the authority of the chair, although suspension requires the agreement of the house. And in the event of grave disorder, the speaker can 'if he thinks it necessary to do so' adjourn the house.

Mr Speaker occupies a position of great historical importance. That position in New Zealand today seems to have lost much power and prestige. The speaker invariably is the nominee of the party in government, a fact which erodes his independence. There is no constitutional reason why the speaker needs to be a member of the governing party; it is so because each party when in power feels the need to have one of its own members presiding over proceedings. The speaker is the chairman of the important debates in the house; he rules on points of order and controls proceedings generally. Impartial chairmanship demands detachment and neutrality. A speaker of real independence would present dangers to a government, as its ability to control proceedings in the house would be reduced. Speakers do protect the rights of the minority and do not accede to every request made by the government members. But it is too much to expect party politicians, whose political survival depends upon the party to which they belong, to treat their adversaries with detachment and neutrality. They actually do much better in that direction than may be expected given the circumstances.

A number of steps could be taken to remedy the current situation. The speaker could be chosen from outside the house. The Social Credit Political League said in its 1978 election manifesto (p. 50) that its policy was to appoint 'a member of the High Judiciary' to be speaker of parliament. The difficulty with the proposal is that a parliamentary background is probably necessary for the chairman of parliament. A more realistic proposal is for a person to be elected to the office of speaker on a free vote. The person could vacate his seat in parliament, sever connection with his former colleagues and continue as speaker for a fixed term of years, regardless of which party was in power. It is my belief that real independence in the chair would contribute to elevating the standard of debate and the conduct of members of parliament.

An independent speaker would be encouraged to use his powers fearlessly to promote dignified standards of conduct in parliament. But more should be done. The standing orders should be altered to limit the time for many of the debates in parliament. No single step would do more to improve their quality. The amount of repetition, irrelevance and tedium which results from an unlimited number of speeches on each side is substantial.

All members of the New Zealand parliament have a large desk in the chamber. Members speak from this desk. They can easily use it for the accommodation of bulky notes and even lean on it during the delivery of a speech. The desks encourage a tendency for members to read their speeches, even though this is prohibited by standing orders. If there were no desks, as in other parliaments, members would say what they wanted to say and sit down. Debates would be crisper and more spontaneous. Mr F. D. O'Flynn Q.C., Member of Parliament, first brought this matter to my attention. He advocates the removal of desks. I think he is right.

Privilege

The ancient and technical matter called parliamentary privilege also needs to be clarified. The New Zealand House of Representatives enjoys the same privileges as the House of Commons in Great Britain as on 1 January 1865. Those privileges seem to include the power to fine and imprison. The New Zealand House of Representatives fined a banker £500 in 1896 for refusing to supply information asked for by a select committee. Journalists have also been fined on two occasions in New Zealand.

Parliament must be able to protect its own proceedings. Outsiders cannot be permitted to interfere with its freedom of debate. But the range of parliamentary privilege and the capacity of parliament to punish outsiders is a vague area of the law. There are unresolved difficulties about the rights of courts to intervene. In recent times, however, the New Zealand House of Representatives has shown an unwelcome tendency to use the procedure for breach of privilege more frequently. Recent examples include the following:

- In 1968 a newspaper headline 'Statistical Claim is made that Four M.P.s in N.Z. are probably Homosexual' was branded a breach of privilege, although in view of the editor's expression of regret no further action was taken. (*New Zealand Parliamentary Debates*, vol. 358, p. 2725)

- Several cases where publication in the news media of what occurred in select committee hearings not open to the public have been held a breach of privilege.

- An editorial saying that the speaker of the house was willing to permit derogatory interjections based on racial prejudice and that he would not intervene to stop them was declared to be a serious breach of privilege and the editor was censured although no further action was taken when the editor expressed his regret.

- Statements in a television interview with a transvestite, in which it was alleged that there was a member of parliament who was a homosexual and a number who were bisexual, were held to be breach of privilege. The house expressed its strong disapproval and reprimanded Carmen, the person who made the statements, but took no further action.

The tit-for-tat quality of privilege is well illustrated by a couple of cases involving members of the house. In 1975 Mr R. D. Muldoon, the leader of the opposition, was held in breach of privilege for publishing an article in *Truth* accusing the speaker in the following terms: 'Even the Speaker, no doubt under the pressures of political adversity, has been leaning far more heavily on the Opposition than on the Government. Indeed, he rarely accepts an Opposition point of order without at the same time delivering a general rebuke which includes the Opposition as well as the Government. His ear on the Opposition side seems to be much better at detecting irregularities than his ear on the Government side. He rarely pulls up a Government speaker unless an Opposition member raises a point of order.' (*New Zealand Parliamentary Debates*, vol. 397, p. 1140) The statement was held to be breach of privilege and Mr Muldoon was censured. Then in 1976 with a new government in office, Mr Jonathan Hunt, an opposition member, was held guilty of a breach of privilege and suspended for one sitting day for saying in a radio programme, 'The first thing of course is to change the Speaker' and 'The Speaker should have been stronger . . .' (*New Zealand Parliamentary Debates*, vol. 407, p. 3157)

Privilege is another of the devices used by the political parties to score points off one another. In the final analysis a breach of privilege is what the majority in the House of Representatives says it is. The speaker has the duty to decide whether a prima facie breach of privilege exists. If he decides in the affirmative the case is referred to the Privileges Committee, upon which the government always has a majority. The report of that committee will be adopted by the house. There is no right to have counsel before the Privileges Committee, although the committee may allow it. There is nothing in the nature of a precise charge formulated as in the criminal courts. The law to be applied to the case is vague in the extreme. Adjudication for breach of privilege is really in the nature of a political trial, for which the penalties are not defined by law, but rather at the whim of politicians.

The antique weapon of parliamentary privilege should be reformed so that it cannot be used for political purposes. Limits should be imposed by statute upon the capacity of parliament to punish people who are not members. The new independent speaker should be the chairman of the Privileges Committee. The committee should comprise two government members and two opposition members. The hearings should be open to the news media.

6
Select committees and legislation

We have been considering parliament. In the next two chapters we begin to consider in greater detail the legislative function of parliament. The select committees form the principal parliamentary machinery for the consideration of legislation, and their role is outlined in this chapter. But before bills come to parliament their content is settled within the executive branch and that process must be understood.

Bills and negotiations

There are several different types of bills which are introduced and debated in Parliament:

1. Public bills – there are two types – those promoted by the government and introduced by a minister and those promoted by a private member. Private members' bills are not usually passed unless taken over by the government.

2. Local bills are those which affect a particular locality only. They are usually passed to allow a local authority to act; for example, to permit a harbour board to engage in a reclamation project.

3. Private bills – these are unusual. They are designed to deal with the particular interest or benefit of a person or group of persons. Two were passed in 1976. One was to facilitate the holding of property by District Grand Lodges of English Freemasons of New Zealand Trustees, after a re-organization of masonic lodges. The other amended the Methodist Charitable and Educational Trusts Act 1911.

The relative importance of each category of legislation in the eyes of the parliamentarians can be appreciated by examining Table 3, which sets out the amount of parliamentary time in the debating chamber devoted to each type.

Table 3 Parliamentary time spent on categories of legislation according to space in *New Zealand Parliamentary Debates*

Legislation	Percentage of space		
	1957	1967	1977
Private	1.0	.1	.2
Local	3.5	3.8	1.4
Public	95.5	96.1	98.4

One of the problems of legislation exists within the executive branch of government itself. The meat grinder of government is so big that it is necessary for the executive to conduct elaborate negotiations with itself in order to decide what the policy should be. Take, for example, a question concerning the reform of the criminal law. The Justice Department will have considerable interest and concern with the shape of the policy. So will the police. Often the perspectives of these two departments on legislation differ; sometimes the debate between them will become harsh and strident. Sometimes the matter will need to be resolved at cabinet level. In all this argy bargy within the executive branch of government it has been the custom to conduct most of the negotiations in secret. In New Zealand very little material relating to such in-fighting becomes public, for if it did there could be political embarrassment. It should happen more often. The public should be aware of important differences between departments of state.

In order that as many anomalies as possible may be ironed out of the legislation before its introduction, printed copies of draft bills are circulated within the executive. This has two advantages. First it enables the sponsoring department to secure agreement from other affected departments or parties. Second, it reduces the number of potential embarrassments by removing the mistakes or oversights. The problem in this procedure within the executive is that by the time the bill is actually introduced to the house it has been the subject of considerable discussion, negotiation and thought in private. Sometimes those negotiations will have included parties outside government who may be vitally affected by it. The result of this elaborate procedure is to reduce the impact of submissions made to parliamentary select committees considering the legislation. Usually by the time the public has been able to consider the legislation the executive branch of government has taken a stance upon it. Frequently the minister in the course of this process will have become committed to important details. The cabinet itself will have considered the legislation prior to its introduction, as will have the government caucus.

The curious result of the procedures within the executive branch of government is that many public servants outside parliament are far better informed about the detailed provisions in a bill than are the parliamentarians formally in charge of passing it. This applies particularly to members of the opposition, who do not see the bill until it is introduced. Their capacity, therefore, to ask questions in the first reading of a bill which they have only just seen is very limited. The practice of keeping secret the terms of proposed legislation until it is introduced in parliament is unfortunate. There seems little reason for the secrecy in most instances and many law reform bodies publish draft bills which are later introduced without any harm occurring. The practice is another example of the thraldom in which parliament is held by the executive branch of government.

All this means that there are powerful interests in favour of the bill as introduced. It is therefore necessary to mount considerable efforts to change details once they have appeared in public. The committed atmosphere surrounding the bill as introduced is compounded by the party composition of select committees. The government always enjoys a majority on any select committee. Select committees are reluctant to reach conclusions, therefore, which are likely to embarrass the government. On important matters the government members of the select committee always seem to consult with the minister, who is also often on the committee, and the result is that no change will be made unless the government agrees to it. And the government often has an interest in demonstrating that what it thought first was perfectly sound. The matter is complicated by caucus and caucus committees which often work in parallel to the select committee; in some ways their work competes with that being done by the select committees.

Nevertheless, there are occasions when drastic and widespread changes are made to legislation following its introduction. They are usually made by the select committee, with the government's concurrence, because the members of the select committee have been able to convince their colleagues in government that the changes are necessary. Examples from recent years include the Accident Compensation Act 1972, the Matrimonial Property Act 1976, the New Zealand Superannuation Act 1974 and the Securities Commission Act 1978.

Select committees

The working of the select committee system is the brightest spot on the New Zealand parliamentary scene. Select committees carry out a number of tasks. The standard type of select committee considers bills referred to it. Sometimes select committees carry out investigative studies; such is the role of the Public Expenditure Committee. The report of the Select Committee on Women's Rights, entitled *The Role of Women in New Zealand Society* and produced in 1975, is a particularly good example of investigation by a select committee into a topic of social concern. But scrutiny of legislation occupies the lion's share of select committee work. Often select committees are set up to look at a particular bill when the subject is large and important. Accident compensation, human rights, broadcasting, town and country planning legislation have all been examined by special select committees in recent years. Such *ad hoc* committees go out of existence once their task is finished; other select committees exist throughout the life of a parliament.

Three committees which always exist carry out specialized functions:

- House – dealing with matters pertaining to the domestic arrangements of the House of Representatives, such matters as the catering arrangements
- Library – to oversee the services provided by the General Assembly Library
- Privileges – adjudicates on breach of parliamentary privilege.
  At the end of the 1978 session other select committees were:
- Ancillary Licences
- Commerce and Mining
- Committee on Bills – to decide for each bill whether it is a public, local or private bill
- Defence
- Education
- Foreign Affairs
- Island Affairs
- Labour
- Lands and Agriculture
- Local Bills
- Maori Affairs
- Petitions
- Private Bills
- Public Expenditure
- Road Safety
- Selection (Private Bills)
- Social Services
- Standing Orders
- Statutes Revision
- Violent Offending

These committees usually consist of between five and ten members, and the government party has a majority. Membership changes a great deal during the life of a parliament. All select committees have power to send for persons, papers and records to be brought before them. Usually select committees cannot sit while the house itself is sitting. The chairman, always a government member, is in charge of procedure. Hearings of select committees are closed to the public and news media unless the house otherwise orders, and the evidence is confidential until the committee reports to the house, unless the proceedings have been open to the news media. Minority reports are not permitted. In the United Kingdom, ministers regularly appear before select committees to defend their policies, but they do not in New Zealand. In New Zealand ministers are members of select committees, a factor which increases the domination of the executive in parliament.

Table 2 in chapter 5 demonstrated how much legislation dominates the work of the chamber. It also dominates the work of select committees, as the same table illustrates by showing the percentage of time devoted to the reports of select committees on matters other than legislation.

The majority of select committees consider bills which have been referred to them by the House of Representatives. In 1978 there were twenty-six bills referred and in eighteen instances the hearings were open to the news media. In the 1977 session forty-three bills were referred to select committees and in thirty-seven instances the hearings were open. In 1976 fifty-two bills were referred and thirty-nine of the hearings were open.

The impact of select committee examination of government bills in New Zealand is substantial and on the whole exerts a favourable influence on the content of legislation. The Justice Department is the department in charge of a considerable amount of important government legislation. In his annual report tabled in parliament in 1978 the secretary for justice observed:

Our own experience is that Parliament through its select committee system is playing a larger role than formerly in the shaping of at least what may be called law reform legislation. In last year's report I adverted to the increasing tendency for interested groups or individuals to make submissions on a particular bill. This is by no means confined to those whose interest is purely a matter of the pocket. I believe too that parliamentary committees are more ready than they were even a few years ago to alter Bills in details and in principles alike. This trend must be a source of gratification for those who wish to see our parliamentary system strengthened but I do not know that the public at large is fully aware of it.

That members of parliament feel that their most constructive legislative role occurs in select committees is indicated by the remarks Dr Martyn Finlay made on the occasion of his retirement from parliament in 1978:

In a committee, however, Opposition members should reconcile themselves to the inevitable and accept the fact that the Government's majority must ultimately prevail and its proposals carry the day. Opposition there ceases to be fruitful, and destructive criticism should give way to constructive suggestions, making the best of a bad job. Similarly, there is a responsibility on Government members in committee to regard the rights of minorities and consider reasonable concessions . . . It pleases me greatly that in committee one can to a very considerable extent put aside party affiliation and all members can work co-operatively.

(*New Zealand Parliamentary Debates*, vol. 421 pp.4299-4300)

There are a number of limitations on the effectiveness of select committees considering provisions in government bills. The first is the obvious fact that a select committee will not change government policy on a provision unless the appropriate minister, and sometimes cabinet, agrees. Select committees in New Zealand are not free agents. Where a case is made on a matter of detail to which a concession can be made easily it often will be made. But on a point of fundamental principle, concessions will be resisted. For example, most of the evidence in 1976 was against the introduction of criminal penalties for strikes, but penalties were introduced. They had to be removed later because the expert opinion proved to be more accurate than the government's prejudice. Secondly, not all bills go to select committees; the majority do not. Professor Keith Jackson of the University of Canterbury has written in an article in the *Parliamentarian* that the decision to refer a bill to a select committee 'is an arbitrary process dependent upon the whim of the government of the day'. (vol. 59, p. 94) It is true that most important bills introducing new schemes do go to select committees, but the mass of amending legislation would also benefit from increased scrutiny. Governments have a habit of resisting reference to select committees when they want to avoid the political embarrassment which can occur in that forum. A third limitation on the effectiveness of select committees is that the time a bill is before a committee is insufficient for a detailed consideration of all the submissions. Complex legislation takes time to comprehend fully. Rapidly changing membership of the select committees in New Zealand's small house causes further problems in the effectiveness of select committees. Many members have too many committee tasks to be effective.

Assessing the impact of select committee scrutiny on bills is not a simple task. Many of the alterations made in select committees are drafting changes designed to remove ambiguity and tidy up the language rather than alter the policy. But even where one entire clause is substituted for another, the impact on the policy or intended policy may not be significant. Conversely, big changes in policy can be made on occasion by small changes to a sub-clause. The drafting changes which occur must be judged beneficial, and it can be anticipated that bills not referred to select committees would also benefit from such scrutiny. Table 4 illustrates the extent of changes made by select committees in 1977, but it makes no attempt to assess the extent of policy changes.

It is of considerable interest to compare Table 4 with Table 5. Table 5 summarizes changes made to bills by the Committee of the Whole House, in which bills are debated clause by clause. It has become common for the government to insert amendments, usually of a more minor nature than those made by select committees, at that late stage of proceedings to rectify policy or drafting problems. This opportunity for amendment can be taken with all bills, not merely those which went to select committee.

Table 4   Changes made to bills by select committees as reported back to the house in 1977*

Category	Change of whole clause	Change of whole sub-clause	Change of part of sub-clause
1 Private bill	2	1	5
9 Local bills	13	15	34
36 Public bills	163	261	554

* Removal of a clause or sub-clause and replacement by a new one is categorized as one change. Consequential amendments have not been counted.

Table 5   Changes made to bills by the Committee of the Whole House in 1977 (reported in *New Zealand Parliamentary Debates*)

Bills	Change of whole clause	Change of whole sub-clause	Change of part of sub-clause
6 local bills and 104 public bills, of which 71 in all had not been to a select committee	66	93	318

The amendments in the Committee of the Whole House are usually printed upon a supplementary order paper. It is hard to trace the precise effect of each change as it is being debated. If all bills were sent to select committee the number of changes made in the Committee of the Whole House would be reduced. That would enable the amendments made to be better considered.

Improvements

A number of measures can be undertaken to improve the working of select committees, their interaction with parliament and their scrutiny of legislation. By strengthening the select committees, parliament can enhance its capacity to check the executive. The key to reform of New Zealand government lies in reform of parliament. And the key to reforming parliament lies in the select committees.

Select committees should be given more power. They should be able to initiate their own inquiries. Some of them should be chaired by members of the party in opposition. Minority reports should be permitted. Perhaps the most important change required is the improvement of administrative facilities and staff available to the committees. Effective investigation by select committee requires an independent, expert staff capable of probing properly the policies and activities of the executive. The staff should be answerable to parliament and not to the executive. The staff should be under the direction of an independent speaker and not subject to orders from ministers.

Increased numbers of members of parliament are necessary for the select committee system to function properly. Specialization is essential and that is difficult to accomplish in a house as small as the one in New Zealand. The demands on members' time outlined in chapter 5 suggest that members would work more effectively if they worked over a narrower range of activities. Increased membership is important, too, in increasing the feeling that parliament is independent of the executive; it is too easy for cabinet to dominate a small house. And increased membership would broaden the base of talent available for cabinet. An increase to 120 members, plus an independent speaker, appears justifiable.

A change in the timetable of parliament would allow select committees more time in which to carry out their work and give proper consideration to legislation. Rushed legislation is an endemic part of the New Zealand scene, as chapter 7 shows. Some say that change in the parliamentary timetable will not cure that; I believe that view is false. Fundamental review of the parliamentary timetable has never been tried. One feature of developments in the last few years has been the introduction of bills before the end of a session so they can be studied, and select committees can deliberate on them, during the recess. The matter has been taken further by amendment to the Legislature Act in 1977; the act provides that bills can be introduced in the life of one parliament and passed by the next rather than lapse, as was previously the case.

There are other arguments which favour a different timetable. When parliament is in session the likelihood of checks upon executive power is higher than when it is not. If everyone – the public, the public servants, the members of parliament and the cabinet – knew that parliament would meet according to a predetermined timetable and not at the whim of the prime minister, constrained only by the need to obtain supply, orderly planning of parliamentary work would be much easier. At the same time there is need for more time away from the chamber to allow select committees to work systematically. At the moment the longer the session continues the further behind the committees tend to become.

A more ordered timetable, running continuously, would reduce the need for government to resort to the urgency provisions in the standing orders. That would mean that it would be possible to prohibit altogether the sitting of parliament beyond midnight. Such changes would enhance public confidence in the institution of parliament.

If parliament were to sit three days a week, three weeks a month, ten months of the year the unseemly scenes which have characterized the New Zealand parliament in recent years would disappear. Parliament would be strengthened. There would be more time for select committee work which could continue on one day of the week and in the vacant week each month. Standing orders should be revised to prohibit absolutely sittings beyond midnight. Parliament should be broadcast all the time it is sitting. News programmes should be permitted to broadcast excerpts from debates, a practice not permitted at present. Television transmissions from parliament should be tried, as in Canada.

To enhance the open nature of proceedings, all select committee hearings should be open to the public and representatives of the news media, although publication of certain material could be prohibited in the public interest by committee decision. At present, committee hearings are open to the news media only if the house (in reality the government) so decides. The presumption against openness should be displaced.

A better method of securing public contribution to legislation must be devised. We have seen that select committee consideration of legislation is beneficial. All bills, except money bills, should be referred to select committees. Committees should examine and receive submissions from the public on all bills. When hearings are held, times and places should be widely advertised. Select committees should hold hearings all round the country, more than they do at present. Standing orders should be altered to allow more time between the introduction of a bill to parliament and its reporting back from select committee; three months should be made a minimum. That would allow those who are likely to be affected by the legislation to have a reasonable opportunity of making their views heard. In turn, steps must be taken to ensure that details of legislation are made known when the legislation is introduced. One simple way would be to send every public library in New Zealand a copy of the bill when it is introduced. A second sensible step would be to advertise, even more widely than is done at present, the agenda of select committee hearings on bills. At present too many select committees are unknown outside parliament and too few private individuals know of their rights to appear before them and make submissions. In this respect, New Zealand seems to be an apathetic democracy. People are not vigilant about protecting their rights as citizens. They take a benign view of government. They do not take advantage of the opportunities they have, even under the existing system, to influence the outcome of government decisions.

One other reform to transform the impact of parliamentary scrutiny of legislation should be undertaken – it lies in the realm of information. The process by which policy and legislation are hammered out in the first instance means that government has a monopoly on much of the information pertinent to the bill. The same situation exists in the United Kingdom. There Professor J. A. G. Griffith in an elaborate study published in 1974, *Parliamentary Scrutiny of Government Bills*, concludes that the following reform should be undertaken:

I suggest that when a bill is first published, it should be accompanied by a document that would set out, in a general introduction, the history of the proposal and the need for the bill. The document would then deal clause by clause with the contents of the bill giving enough information to enable Members and other interested persons to understand the purpose of each clause and why (this being particularly important) the particular means used by the clause to achieve that purpose had been adopted. The document would also be accompanied by appendices setting out relevant statistical and other background material.

The purpose of this document – and this could be used as a yardstick to determine whether or not to include or exclude material – would be to ensure that Members and others were as well-informed as the Minister, no more and no less. The additional departmental work involved in producing such a document would be slight as the information needed would all be most easily and readily to hand in the process of building up the brief from which the Minister presently speaks. The size of the document would be determined by the size of the bill. I would expect that a bill of thirty clauses and schedules would require a document (with introduction and appendices) of about fifty to eighty pages. (p. 247)

That particular suggestion is directly applicable to our own parliamentary procedure, although it will hardly be popular in certain quarters. It goes far beyond the explanatory notes which are appended to bills at present. Coupled with increased use of select committees, and advertising of the fact that the public can make submissions, it would go a long way towards ensuring that people have a real chance of participating in the legislative process.

7

The fastest law in the west

New Zealand passes too many laws and it passes them too quickly. Legislative overload is not unique to New Zealand, although it is more pronounced here than in most other countries.

In 1977 B. Manning, a respected American authority, wrote in the *Northwestern University Law Review*: 'Hyperlexis is America's national disease – the pathological condition caused by an overactive law-making gland.' (vol. 71, p. 767) But in no United States legislature, and there are fifty-one of them, is it so easy to pass statutes as in New Zealand. All but one of them have two houses; all have legal restrictions upon what they may pass laws about; and in none does strong party affiliation influence legislation to the extent it does in New Zealand. In the United States the executive branch can never be sure how its proposals will end up when the legislative branch has dealt with them.

Lord Hailsham has been Lord Chancellor of England, the top judge, and a respected elder statesman of the Conservative Party. Speaking in a House of Lords debate in 1978 he said:

. . . we do not know what the new sections mean. The statute book is growing and growing. Nobody understands it and one wonders whether the exercise is worth the pain of legislation and the trouble the judges will have in understanding it. The more words you put into a statute the more cases will go to the House of Lords. Year after year we pass 3,000 pages or more of Acts of Parliament and another 10,000 pages of subordinate legislation and nobody knows what the law is, or can know, because it is so voluminous.

(*The Times*, 1 February 1978, p. 7)

The *Australian Law Journal* commented in 1976: 'There are no visible signs that the output of Australian legislatures is tending to diminish. The tide of legislation continues to roll unceasingly and complaints are general that too much legislation is being enacted.' (vol. 50, p. 108) In March 1978 the president of the New Zealand Law Society, Mr Laurie Southwick, Q.C., was moved to remark that in the past ten years parliament had passed no fewer than 1700 Acts, many of which had reached the statute book by a very hasty path. 'The Acts which included many amendments and some 3000 regulations imposed a difficult problem of interpretation for lawyer and judge alike,' Mr Southwick said.

In all the countries mentioned the opportunities for holding up legislation are greater than in New Zealand as, with the exception of the states of Queensland and Nebraska, all have two houses in their legislatures. In all countries the scrutiny is likely to last longer and be more searching than it is in New Zealand.

We can read today with a wry smile the complaints which were made about inadequate consideration of legislation in New Zealand nearly fifty years ago. In 1932 the editor of the *New Zealand Law Journal* wrote:

We have recently witnessed our Parliament spending eleven weeks in session. At the end of ten weeks, five new legislative enactments were added to the Statute book. Then, after setting out to break previously deplorable records with a last minute endurance test of continuous sitting – with only intervals for meals, for even legislators must feed – four days' sitting resulted in the passing of seven Acts, containing nearly two hundred clauses, all of a highly technical nature and most of them of far-reaching importance.

The system is entirely wrong and fraught with all kinds of danger and possibility of injustice. The time has long since passed when proposed legislation should be available for a reasonable period before its final consideration by Parliament. (p. 117)

Deplorable as it may have seemed then, the machine is capable of much more speed now. The amount of material passed in 1932 must have been examined closely compared with the brief scrutiny which goes on today. Of course, the machine has been made to run faster since that time too, by the abolition of the second chamber.

New Zealanders exhibit an innocent and misplaced faith in the efficacy of legislation. We also undervalue the importance to the community of good law flowing from good law-making procedures. We seem to be addicted to passing legislation for the sake of it, and to believe that legislation can cure our innermost ills. Not infrequently we try to legislate the impossible. For instance, after criminal penalties were introduced in the industrial relations field, some prosecutions were launched. Then it was decided to offer no evidence and change the law. The criminal penalties were taken out less than two years after they went in. Then in 1978 a law was passed about massage parlours, a law which is unlikely to have its intended effect. This superfluity of legislation is in part a response to political demands. In a period of considerable social upheaval, the government must be seen to be reacting; if it passes a law it can be said to be doing something. In response to other pressures, legislation is passed for which there is no legal need – for example, the legislation which established the Planning Council and the Commission for the Future. These organizations could have existed without legislation, but legislation was passed. Some legislation results from pressure groups which wish to enhance their status by legislation – for example, the Music Teachers Registration Act 1957. For many occupational groups it is not the public interest which requires legislation, it is their own private interest.

The New Zealand attitude seems to me to be dangerously close to that summed up by M. Dalloz, a distinguished French jurist:

When ignorance reigns in society and disorder in the minds of men, laws are multiplied, legislation is expected to do everything, and each fresh law being a fresh miscalculation, men are continually led to demand from it what can proceed only from themselves, from their own education and their own morality.
(quoted in the *New Zealand Farmer*, 10 August 1978, p. 66)

There are a good many things about which it is better not to legislate. The wholesale creation of new criminal offences in an effort to regulate behaviour often creates great problems in the enforcement of the law and it leads to an atmosphere of community disrespect for the law. The limits upon legal sanctions as a means of ordering society have been but dimly appreciated in New Zealand; moral purity cannot be brought about by legislation. Not only should we pass fewer laws, we should go through the statute book and see what can be cut out.

Too much law

There are three major species of New Zealand legislation:
- statutes
- regulations
- by-laws

Statutes are passed by parliament. Regulations are made under the authority of statutes; a statute will state that regulations can be made on various topics. A fairly typical example comes from the Poultry Board Act 1976. (Put on one side for a moment the question whether a Poultry Board is really necessary and, if it is, whether it needs to be created by statute.) The Poultry Board Act is neither long nor complex. But it does include a regulation-making power. The provision says:

The Governor-General may from time to time, by Order in Council, make regulations for all or any of the following purposes:
(a) Registering poultry farms:
(b) Prescribing any form required for the purposes of this Act:
(c) Prescribing purposes for which the money of the Board may be expended:
(d) Prescribing the amount of any fees (except registration fees) payable under this Act:
(e) Providing for such matters as are contemplated by or are necessary for giving effect to the provisions of this Act and for its due administration.

'Order in Council' means that the governor-general and the cabinet ministers have a meeting and the governor-general signs the regulations proposed by the ministers. These are meetings of the executive council, as distinct from cabinet which the governor-general does not attend.

Actually, regulations are approved by cabinet before being sent to the executive council. Meetings of the executive council do not need to be attended by all ministers. Three ministers constitute a quorum.

By-laws can only be made where an act of parliament confers power upon an organization to make them. The most common source of by-laws in New Zealand are local authorities. Most by-laws deal with matters which come under the control of local authorities.

It is the job of the courts to interpret what statutes mean in the event of a dispute. With regulations, the courts have wider powers. Not only can the courts interpret regulations, but they can also declare a regulation to be invalid and of no effect if the regulation is outside the ambit of the power laid down in the enabling act. For example, a regulation made under the Poultry Board Act which attempted to control the price of television sets would be struck down. No power is given by the act to make regulations for that purpose. With by-laws the powers of courts stretch even further. Not only can a by-law be declared invalid because it is outside the power, it can be struck down for 'unreasonableness'.

Statutes are often said to contain the most important laws and that regulations contain only administrative detail, but the distinction is not true for New Zealand. Important facets of our national life can be and are controlled by regulation. The powers given to the executive by the Reserve Bank Act and the Economic Stabilization Act allow the government to control prices, wages and take almost every economic measure conceivable (short of raising taxes) by regulation. There is even power, in effect, to nationalize the insurance companies by executive act under the Reserve Bank Act by requiring their assets to be held in government securities.

There is a tendency in the executive branch of government to prefer regulations to statutes. They attract less discussion. They are hardly ever debated in parliament. They can be brought in at any time of the year whether parliament is in session or not. They can be changed rapidly. And even if they are invalid it will be a long time before anyone gets around to challenging them in the courts. And most regulations cannot be successfully challenged anyway because wide powers have been given in the first place to make regulations. The power to make instant law by regulations is one of the most fearful instruments of executive domination in New Zealand. For sheer speed, lack of warning and absence of consultation, nothing beats regulations.

There is one school of thought which says that our fast law-making procedures allow our laws to be kept up to date easily and encourage a flexible approach. The other view is that the speed and simplicity of our legislative procedures make it too easy for the executive branch of government to do what it likes, to take power that it does not really need and smother us all in red tape. Although both views contain important elements of truth, New Zealand has now reached the situation in which the benefits of flexibility are outweighed by the threat of oppression flowing from an insufficiently controlled law-making power.

Statistics alone do not say everything about the bulk of New Zealand legislation. They must be used with caution. Not all acts of parliament are long and complex, although many of them are. And many of the acts passed by the New Zealand parliament each year are amending acts, patching up anomalies which have been discovered or making provision for new policies and developments. But to give some impression of the volume of New Zealand legislation, Tables 6 and 7 show the pattern for the same years examined in previous tables.

Table 6　Numbers of statutes and regulations

Year	Total number of bills passed	Days parliament sat	Total number of regulations made
1956	123	67	224
1957	124	80	281
1966	140	78	222
1967	182	99	289
1976	182	96	332
1977	206	118	337
1978	120	87	340

Table 7　Printed pages of statutes and regulations

Year	Statutes	Regulations
1956	1355	1202
1957	1173	1134
1966	1969	1339
1967	1563	1942
1976	2361	1960
1977	2872	1526

Parliament sits on average about a hundred days a year. For every day that it was in session 1976–8 it passed 1.6 statutes. And for every day parliament sat, on average more than three regulations were made. That may be acceptable if parliament scrutinized those laws properly, but it does not. Regulations are hardly looked at and many are made when parliament is not sitting. The statutes are not looked at sufficiently closely. Parliament, of course, does much more than pass legislation. For example, in 1976, 2,420 questions were asked of ministers. And 485 papers were laid on the table of the house, presumably for consideration by members of parliament. The address and reply debate in which almost every member of the house usually speaks takes up a lot of time, but covers no legislation. The budget debate is similar. Much of the argument which goes on in the debating chamber is of a generalized party political nature and does little to improve the quality of the legislation. The scrutiny that parliament does carry out is done for the most part in select committees, but many bills do not go there, as shown in chapter 6; for example, the Security Intelligence Amendment Act 1977, a most important measure taking wide powers to intercept communications, was not referred to a select committee. No doubt parliament could do a better job of probing and scrutinizing the legislation which comes before it if there was less of it. Part of the increase in the last few years in New Zealand may be due to the election of new governments in 1972 and 1975, which felt the need to legislate the programmes upon which they were elected. We may perhaps anticipate a decrease in the number of laws to be passed in the coming three years.

With the new law which is added each year must be considered the law which remains from previous years. Professor K.J. Keith, in an article in *Reform of Parliament,* gave a graphic description of the bulk of the New Zealand statute book:

The New Zealand Statute book is enormous. It now runs to well over 60 volumes of an average of 800 pages each. In 1931, 29 volumes were consolidated into eight volumes (which were annotated and had an index volume), in 1957 those eight volumes plus a further 33 were reprinted in 16 volumes and in the last 19 years we have had a further 54 volumes. There is some relevant legislation not included in those volumes – including applicable British statutes. Not every page of those 70 volumes – which must contain something like 15,000,000 words – is still part of the law; indeed a few volumes are completely superseded. The basic 1957 reprint does however still contain much extant material – about one third of the more than 600 principal public Acts which are in force. (p.26)

Professor Keith goes on to point out that the whole statute law of the Canadian province of Ontario was contained in a five volume reprint plus one or two volumes for each subsequent year. Add those to the Canadian Federal Acts and the total number comes to about twenty-five volumes and covers six feet of shelf space; more than sixty New Zealand volumes take up fourteen feet of shelving. The State of Iowa in the U.S. contains all its relevant statute law in a code which is reprinted in its entirety every year incorporating all the changes which have been made that year. That code fits in two thick close-printed volumes. A third volume contains a comprehensive index. That means that many people in the state can have the laws in their office. They are cheap, easy to use and easy to house. You do not need to be a lawyer to find your way around the Iowa code, whereas few lay people could find their way around the cumbersome New Zealand system.

Drafting

Not only is law made quickly in New Zealand, much of it is incomprehensible to ordinary people. Canadian writer M.L. Friedland, in his book *Access to the Law*, has asserted: 'The state has an obligation to ensure that its laws are available in an understandable fashion to laymen.' (p.1) That should be our goal.

The drafting of all public bills and all statutory regulations in New Zealand is in the hands of the parliamentary counsel office. The office is established under its own statute. The office in 1977 had ten lawyers engaged on drafting work. Each person in the office that year had to draft over 400 pages of law. The amount is staggering when the complexity and difficulty of the work is considered. First, the parliamentary counsel must be a skilled and experienced lawyer. Then he must be skilled in the specialized work of drafting, a skill which takes years to acquire. To do a good job he must become immersed in the subject matter with which the bill deals. Then it is necessary to get sensible instructions as to what should be in the bill, no easy task on many occasions. Then the bill must be drafted and examined in a rigorous fashion to detect flaws in it. That is time consuming. Bills and regulations should never be drafted by departmental officers, as they sometimes are in New Zealand.

Drafting cannot be rushed. But often government demands that it be rushed. Bills to be passed by parliament are legal documents which need to spell out the law clearly. They are also political documents aiming to achieve a political purpose. Frequently politics demands that they be prepared and passed with haste. On one celebrated occasion in 1978 when the government wanted to amend its industrial relations law, parliamentary counsel appeared to have had only the weekend to draft what was quite a difficult bill. (Actually the job was achieved with great skill.) Better drafting is essential in New Zealand legislation, and a key to better drafting is more time.

The New Zealand approach to drafting statutes is similar to that of the United Kingdom. Both use what is known as the detailed approach. Statutes in New Zealand do not confine themselves to general principle. They spell everything out, often in detail of tedious and incomprehensible prolixity. The approach is not taken in every instance, but it is taken frequently enough to inflate the pages of the statute book considerably. The difference between the general and the detailed approaches can be seen in the two following examples.

Section 138 of New Zealand's Accident Compensation Act 1972 deals with the situation where a person has died by murder or manslaughter and the person who did the deed claims compensation arising out of the death. If nothing was said it may be thought that the murderer could benefit from his own crime. For example, a woman dependent on her husband might make herself a widow by murdering her husband and then claim compensation. Here is how the New Zealand act deals with the problem:

138. Disqualification through conviction of murder or manslaughter – (1) No compensation shall be payable under any of the provisions of sections 121 (2),

121(4), 123, 124, and 125 of this Act to the spouse or a child or other dependant of any person by reason of the death of that person if that spouse, child, or dependant has been convicted by a Court of law in New Zealand or any other country of the murder or manslaughter of the deceased person:

Provided that the Commission may pay compensation under any of those provisions to any such spouse, child, or dependant who has been convicted of the manslaughter of the deceased person if it is proved to the satisfaction of the Commission that the convicted person had no intention of killing or causing grievous bodily harm to the deceased person or any other person at the time when he killed the deceased person.

(2) In any case where the widow or widower, or a child or other dependant, of the deceased person is disqualified from being paid compensation under sections 123 and 124 of this Act, those sections shall be read as if the disqualified person had died before the deceased person.

(3) Where the Commission has reason to suspect that the death of any person was due to murder or manslaughter, and has reason to suspect the spouse or a child or other dependant of the deceased person of the murder or manslaughter, the Commission may refuse to make any payment of compensation to that spouse or child or dependant under any of the provisions of sections 121(2), 121(4), 123, 124, and 125 of this Act until the expiration of 6 months from the date of the death of the deceased person.

(4) Where any compensation is paid by the Commission under any of the provisions of sections 121(2), 121(4), 123, 124, and 125 of this Act to the spouse or a child or other dependant of any person by reason of the death of that person, and that spouse, child, or dependant is or has been convicted by a Court of law in New Zealand or any other country of the murder or manslaughter of the deceased person, the Commission may recover the amount of the compensation so paid from that spouse, child, or dependant as a debt.

(5) In this section—

'Dependant' includes a person who is entitled to compensation under subsection (2) of section 121 of this Act: 'Manslaughter' means manslaughter within the meaning of the Crimes Act 1961; and includes any killing of a human being outside New Zealand that would, if done in New Zealand, have amounted to manslaughter:

'Murder' means murder within the meaning of the Crimes Act 1961; and includes any killing of a human being outside New Zealand that would, if done in New Zealand, have amounted to murder.

Legislation was prepared in Australia to accomplish the same purpose as in New Zealand's Accident Compensation Act. The parallel provision in the Australia legislation was as follows:

A benefit is not payable under this Act to a person by reason of the death of another person if the first-mentioned person has been convicted of the murder of that other person.   (National Rehabilation and Compensation Bill 1977)

The policy differs to some degree between the two sections. The Australian provision makes no reference to manslaughter, as a deliberate policy. But had that matter been included, the provision need not have been much longer. The question that must be asked is whether the extra words in the New Zealand provision really add anything?

Certainly, they include more detail; but do they really make the outcome of cases easier to predict and the application of the act any more clear?

A powerful argument can be made that the more detail that is included the more opportunity for dispute exists. The attempt to deal with all problems in advance is often self defeating because not every eventuality can be anticipated. The detailed approach tries to purchase certainty at the expense of clear, succinct statements. If our statutes were drafted in a clear and concise way many more people could consult the statute book with profit than can do so at present. I do not say that it is possible to draft a statute so that every implication will be clear to a lay person. Some legislation deals with subject matter which is itself so complex that the legislation will reflect the complexity. What I am saying is that it is desirable that statutes be written in terms which are comprehensible to ordinary people as far as possible. The New Zealand example above fails that test, while the Australian one passes.

Many complaints have been made about the drafting techniques that have come to be employed in modern times. In England, two leading authors, Megarry and Wade, wrote in their book *The Law of Real Property*: 'Statutory draftsmanship has now attained a level of professional technique which too often endangers clarity and logic.' (p.v.) Lord Scarman, in a celebrated lecture delivered in England, remarked that 'statutes are complex and detailed often to the point of unintelligibility and seldom contain any broad declaration of principle.' (*English Law – The New Dimension*, p.4)

Sir William Dale, in a comparative study of legislation in England and certain continental countries, *Legislative Drafting – A New Approach*, concluded that United Kingdom acts came out badly by comparison. He concluded:

Features making for obscurity or length, usually both, in United Kingdom Acts are –
(a)   long, involved sentences, and sections;
(b)   much detail, little principle;
(c)   an indirect approach to the subject-matter;
(d)   subtraction – as in 'Subject to . . .', 'Provided that . . .';
(e)   centrifugence – a flight from the centre to definition and interpretation clauses (''the famous freak of modern law givers'');
(f)   poor arrangement;
(g)   schedules – too many and too long;
(h)   cross-references to other Acts – saving space, but increasing the vexation. (pp.331-2)

Sir William Dale suggests that a new technique of drafting be introduced.

We need at least to reduce the verbal impedimenta; to be less fussy over detail, to be more general and concise; and to situate each rule where it belongs, in an orderly and logical development. On this level, the question is largely a matter of style and arrangement. A more profound change is also desirable: a determination to seek the principle, to express it, and to follow up with such detail, illuminating and not obscuring the principle, as the circumstances require. (p.335)

In my opinion the changes called for by Sir William Dale should be implemented in New Zealand. The attorney-general should so instruct parliamentary counsel. New Zealand statutes furnish plenty of examples of obscure language, over-elaboration in the illusory desire for certainty, repetition, inconsistency and illogical structure. These points have been amply demonstrated in Professor K. J. Keith's paper, 'A Lawyer Looks at Parliament', published in 1978 in *Reform of Parliament*.

The counter-arguments that parliamentary counsel would advance for their present approach are:

- the general approach often does not fit the specificity of the purpose wanted by the government
- lack of detail would lead to substantial doubt continuing until resolved by the courts
- litigation is expensive and should be avoided where possible
- leaving the matter to the courts detracts from the power of the House of Representatives whose job legislation is. The general approach gives too much power to the courts to 'legislate'
- the courts have become accustomed to the detailed approach and change now would be difficult for them

Some of these arguments are valid. Undoubtedly the new approach to drafting outlined above would require a new approach to interpretation by the courts. We must have confidence that the courts would try to further the real policies behind the legislation, rather than cutting them down or approaching them in a pedantic fashion or in an unrealistically narrow way.

My own view is that we can and should trust the courts. In some areas they have shown themselves to be capable of faithfully trying to implement parliament's intention; town and country planning law is an example. In other fields, doubts exist. Some have suggested that, in the field of matrimonial property, the courts were less than generous in their approach to construing the 1963 legislation on that topic. In other words, the courts gave wives an unfair deal under the legislation presumably because the judges did not take an up to date view of the rights of female parties to a broken marriage. New legislation was passed in 1976 based on the principle of equal division of matrimonial property between the parties to a marriage. The new act contains considerable detail, presumably to ensure the courts do not go wrong. But before the old law was done away with there were signs the courts were changing their views; indeed a privy council case placed interpretation of the legislation on a new path. It often takes time to see how an act will work in practice. Already there are efforts being made to change the 1976 act, but it is too soon.

86

The composition of the judiciary has changed a great deal in the last twenty years. Some of the new judges are much more aware of social reality than some of their predecessors were. They are less wedded to technical solutions based on precedent. I think we have arrived at the stage where we can put more trust in the judges by changing the basis upon which we legislate. A further argument in favour of that course is that by so doing we remove some control from the executive branch of government (which in substance does all the legislating) and place more power into the hands of courts.

Presentation

Not enough attention in New Zealand has been given to providing aids to finding the law. In 1978, for the first time, the tables setting out the names of the public acts of the New Zealand parliament and the statutory regulations were published as a separate volume. That list covers 176 pages, which itself gives some indication of the volume of law we have. For the most part the tables list the statutes and regulations in alphabetical order by name; there is some cross referencing, but unless you know the name of the act or regulation you are looking for there is a good chance you will not find it. Let us say, for example, that I wanted to know what laws we had in New Zealand against discrimination. I look up 'discrimination' in the tables and there is no reference to it. But we have a Race Relations Act, a Human Rights Commission Act and an Equal Pay Act, all of which deal with discrimination. The difficulty does not arise all the time. For example, if I want to find what laws we have about prisons and I look up 'prisons' in the tables, I am referred to 'penal institutions'. But these tables are rudimentary compared with the digests and indexes which are available in some overseas countries to provide access to the statute law.

The State of Iowa reprints the entire statute law every year together with a comprehensive index. The compiler divides up the code into topic headings, and ensures that the index contains every conceivable cross reference to the headings. The headings will include such topics as education, social welfare, environment, commerce and so on. Within each chapter there is room for sub-division. Each section of the law within such a code has a unique number, so that identification of the particular provision a person is referring to is simple.

In New Zealand we have a number of different statutes which bear upon each of these topics above and they are to be found throughout sixty-five volumes or more of statute books that we have. If the Iowa system were adopted, when new statutes are passed each provision would be slotted into its appropriate place in the code and repealed provisions taken out. Indeed, with the use of computers it should be possible to store all New Zealand statute law on computers, punch in the changes each year and print out a complete code afresh each year. This method of presenting the law would be simpler than the one employed at present. It would give the public a real chance of finding the law for themselves when they needed it.

More resources need to be devoted to the compilation of statutes, not just their drafting. There was a staff of only three in the compilation department of parliamentary counsel's office in 1977. They concentrated on the reprinting of statutes which have been heavily amended. That process is useful because after five or six extensive amending acts have been made to a principal act, fitting the pieces together is like a difficult jig-saw puzzle. But if the method suggested above were adopted there would be no need for the continuous reprinting that is done now. The logic of that approach is to reprint everything every year, which is what I am suggesting.

The day is long past when a lay person could attempt to keep abreast of changes in our legislation. For one thing it would cost too much. A full set of annotated New Zealand statutes cost $985 in 1978. It is impossible to buy a complete set of New Zealand's regulations from the government printer. Some of them are simply out of print and there are no current plans to remedy that situation. The government apparently takes the view that citizens do not need to be able to ascertain the content of the laws which govern them. The bound volumes of statutes are not usually available until nearly a year after the conclusion of the parliamentary session in which they were passed, although individual copies will be available before that time. It is common, unfortunately, that statutes come into effect before they are generally available to the public. Ignorance of the law, of course, furnishes no defence to a criminal charge.

Happily the matter shows signs of becoming a political issue. In 1978 the Labour Party policy on parliamentary reform promised: 'Every effort will be made to write laws in language everyone can understand.' It pointed out that: 'Parliament passes too many laws and it passes them too quickly.' The party promised to appoint a law reform commissioner whose first priority would be to recommend how 'New Zealand's laws can be made more understandable to the general public'. (*New Zealand Labour Party Policy*, p.1) The National Party later echoed the approach by expressing concern that 'some statutes and regulations are outdated or irrelevant' and promising to review them. It also said the review 'will be facilitated by a new method of reprinting statutes'. The method is apparently to be by a new continuous reprint of statutes. 'When completed, this will mean that all statutes will have been reprinted in the previous ten years – and this cycle will be maintained on a continuous basis.' (*National Party Election Manifesto*, p.31) If it happens, it will be an improvement, although in my opinion it is not good enough.

A key proposal in the Labour manifesto, imported from the United States, was the sunset law idea. Labour promised that 'new legislation will be passed with the inclusion of specific expiry dates. No law should remain on the statute book without periodic review.' (p.2) The purpose of that proposal was to ensure that those responsible for administering a law faced up to the task of reviewing and revising it systematically. No longer should a law continue for ever without review. Unless positive steps were taken, it should expire. Such a provision would encourage greater watchfulness on a more continuous basis than at present. Where a law is working well it can be re-enacted with little alteration. Where the law no longer serves any useful purpose, the sunset provision would kill it off. Where a law serves a need but is defective, it should be repaired. The sunset provision would encourage revision and would provide political obstacles to governments which fail to carry out the reviews effectively. About ten years would be long enough for most statutes. The fact of review within a reasonable time would discourage amendments before the time of expiry. Sunset laws would force parliament to examine periodically its creations and see whether they measure up.

A further reform would be to increase the number of parliamentary counsel. It we doubled their number and halved the number of laws they were asked to draft the quality of our law would improve.

Another irritating feature of New Zealand statutes is that the reader often cannot tell by looking at them when they come into effect. Some acts come into force on a date mentioned in the act itself. Others, probably the majority, come into force on the day they receive the royal assent by being signed by the governor-general. Frequently that occurs before any copy of the act is procurable from the government printer. That is quite understandable when it is considered that thirty-eight royal assents were given in one day in 1978. Obviously it is undesirable and unfair that a law should come into effect without the public being able to secure copies of it. Other acts, usually those for which considerable administrative preparation is required before they can begin to work, do not come into force until an order-in-council is passed bringing them into force. None of this is satisfactory; it creates uncertainty and confusion. It would be best if all statutes passed in each year came into force on 1 April of the following year. For those requiring elaborate preparations a certain date in the future should be set in the act itself. Such a change would prevent uncertainty and confusion. It would enable people to become conversant with a provision before they were required to obey it.

Some examples of how New Zealand legislates

Amendments

A further qualification should be made to the figures on statutes given in Table 6. The number of statutes in New Zealand is increased by a unique New Zealand institution known as the Statutes Amendment Bill. This annual bill is much prized by the public servants. It allows them to have amendments made to legislation they administer. The amendments are always non-controversial; if they are not, they cannot be introduced in the Statutes Amendment Bill. They are examined by a select committee. Any member of parliament can object to anything in the bill and it will be taken out. The 1978 bill had 133 clauses and amended fifty-six different statutes.

Reference has already been made to the Poultry Board Act 1976. The Statutes Amendment Bill 1978 contained a provision to provide for staggered retirement dates for the members of the Poultry Board. Because members of the board 'are required to be members of the Egg Marketing Authority, the retirement dates of both bodies have been brought into line', the explanatory note (p.v.) accompanying the bill observed. That simple amendment illustrates two things which are typical of New Zealand statute law. The difficulty with which the amendment dealt would have been just as obvious at the time the principal act was going through the legislative process in 1976 as it was in 1978, if anyone had thought of it.

When the Poultry Board Bill was passed in 1976 there was not much time to consider it. It was introduced on 16 November. It did not go to a select committee for consideration. It attracted little discussion in parliament. On 30 November the government took urgency in the House of Representatives and the Poultry Board Bill was included in the list of items to which urgency was accorded. The bill received its main parliamentary debate beginning at about midmight while parliament was off the air. The debate concluded at 12.57 a.m. after what the speaker described as 'a protracted and unhappy discussion' as to when the members of parliament could go home to bed. (*New Zealand Parliamentary Debates,* vol. 408, p.4366) Hansard demonstrates that the house was in an unruly mood and gave scant consideration to the provisions of the bill. The third reading took place on 7 December, again when the house was proceeding under urgency. So with that sort of scrutiny being given in parliament to the Poultry Board Bill it was not surprising that the defect in it which required the 1978 amendment was not detected. The story shows that inadequate scrutiny of bills leads to demand for amendment. And the amendments themselves are not adequately scrutinized either. A vicious circle develops – the more amendments that are made the more there need to be made.

Detailed drafting also leads to amendments. If you have a bill which spells out in considerable detail procedures which later are found to be inconvenient, another source of pressure for amendment builds up. It all leads to New Zealand's law of legislation: the more you have, the more you need. All sorts of quangos are appointed under statutes. These statutes spell out appointment terms. First, why do it by statute at all? And if it is done by statute, why spell out the terms of appointment in a way which causes trouble later? Why not make all appointments at the pleasure of the government? After all, the short terms laid down for most of these bodies mean that government is interested in putting on people who can be relied upon to do the sort of things the government wants.

There is another feature of the amendment avalanche. An examination of amending bills shows a strong tendency to favour amendments which make things more convenient for those who have the running of the legislation. Take the Accident Compensation Amendment Act 1978. Most of the provisions in that act were proposed by the Accident Compensation commission and accepted by government – they were to do things which the Accident Compensation Commission thought should be done. Many of them were not steps which necessarily assisted those whom the Accident Compensation scheme is designed to help, the injured. The example suggests that all too much of the legislation which goes through in New Zealand is legislation by the executive for the benefit of the executive.

A perusal of the Statutes Amendment Bill also suggests that many of the changes are unnecessary; great hardship will not occur if they are not made. The attitude to legislation which the Statutes Amendment Bill encourages is a happy-go-lucky one: if we make a mistake or don't think things through properly we can always patch it up by amendment. If the procedure were not available departments and other agencies might be a great deal more careful when the principal act is being hammered out.

The current practice leads to a departmental attitude where a book is kept of all the amendments the department would like to see made and a couple are poked in the Statutes Amendment Bill each year. Tinkering around with the detail achieves little for anyone except the executive branch of government; it threatens to allow the law to be changed at will, something for which people who deal with government must be constantly on their watch. In New Zealand the ultimate bargaining ploy of government is legislation. It would be better if legislation were investigated thoroughly to begin with and then left alone until the whole policy dealt with by the principal act was reviewed as discussed earlier. Then everyone would know where they stand. There has been too much legislative cut and fill in New Zealand.

The end of session rush

To the problems ensuing from the quality of legislation passed must be added one that has become endemic to New Zealand. It is known as the 'end of the session rush'. The end of session rush is the product of two powerful weapons in the government's legislative armoury. The standing orders of the house give the government the right to claim 'urgency in the public interest' on any bill or other matter on the order paper. When urgency is accorded the house remains in session until the business has been concluded, except that the house cannot sit on

Sunday. In fact, there does not need to be an element of urgency present in the circumstances at all for urgency to be claimed. The government controls the numbers in the house so it can claim urgency when it pleases. Standing Order 203 provides for closure of debate. Where a member moves 'That the question be now put' and the speaker accepts it (which he will not do if it is 'an infringement of the rights of the minority') and the motion is carried, the matter can be debated no further. Those two standing orders mean that the government can ram through the House of Representatives anything it wants and all the opposition can do is delay for a day or two until they come to the limits of their physical endurance. Much legislation passes the New Zealand House of Representatives under the urgency provisions. With a new timetable, urgency provisions should be deleted from standing orders.

The 1978 session of parliament affords a particularly sad example. At the end of the session urgency was taken on seven successive days. Parliament sat sixty-two hours after midnight in 1978 compared with fifty-one hours in 1976 and thirty-nine in 1977, and in both those previous years much more legislation was passed and parliament sat more days. The statistics for the last week of sittings in 1978 are shown in Table 8.

Table 8   Parliament's last week of sittings in 1978

Day	Hours house sat	Bills handled
Tuesday	10	8 third reading debates 7 second reading debates
Wednesday	27*	1 bill through all its stages committee stages on 17 bills 4 second reading debates
Thursday	8.5	15 bills from second reading through all stages 22 bills put through third reading.

*Only in parliament can a day have more than 24 hours!

Often the third reading debate of a bill is short, but where the bill is contentious the debate will be longer. At one stage during the week illustrated in Table 8, I witnessed eleven third readings disposed of in seven minutes. Obviously when the government has taken urgency a long way down the order paper, an opposition is placed in a dilemma. Should it continue to say all the things it wishes to say on bills and therefore keep the house sitting around the clock or should it allow things to be pushed through with only perfunctory debate to allow members to get home at a reasonable hour each night.

The strange thing about the 1978 end of session rush is that there was absolutely no need for it. Parliamentary business earlier in the year had been light. The house rose on 6 October, the general election was not until 25 November. To ram through legislation at the rate that was done in the last week of the 1978 session defies all explanation. It is a sign that parliament is in decline and that the government does not take seriously the contribution parliament can make to legislation.

Major legislation not properly considered

The Town and Country Planning Act was passed in 1977. That legislation and its predecessor, which was passed in 1953, governs the way in which permission is obtained to use land. It deals with the zoning of land for certain uses. District schemes for development are prepared. Important issues relating to the nature of the environment in which all New Zealanders live, and the use people may make of their land fall to be determined under the legislation. Few pieces of legislation can be as important in their impact on everyday life for so many people.

In 1973 a special committee which had been appointed to review the operation of the legislation and make recommendations reported. Important changes were recommended. The Labour government began work on preparing a new bill. According to the minister who was then in charge: 'The bill had top priority and drafting was well advanced at the time of the change of Government.' (*New Zealand Parliamentary Debates,* vol. 413, p.2411) Nothing occurred in parliament in 1976 although no doubt the department was busy. In 1977 the new bill was introduced in parliament. The scenario was as follows:

24 August	Town and Country Planning Bill introduced, 115 pages long, with seventeen pages of explanatory notes; A select committee on the bill was set up.
3 October	The date by which submissions by the public were to be in to the committee.
17 October	The extended date for receipt of submissions. Local body elections were held during the month which made it dificult for local authorities to formulate submissions. Copies of the bill were difficult to obtain. 237 submissions were received – forty were heard before the government decided no more should be heard. Many others had indicated a wish to be heard.
7 December	The bill was reported back to parliament by the select committee. Extensive changes were added to the bill by the select committee. (The bill now numbered 159 pages.) The government printer did not have more than a handful of the amended bills available.
8 December	The bill was given a second reading under urgency. Debate concluded at 12.06 a.m. after less than three hours discussion. The changes made in the bill were substantial – whole parts were rewritten.

Mistakes were contained in the new material.

The 159 page bill was not available to opposition members until just *ten hours* before the second reading.

The opposition tried hard to have the bill deferred for recess study.

Many interest groups wanted to comment on the new, rewritten parts.

16 December The bill went through its committee stages and was given its third reading on the last day of the session, under urgency.

Unfortunately neither governments nor their leaders seem embarrassed by the methods to which they resort to pass legislation. There appears to be no pride taken in the fact, for example, that it has not been necessary to use the urgency provisions of standing orders. Indeed there is evidence to suggest that in New Zealand both major political parties derive some satisfaction from the contest that ensues when the government takes urgency and a round of marathon sittings occur in which many bills are dealt with. It appears to satisfy the fighting instinct of politicians; it lifts their morale and makes their adrenalin flow. We have arrived at the stage in the New Zealand parliament where legislative scrutiny is the poor relation of political confrontation.

Conclusion

Law-making should be a solemn and deliberate business. It ought to permit time for reflection and sober second thought. It ought to be organized so that people have a chance of knowing what is happening and making representations about it if they wish. It ought not to be rammed through the House of Representatives in the dead of night when parliament is off the air, by ruthless use of the urgency provisions in the standing orders.

The dangers which flow from the rapid passing of legislation are obvious enough:

- the legislation is not sufficiently scrutinized to detect flaws, omissions and anomalies
- there will not be enough time for the public to participate in the parliamentary process by making their views known
- inadequate scrutiny produces more amending legislation later
- it brings parliament into public disrepute and lessens the faith of people in it as watch-dog on government and a place where the opinion of the public will be listened to
- changes in the law come less to the attention of the public
- the passage of law comes to depend less on reasoned argument
- it brings the law itself into disrepute

Few of the ills from which New Zealand suffers can be easier or cheaper to cure than the problem of producing too many laws too quickly.

8
More fast law – regulations

Regulations are sometimes called 'subordinate' legislation. Although that statement is technically true in New Zealand, it wrongly suggests that regulations are always concerned with minor matters. Often they are. But the New Zealand parliament has passed acts allowing for regulations to be made on all manner of things. The purpose of this chapter is to explore the use of the regulation-making power in New Zealand, assess the strength of the protections which are available against it, and suggest improvements.

Regulations are inevitable in a modern and complex state where high technology, often dangerous, is in use. The grant of some legislative power to the executive branch of government is an inevitable feature of all modern democracies. A number of reasons are advanced to justify the use of regulations. Parliament does not have the time to consider everything so it should leave detail to the executive branch. Then there is the technicality of much subject matter, which is not fit for statute law. Flexibility and the opportunity to experiment are desirable and regulations provide these. And, it is suggested, emergency conditions requiring instant action can best be handled by regulations.

To grant the above points is not to say that we need as many regulations as we have. Figure 2 sets out the number of regulations published each year since systematic publication began in 1936. It can be seen that the years of the second world war produced a great many regulations, and we have been approaching those levels again since 1973. Of course mere numbers do not mean very much and Figure 2 does not include the regulations which have been repealed each year; that number has been considerable in recent years.

Also, to concede that regulations are necessary does not mean that the manner in which they are made is satisfactory, or that the protections available to the citizen against regulations are adequate. Regulation-making forms one of the most important sources of executive power in modern governments, the power to make law instantly. Against that

Figure 2   Regulations published annually since 1936

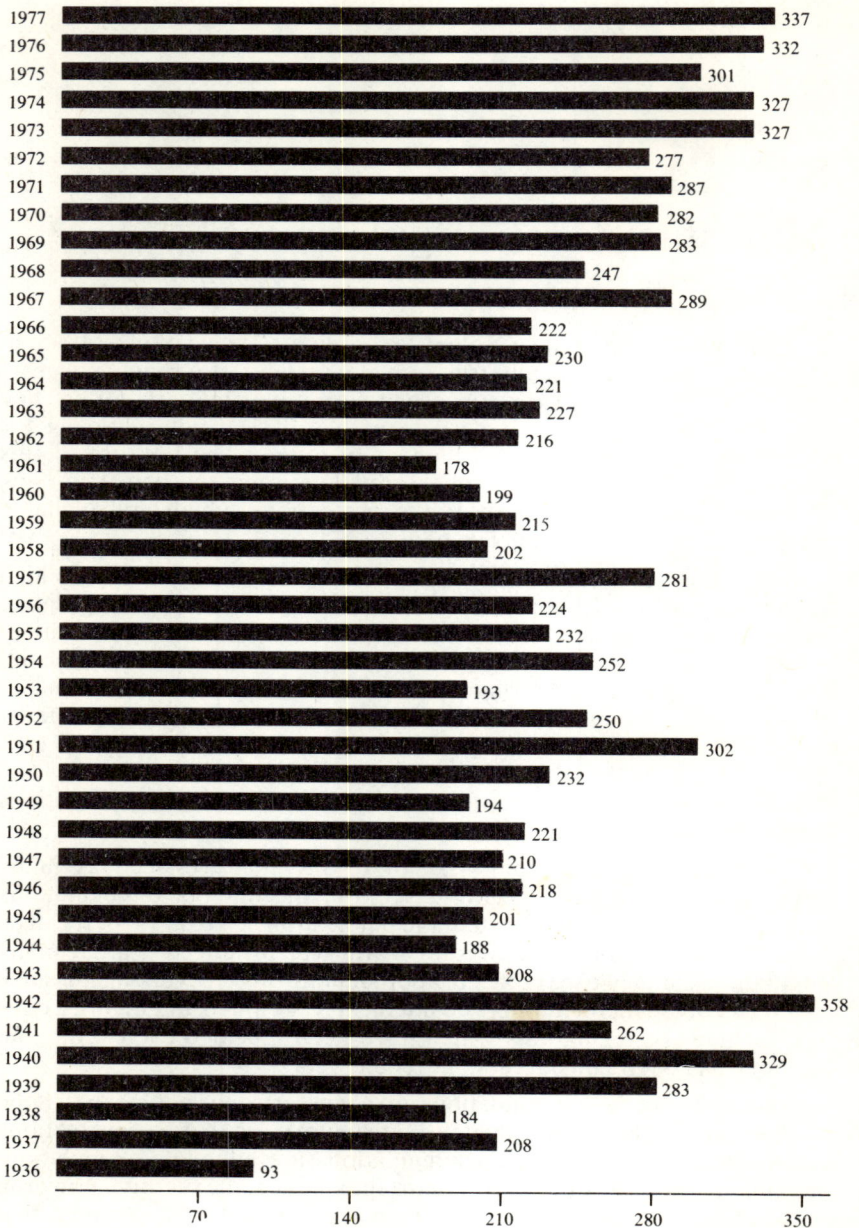

Year	Value
1977	337
1976	332
1975	301
1974	327
1973	327
1972	277
1971	287
1970	282
1969	283
1968	247
1967	289
1966	222
1965	230
1964	221
1963	227
1962	216
1961	178
1960	199
1959	215
1958	202
1957	281
1956	224
1955	232
1954	252
1953	193
1952	250
1951	302
1950	232
1949	194
1948	221
1947	210
1946	218
1945	201
1944	188
1943	208
1942	358
1941	262
1940	329
1939	283
1938	184
1937	208
1936	93

70   140   210   280   350

power New Zealand has fewer protections than many other democratic countries.

Of course I am being a little unfair when I stress the instant quality of regulations. The speed of law all depends on your point of view. To the unwary citizen a regulation may come like a bolt out of the blue. To the public servant who has been plodding away in his specialized area for years trying to get his department, parliamentary counsel and cabinet to make the regulation he believes to be essential, it may seem to be a very different process. There are plenty of cases of draft regulations languishing in departments for years because they do not have enough priority to rate action. All of which suggests that we should experiment more with alternatives to the coercive power of regulations, which are backed by the sanction of a criminal offence. We should try codes of practice which depend for their force upon community acceptance and knowledge. As it was put in a famous report in the United Kingdom by the Committee on Safety and Health at Work: 'Much greater use should be made of agreed voluntary standards and codes of practice to promote progressively better conditions.' (paragraph 453)

Generally we have relied too much upon legal controls and too little upon other approaches to control behaviour. Regulations should be used as a rapier rather than a broadsword. Unfortunately, the tendency in New Zealand has been to resort to regulations first, thereby avoiding the need to think about more creative approaches. I often wonder whether our penchant for regulations has done us much good. Is it not possible that our economy could be in a more healthy condition than it is if our politicians did not have the capacity to interfere with it as outlined in the next four paragraphs?

Consider two of the most potent sources of regulations in New Zealand. First let us look at the Economic Stabilization Act 1948. Section 11 provides:

(1) The Governor-General may from time to time, by Order in Council, make such regulations (in this Act referred to as stabilisation regulations) as appear to him to be necessary or expedient for the general purpose of this Act and for giving full effect to the provisions of this Act and for the due administration of this Act.

The act then goes on to authorize regulations for all or any of the following purposes:

- regulating the marketing of any goods or classes of goods for the general purpose of the act
- equalizing as far as possible the net returns received or payable in respect of any goods or classes of goods, and for that purpose imposing levies in respect of any goods or classes of goods
- the recovery of subsidies paid out of public monies in respect of any goods or classes of goods

- providing for the appointment of officers and committees and other bodies, and defining their functions and powers

These were the powers of which Mr Muldoon was thinking when he said in April 1976 that 'you can do anything provided you can hang your hat on economic stabilization' (*The Times*, 14 April 1976, p. 18); a chilling prospect even allowing for over-statement. Regulations made under the Economic Stabilization Act have had some nasty features: they tend to be retrospective and they purport to over-ride acts of parliament inconsistent with them. Regulations have been issued which are probably outside the scope of the act but challenges in the courts have unfortunately been rare.

The Reserve Bank of New Zealand Act 1964 gives important powers to make regulations to control the economy. Section 28 of the Reserve Bank of New Zealand Act 1964 provides that regulations may be made on a wide range of matters 'for the purpose of safeguarding in the public interest the credit, overseas resources, or development of New Zealand'. Matters about which regulations may be made include

- any overseas exchange transactions
- dealing in foreign securities
- commencement of business in New Zealand by overseas companies
- the methods of payment for exports
- disposal of foreign currency and foreign securities held by New Zealand residents
- the power to search people about to leave New Zealand

These powers are very considerable and should be in statute rather than regulation. (The matter was improved in that respect by the Overseas Investment Act 1973.) Elsewhere the Reserve Bank of New Zealand Act gives power to control interest rates by order in council, prohibiting, restricting or regulating dealings in gold, requiring financial institutions to hold assets of a certain type and in specified amounts. It is this latter provision which allows the government to control the business of banks and insurance companies to a very substantial degree. New Zealand statutes give the government power to make regulations of a breadth and range with which an economic dictator would think himself well served.

Regulations in New Zealand

Complaints against regulations in New Zealand go back a long way. They parallel the complaints about rushed legislation and they have produced the same effect. Despite constant complaint the position has deteriorated despite efforts to turn the tide in 1961 and 1962. At a Law Society Conference in 1928 the following resolution was passed:

That this Conference expresses its strong disapproval of the growing practice of legislating by regulation in important matters, and also of the tendency of recent legislation to entrust to officials wide powers not subject to control by the Courts and, in particular, the power of deciding questions affecting private rights, without allowing the constitutional right of appeal to the Courts.

('Proceedings of First Annual Legal Conference', *New Zealand Law Journal*, vol. 4, p. 51)

The discussion was carried on and in 1933 the prime minister of the day, George Forbes, felt constrained to defend the practice. But he did concede some ground:

It is always possible that mistakes have been made and the Government is as much concerned as its critics to ensure that Parliament does not lightly delegate its powers, and welcomes constructive criticisms of recent delegations by Parliament. To be constructive this criticism must be specific and not in vague general terms of condemnation.

(in *New Zealand Law Journal*, vol. 9, p. 92)

Through the gap left open by the prime minister ran Professor R. M. Algie, then a professor of law at the University of Auckland. He provided the prime minister with examples. In 'A System Open to Abuse', he concluded that the right to resort to delegated legislation 'has been very definitely abused in New Zealand'. The tendency to confer regulation-making power in wide and general terms was a 'deliberate and poorly concealed device for ousting the jurisdiction of the Courts', he said. And the power to make regulations was inserted in statutes 'on every possible occasion as a piece of convenient machinery irrespective of whether or not a pressing need for such a power actually exists'. (*New Zealand Law Journal*, vol. 9, p. 93).

There followed the period of the first Labour government and the second world war, both of which called for expanded use of regulations. The war, especially, produced many regulations. Indeed the record number of regulations passed in any year in New Zealand was 358 in 1942. But the Labour government had an attorney-general, H. G. R. Mason, who was interested in these matters and a Regulations Act was passed in 1936 which provided for the printing, publication and sale of regulations. And from 1936 regulations could be purchased from the government printer and annual volumes of regulations were made available. This was a great improvement upon the previous practice where it was necessary to search through the New Zealand *Gazette* to find regulations and indeed some regulations had not been published at all. And Mr Mason instructed that henceforth all regulations should be drafted in parliamentary counsel's office (as it is now called) and not in the department, a step which improved the drafting considerably. It should be observed, however, that publication of regulations before they come into force is not yet required in New Zealand. And the attorney-general can exempt regulations from publication, an unfortunate provision which could well be dropped. The fact that proper publication was not required until 1936 can still cause trouble as the following question and answer from parliament in 1977 illustrates:

Mr LANGE (Mangere) asked the Attorney-General: Has he noted the number of questions asked during the session about obsolete regulations that departments are ignoring, and about which Ministers commenting have said that their regulations should be reviewed, and, if so, will he take steps to ensure that departments review the regulations for which they are responsible, repeal those no longer needed, and consolidate those such as the Stock Importation Regulations 1915, which are in 28 separate places, including 14 in the *Gazette* prior to 1936, so that it will be possible to consider a reprint of the regulations?

Hon. P. I. WILKINSON (Attorney-General): I am aware that a number of questions regarding regulations have been asked this session. The review of regulations is a continuing and time-consuming process, which has proceeded in each department as resources have permitted. Unfortunately, a number of regulations published before 1936—including the Stock Importation Regulations 1915—are still to be found only in the *Gazette* . . .

(*New Zealand Parliamentary Debates*, vol. 416, pp. 5354–5)

Although these publication measures improved the situation, complaints did not cease. At a Law Society Conference in 1947 a lawyer, Mr A. C. Stephens, gave a paper entitled 'The Abuse of Delegated Legislation' in which he described regulations in strong language:

. . . this insidious evil on our community, for that is what it is, an insidious evil. It is insidious because it is creeping all around us, slowly, silently, and steadily, ever-increasing its scope; and it is an evil because, if unchecked, it will filch from us the freedom which we at present enjoy under the law . . .

(*New Zealand Law Journal*, 1947, p. 80)

The suggestion was made that parliament should have a special committee to scrutinize regulations.

It was Professor Algie who finally made the rescue attempt; he was in 1962 a member of parliament and speaker of the House of Representatives; he had been a minister of the crown. A book published in 1960, *Parliamentary Supervision of Delegated Legislation* by J. E. Kersell, had examined parliamentary supervision of delegated legislation in a number of Commonwealth countries and concluded that: 'the Parliament of New Zealand has been most lax in not providing protection to persons who find themselves subject to subordinate laws.' (p. 162)

Mr Algie (later Sir Ronald) chaired a parliamentary select committee which considered the situation in New Zealand and made some recommendations for change which were adopted. The committee praised the new form of regulation-making power which government had approved in 1961. The new form was designed to ensure that the courts could review whether a regulation fell within the scope of the power given in the act to make regulations. The courts, not the executive which made the regulation, would be the ultimate judge. And it was designed to ensure that 'the precise limits of the law-making power conferred by Parliament are set down as clearly as possible . . . .' ('Report of the Delegated Legislation Committee 1962', p. 12)

The Algie committee also considered that all regulations made should be laid upon the table of the House of Representatives so that they could be discussed there if members wished. The Regulations Act 1936 was amended to provide that all regulations 'shall be laid before Parliament within twenty-eight days after the date of the making thereof if Parliament is then in session, and if not, shall be laid before Parliament within twenty-eight days after the date of the commencement of the next ensuing session'. (s. 8)

A major recommendation of the Algie committee was that the Statutes Revision Committee, a select committee of parliament, be empowered to consider regulations referred to it with a view to determining whether the special attention of the house should be drawn to the regulation on the grounds:

(1) That it trespasses unduly on personal rights and liberties;
(2) That it appears to make some unusual or unexpected use of the powers conferred by the statute under which it is made;
(3) That for any special reason its form or purport calls for elucidation.
('Report of the Delegated Legislation Committee 1962', p. 13)

The standing orders of parliament were amended to make such provision, with a procedure for allowing the regulation to be referred to the committee if five members of the house request it during a parliamentary recess.

The procedure has existed for more than fifteen years, but until 1978 it had been employed on only three occasions, twice in 1977. These occasions were:

• an examination of the food hygiene regulations in 1964
• a review of a 1976 amendment to the rock lobster regulations, which placed an absolute prohibition on the hand-picking of rock lobsters on the part of fishermen who earned their living thereby
• reference of an order bringing into force the Wanganui Computer Centre Act 1976 after the computer was in full operation and some unauthorized dissemination of information had occurred;

In all of these cases the Statutes Revision Committee took a modest and cautious view of its power. Nevertheless, it was made clear that the power to report adversely to the house upon a regulation was one which would be availed of on the appropriate occasion. In the computer case, the committee found there was no matter requiring the special attention of the house. In the rock lobster case, on the other hand, the committee took the view that the regulation went further than was necessary and was an undue trespass on personal liberty. It recommended that the regulation be amended, revoked or replaced, a recommendation which was implemented by the replacement of the total ban on the picking of rock lobsters by the introduction of a closed season.

The two most recent commentators on the review of regulations in New Zealand, A. Frame and R. McLuskie, have 'welcomed the emergence from relative obscurity' of the procedure. (*New Zealand Law Journal*, 1978, p. 423) But I do not think it yet amounts to a sufficient protection for the citizen. The difficulties of getting a regulation referred to the committee are considerable, and indeed may be greater when the house is in session than when it is not. The difficulties are not helped by the fact that copies of regulations are not supplied to members of parliament unless they request them. One recent commentator, D. C. Pearce, who has examined the position in detail in all the Australian states and in New Zealand comments on 'the limited ability of the New Zealand parliament to exercise any control over regulations . . .' (*Delegated Legislation in Australia and New Zealand*, p. 80) It should be stressed, however, as is more fully described in chapter 9, that since 1963 the ombudsman has had considerable success in investigating and reporting upon unfair provisions in regulations and acts and causing them to be altered. And since 1978 the Human Rights Commission has been charged with reporting to the prime minister: 'The implications of any proposed legislation (including subordinate legislation) or proposed policy of the Government which the Commission considers may affect human rights'. (s. 6) How that might work remains to be seen.

There are occasional regulations in New Zealand which require confirmation by statute. For example, the Primary Products Marketing Act 1953 provides that all regulations made under the act shall be laid before parliament and shall expire on the last day of the session in which they are laid 'except so far as they are expressly validated or confirmed by an Act of Parliament passed during that session'. (s. 4) In 1978 three sets of regulations were confirmed by the Primary Products Marketing Regulations Confirmation Act of that year. Such provisions are not popular with governments as they can forget to sponsor the appropriate legislation; if that happens some regulations will lapse. In 1977, for example, it was necessary to pass the Primary Products Marketing Regulations Validation and Confirmation Act 1977 saying that certain regulations 'are hereby declared to be valid and to be in force, and to have always been valid and to have continued in force, in all respects as if they had been laid before Parliament' (s. 2) as required by the Primary Products Marketing Act. That was necessary because validating legislation had not been passed when parliament met for one day in February of 1977 when Queen Elizabeth was in New Zealand.

One other safeguard existed in New Zealand of which the Algie committee approved. Before the regulations are submitted to the governor-general in council the attorney-general must certify that they are in order. In practice the attorney-general used to take independent counsel's opinion whether the regulations would restrict liberty or were otherwise within power. That practice has lapsed and the attorney-general now relies upon a report from parliamentary counsel. The development can hardly be counted a desirable one.

In New Zealand the great majority of regulations come into force on the day after their notification in the *Gazette*. For example, the Hire Purchase and Credit Sales Stabilization Regulations 1957 Amendment No. 29 were made on 28 March 1977. They were notified in the *Gazette* on 31 March 1977. That is the usual lapse of time. A regulation sometimes becomes law before it is published and publicly available around the country.

In the United Kingdom quite a number of acts which authorize the making of regulations require consultations to be held with interested parties likely to be affected by the regulations. These requirements provide some opportunity for people likely to be affected by the regulations to put their point of view. It does not go as far as the American practice of publishing the draft regulation and receiving submissions or holding hearings on it, but it does provide some protection. In the United Kingdom, too, many regulations can be disallowed by resolution. In other words the regulation takes effect immediately, subject to annulment by resolution of either house. Such a procedure enables those affected adversely by a regulation to mount some sort of political protest against it and possibly succeed in having it thrown out. There are also some regulations in the United Kingdom which need to be laid before parliament in draft and require affirmative resolution before they can become law.

New Zealand regulations require consultation in only a few instances, although in practice there is often consultation. A novel procedure is contained in the Securities Act 1978. Regulations under that act are made in accordance with recommendations of the Securities Commission. Before it makes recommendations the commission is required to 'do everything reasonably possible on its part to advise all persons and organisations, who in its opinion' will be affected by the regulation. (s. 70) Such people must be given the opportunity to make submissions to the commission. And before making any recommendation the commission must give not less than fourteen days' notice in the *Gazette* and state briefly the matters to which the recommendation relates. The procedure for consultation is a real advance on anything tried in New Zealand before and it is to be hoped that the example will be adopted in other fields.

Emergency regulations

The most potent variety of regulation relates to emergencies. Regulations can be made under the Agriculture (Emergency Powers)

Act. And it is significant that some of these regulations are more difficult to challenge before a court than are usual regulations. For example, the Civil Defence Act 1962 provides a formula which empowers the governor-general to make regulations 'as appear to him to be necessary or expedient for the purpose of securing the public safety and generally safeguarding the interests of the public during any state of national emergency . . .'. (s. 55) The Public Safety Conservation Act 1932 is potentially the most dangerous and repressive piece of legislation on the New Zealand statute books. The act has been used only twice in forty-four years, once at the outbreak of war in 1939, when regulations were promulgated under the act; these were later brought under the authority of the Emergency Regulations Act 1939. The second occasion was the 1951 waterfront strike, an episode which can hardly be classed as one of the finer moments for the rule of law in New Zealand.

Section 2(1) of the Public Safety Conservation Act 1932 provides:

If at any time it appears to the Governor-General that any action has been taken or is immediately threatened by any persons or body of persons of such a nature and on so extensive a scale as to be calculated, by interfering with the supply and distribution of food, water, fuel, or light or with the means of locomotion, to deprive the community or any substantial portion of the community of the essentials of life, or if at any time it appears to the Governor-General that any circumstances exist, or are likely to come into existence, whereby the public safety or public order is or is likely to be imperilled, and a state of national emergency or of civil defence emergency has not been declared under the provisions of the Civil Defence Act 1962 in respect of those circumstances, the Governor-General may, by Proclamation approved in Executive Council . . . declare that a state of emergency exists throughout New Zealand . . .

When a proclamation of emergency has been made the act gives power to the governor-general 'to make all such regulations as he thinks necessary for the prohibition of any acts which in his opinion would be injurious to the public safety, and also to make all such other regulations as in his opinion are required for the conservation of public safety and order and for securing the essentials of life to the community'. (s. 3)

The 1951 regulations made pursuant to the Public Safety Conservation Act 1932 contained provisions of an unduly onerous type. The definition of strike included failing to work overtime. The minister was empowered to end strikes by notice in the *Gazette*. Freedom of expression in relation to declared strikes was prohibited. There was provision for the prohibition of processions, public meetings and the display of posters. The publication of statements made at public meetings which were likely to aid or abet the continuance of a declared strike became a criminal offence. The regulations placed all the funds of unions which were parties to a declared strike in the hands of a receiver. The minister was empowered to suspend awards and industrial agreements. The regulations authorized the temporary employment of members of the armed forces for any kind of work specified by order of the minister in writing. Picketing was made an offence. Special powers of entry without a warrant were given to the police.

In 1951 an unsuccessful attempt was made to challenge in the Supreme Court the use of the act and the validity of the regulations made under it. The climate for judicial review of subordinate legislation has changed considerably since then and it may very well be that a court might embark upon judicial review in an appropriate case. It would probably be difficult to persuade a court to interfere, but it might be possible in some circumstances.

An amendment made to the Public Safety Conservation Act in 1960 offers some check on the arbitrary use of the act. If parliament is not sitting when the proclamation declaring the emergency is made then parliament must be called together and sit not later than seven days after the date of the making of the proclamation of emergency. And the regulations expire after fourteen days from being tabled in the house unless they are confirmed by resolution.

Whether the courts or parliamentary debate could save us from abuse of the Public Safety Conservation Act is problematic. It may be that the apt legal description for the state of civil society undergoing a proclamation of emergency under the Public Safety Conservation Act comes from the Duke of Wellington's description of martial law. 'Martial law is neither more nor less than the will of the general who commands the army. In fact martial law means no law at all.'

It is a fact, which may be unpalatable to some people, that there are occasions when the public good requires the use of repressive powers. Who could argue in New Zealand that an outbreak of foot and mouth disease would not warrant taking drastic steps? That does not mean that the taking and using of drastic powers should be beyond all control or review either in parliament or in the courts. Such review must be available to ensure that when great powers are used the occasion for their exercise is appropriate. The people who have used them should not be the judge.

Parliamentary scrutiny of regulations overseas

In the United States the Administrative Procedure Act provides minimum standards which all federal agencies must meet when they are making 'rules', as regulations are called in the United States. With certain specified exceptions, general notice of proposed rule-making must be published in the federal register. Every such notice must include a statement of the time, place and nature of public rule-making proceedings. It must include a reference to the authority under which rules are proposed. And it must include 'either the terms or substance of the proposed rule or a description of the subjects and issues involved'. (*United States Code Annotated*, vol. 5, s. 553) Usually draft rules are published. After that interested persons must be given an opportunity to participate in rule-making by making submissions in writing and often there is the right to present views at a hearing as well. When the agency, having followed those procedures, decides upon the final content of the rules they must be published not less than thirty days prior to their coming into effect. Anyone can petition for the amendment, repeal or making of a rule at any time. Notwithstanding the act, rule-making even within the federal system of the United States is diverse. It can be seen, however, that the nature of the protection offered by the minimum safeguards of the Administrative Procedure Act far outweigh anything available in New Zealand, although the Securities Act 1978 takes a welcome step in the right direction.

In the United Kingdom most regulations are examined by a Joint Committee on Statutory Instruments which comprises members from both the House of Commons and the House of Lords. Each house has separate committees as well. The committee cannot review the merits or policy of the regulation, but can report on a wide range of other matters relating to it. Between 1966 and 1972, for example, the House of Commons select committee reported to the House of Commons on fifty-seven regulations.

Grounds for report include: that the regulation imposes a charge on public revenues; that there are features which exclude it from challenge in the courts; that it is retrospective; that there has been a delay in publishing the regulation or laying it before parliament; that there is doubt whether it is within the statutory power; that it makes unexpected use of power or that the drafting is defective. Before drawing the attention of the house to a regulation the committee must give the department concerned the opportunity of putting its case.

The Joint Committee on Statutory Instruments has made reports which are highly critical. In 1978 the committee stated: 'So far as we are able, we shall continue to assist in ensuring that delegated powers are not abused and will not fall into disrepute.' (*The Times*, 9 February 1978, p. 3) The report condemned the recurring tendency of ministers to by-pass parliament by making regulations which omitted details the public had a right to know and left the way open to wide ministerial discretion. The report was critical of several aspects of the manner in which the executive had used regulations. In commenting on the short interval between the publishing of regulations and their coming into force, the committee said:

We have on occasions been disturbed by what appears to be an astonishingly casual attitude on the part of the executive in this respect, amounting on the face of it to a cynical disregard of the rights of the subject . . .

(*The Times*, 9 February 1978, p. 3)

In all the Australian states and the commonwealth parliament at Canberra, parliament has greater power to scrutinize regulations than exists in New Zealand. Canberra has the most developed system, which has been an influential model for the Australian states. There, after regulations have been formulated, they must be laid before both houses of parliament within fifteen sitting days of each house; otherwise they are void. Either house may pass a resolution disallowing the regulation. In practice, the Australian Senate takes the active role in examining regulations. It has a standing committee devoted exclusively to the task. The committee has seven members, four senators from the government and three from the opposition; but the committee seems to have been little affected by party divisions. The committee scrutinizes regulations to see that:

- they are in accordance with the statute
- they do not trespass unduly on personal rights and liberties
- they do not unduly make the rights and liberties of citizens dependent upon administrative rather than judicial decisions
- they are concerned with administrative detail and do not amount to substantive legislation which should be a matter for parliamentary enactment

It might be observed at the outset that there are many New Zealand regulations which simply could not survive scrutiny under those headings. We often use regulations in situations where the Australians do not even have the power to pass a statute.

The Australian Senate committee receives copies of all regulations immediately after they have been made, together with an explanatory memorandum from the department responsible for administration of the regulations. The committee also has a law practitioner as legal adviser. It frequently summons before it departmental officers and the draftsman of the regulations. The committee can report to the Senate that any regulation be disallowed. D. C. Pearce, a reader in law at the Australian National University, reports: 'If the Committee has recommended that a regulation be disallowed, the Senate has disallowed it.' (*Delegated Legislation*, p. 38)

The existence of this committee and the way in which it carries out its work exercises considerable influence on the manner in which both ministers and public servants regard regulations. In Canberra the view is that regulations are to be avoided. The regulations will have to be justified to the Senate committee, officers may be questioned in a searching way before the committee and it will be necessary to think carefully about what the regulations contain. Once a regulation has been disallowed, a second regulation in like form cannot be made within six months. The committee has, over the years, been explicit about the type of features it does not want to see in regulations and this has exerted a considerable effect on the shape of regulations in Australia. If such a practice were adopted in New Zealand it could be anticipated that the number of regulations would fall and that the content of those which were made would be rather more carefully considered than it is now.

Conclusion

Opinions will differ on how much protection is appropriate from the regulation-making power of the executive in New Zealand. What does seem clear, on any view of the matter, is that the protections in New Zealand now are little short of derisory.

Attention can be focussed on a number of areas when it comes to deciding how to improve the system of checks and balances. It would be possible to give advance notice that a regulation was to be made and allow those with views to be heard. It would be possible to force ministers to make draft regulations available in all cases prior to their becoming law and to allow a parliamentary select committee to conduct hearings on them. But such a proposal would seem to go too far and create too much difficulty for government. The best model for our sort of government would seem to be the Australian one. We should develop a special parliamentary select committee to consider all regulations. We should give the committee power to investigate the background of the regulation thoroughly and to disallow the regulation by majority vote. At present not even parliament has power to disallow regulations.

It was good to see the issue of regulations come alive in the 1978 election campaign. Labour was first in the field and offered a select committee of parliament to review all regulations within three months of their being gazetted. Public hearings on regulations would be held. National promised to 'consult as widely as possible with interested parties regarding draft statutory regulations . . .'. (*Election Manifesto*, p. 31) Social Credit promised that regulations would have to be 'subject to a resolution affirming' of the House of Representatives in order to become law, and that it would also set up a select committee to scrutinize and report on regulations. (*Election Manifesto*, p. 51) Social Credit also promised to amend the law so that a regulation would have to be published before coming into effect.

9
What the courts can do

New Zealand has long enjoyed a judicial system based on British justice. Some complain of the rather formal way in which courts conduct their business, or the delays; others contend that lawyers speak a strange mumbo-jumbo that only confuses and makes things worse. And going to law can be expensive. But whatever charges are levelled against our system of justice, the courts enjoy a high reputation for fairness and impartiality. What people do not realize about the courts is that they are one of the arms of government, and exert an important checking function on the executive and on parliament. Alexander Hamilton, one of the founding fathers of the United States constitution, wrote long ago that 'the judiciary, from the nature of its functions, will always be the least dangerous' branch of government. (*The Federalist*, no. 78, p.483) The same is true in New Zealand. Not only is the judicial branch of our government the least dangerous branch, it is likely to be the most reliable in its adherence to principle, neutrality and rationality.

Most people when they think of the courts think of important criminal trials which are conducted before a jury. The criminal trial, of course, remains central to our system of justice. It provides fundamental protections for the accused person against the might of the state. The accused person has the right to be represented by counsel. He has the right to have the evidence against him heard in open court and tested by cross-examination. The case against him must be proved by the crown to a high level: beyond a reasonable doubt. The nature of the charge must be clear – it must be an offence against the law as written down in a statute. Upon conviction the person will be sentenced in accordance with the law. There is a right of appeal against both conviction and sentence.

The courts also carry out a wide range of other duties. They hear civil cases which are disputes usually involving money, between one citizen and another, or between a citizen and the government. A great many important matters come before the civil courts: questions relating to taxation; business contracts; a wide range of commercial affairs:

questions about wills, trusts and inheritance; family disputes over divorce, custody, separation and matrimonial property; cases where negligent conduct has caused another to suffer a loss; disputes over land and other property. With these cases we are not concerned. The focus here is upon the courts as a check upon abuse of power by government. The courts, coupled with the most important powers of the ombudsmen to examine the propriety of a whole range of government decisions, go a considerable distance towards checking excesses on the part of government and preventing arbitrary and unfair decisions being made. The New Zealand courts have shown themselves able in some situations to strike lethal blows at the aggrandizement of power by government.

The courts and the constitution

New Zealand has no written constitution – no set of principles against which legislation is judged and struck down if it does not conform with the principles. New Zealand has no federal system, which would require the courts to act as umpire between federal government on the one hand and state governments on the other. The basic legal rule of our constitution is that parliament is supreme. When it passes legislation that is the law. There is no higher law. There can be no argument that any statute parliament passed is unconstitutional. For these reasons the courts in our system of government do not often have the opportunity of deciding cases which involve the fundamental relationships between the elements of our government. Such a case did occur, however, in 1976. It is worth examining in some detail as it tells us something about what the courts can be expected to do.

The decision of the Chief Justice Sir Richard Wild in *Fitzgerald* v. *Muldoon* (Wellington, 11 June 1976) was an occasion for dancing in the streets. The case demonstrated that the courts can be bold in checking the excesses of executive power. It was an example of how the courts can uphold fundamental principles.

Three days after the prime minister was sworn in he issued a press statement (15 December 1975) purporting to give effect to the National Party's election policy to abolish the New Zealand Superannuation Scheme and refund all contributions to employees. The offending paragraph of the statement was:

The compulsory requirement for employee deductions to the New Zealand Scheme will cease for pay periods ending after this date. Mr Muldoon said that he recognized that because of arrangements made for payment of wages and salaries in advance through computer systems or by other means, deductions would in some cases continue for limited periods. All deductions and contributions, including any which may be made from now until 31 March 1976, will be returned to employees through the income tax refund system or could be transferred to another scheme. Similarly, the compulsory requirement for employer contributions will cease as from today in respect of salaries or wages paid from now on.   (*Fitzgerald* v. *Muldoon*, pp.616-7)

In a further statement on 23 December 1975 the prime minister said:

... the government had already made it clear that the superannuation scheme finished on December 15 and the compulsory requirement for employee deductions and employer contributions ceased for pay periods ending after that date. Empowering legislation, with retrospective effect, would be introduced early in the 1976 Parliamentary session.

(Fitzgerald v. *Muldoon,* p.617)

At the time the proceedings were issued and the case was decided parliament had not been called together so no legislation implementing the government's policy had been passed. Parliament had been summoned for 22 June 1976, ten days after the date of the court decision.

The New Zealand Superannuation Act 1974 had established an earnings-related superannuation fund. The scheme was a compulsory one. The act required that contributions be made at a prescribed rate by employees on their earnings with matching contributions by their employers. The employer was required to deduct the amount of the employee's contributions from the gross earnings of the employee. The plaintiff in the court case, a clerk in the Department of Education, was not a member of the Government Superannuation Fund established under the Superannuation Act 1956, neither was he a contributor to any approved alternative scheme referred to in the New Zealand Superannuation Act 1974. Accordingly, when the plaintiff became an employee of the crown in June 1975 he began to make contributions to the New Zealand Superannuation Scheme. The evidence showed that from and including the pay period ending 11 February 1976 no employer's contributions were paid in respect of the plaintiff's employment. The learned chief justice found: 'To that extent he has a direct interest and he has suffered a loss which, though small, is of monetary value. In all the circumstances of this case I think he is entitled to sue.' *(Fitzgerald* v. *Muldoon,* p.623)

The plaintiff sued the prime minister, the New Zealand Superannuation Board, the attorney-general, the controller and auditor-general and sought various remedies.

The chief justice vindicated principle by declaring that the prime minister's announcement of 15 December 1975 was illegal as being in breach of s.1 of the Bill of Rights 1688, an English statute which is part of New Zealand law and which states:

That the pretended power of suspending of laws or the execution of laws by regall authority without consent of Parlyament is illegall.

(6 Halsbury's Statutes, p.490)

He issued a declaration to that effect. He held that by making the statements he did the prime minister was purporting to suspend the law without the consent of parliament. Having issued the declaration all other matters were adjourned for six months because 'it would be an altogether unwarranted step to require the machinery of the New

Zealand Superannuation Act 1974 now to be set in motion again, when the high probabilities are that all would have to be undone again within a few months.' (*Fitzgerald* v. *Muldoon*, p.623)

Sir Richard Wild's disposition of this potentially embarrassing case resolved neatly the tension between principle and expediency. On the one hand he stared in the face a frontal attack upon the power of parliament to legislate and the rule of law. Without compromise he branded the occasion for what it was. On the other side he faced the practical problem of potential administrative chaos in setting the Superannuation Act going again when everyone knew that not only was it the government's intention to abolish the scheme but that they had the numbers in parliament to do it. He avoided that problem by the common sense solution of adjourning the proceedings for six months.

The avenues by which Sir Richard Wild might have escaped making a decision so unpalatable to the government were many. He flirted with none of them. He did not delay until parliament changed the law. The issuance of a declaration is discretionary, but it was issued. He rejected arguments, based on a construction of the press release, that there was no assertion that the act was being lawfully suspended. He made it clear, too, that while the prime minister gave no instructions to officials 'it is perfectly clear that they acted because of his public announcement of 15 December. Had it not been made they would have continued as before.' (*Fitzgerald* v. *Muldoon*, p.623)

The chief justice followed his citation of the Bill of Rights with a sustained statement of rhetorical power.

It is a graphic illustration of the depth of our legal heritage and the strength of our constitutional law that a statute passed by the English Parliament nearly three centuries ago to extirpate the abuses of the Stuart Kings should be available on the other side of the earth to a citizen of this country which was then virtually unknown in Europe and on which no Englishman was to set foot for almost another hundred years. And yet it is not disputed that the Bill of Rights is part of our law. The fact that no modern instance of its application was cited in argument may be due to the fact that it is rarely that a litigant takes up such a cause as the present, or it may be because governments usually follow established constitutional procedure. But it is not a reason for declining to apply the Bill of Rights where it is invoked and a litigant makes out his case.

(*Fitzgerald* v. *Muldoon*, p.623)

The chief justice went on to rely upon Dicey's dictum that under the English constitution parliament 'has the right to make or unmake any law whatever, and further, that no person or body is recognized by the law of England as having a right to override or set aside the legislation of Parliament'. (*The Law of the Constitution*, p.39)

In tainting with illegality a press statement the chief justice was instructing the nation. His message was that no one was above the law, that it applies to the mighty as to the humble. The point was also procedural. No one doubts the legitimacy of a legitimately elected government changing the law. But the means by which change must be achieved continues to be of utmost importance to our democracy. Many of our protections in the law are procedural, a characteristic of Anglo-American jurisprudence. The proper forms must be observed.

In the broadest sense the case of *Fitzgerald* v. *Muldoon* is significant for reasons discussed in chapter 1. It demonstrates perhaps more than any case ever decided in New Zealand the division of governmental powers between the three great components of the constitution: parliament, the executive and the judiciary. Each has its role to play. The preservation of balance in the system requires that the activities of each in relation to the others remain within proper boundaries. In the final analysis the courts will say what those boundaries are.

For the sake of completeness it should be recorded that the prime minister did not take the decision in good grace. He suggested that the chief justice had 'misunderstood' the position, although it is significant that no appeal was taken. The prime minister accused counsel for the plaintiff of having taken the initiative in instituting the action, rather than acting as mere professional adviser. That accusation was refuted in open court on the occasion when the chief justice awarded $2,500 in costs to the plaintiff against the prime minister.

In May 1977 the government began collecting, through the Post Office, increased licensing fees for motor vehicles. The collections began before the bill authorizing the increases had been passed by parliament. The Bill of Rights says 'Levying money for or to the use of the crowne by the pretence of prerogative, without grant of parlyament for longer time, or other manner than the same is or shall be granted is illegal.' (s.4) The point was plain enough. The government in parliament took the unusual step of suspending standing orders so that the legislation to legalize the collection of the increased fees could be passed. This was followed by a legally dubious attempt to merge N.A.C. and Air New Zealand by ministerial directive when the relevant statute, the New Zealand National Airways Act 1945, ordered N.A.C. to 'satisfy the need for air services within New Zealand', (s.13) something the directive ordered it to stop doing. That mess had to be sorted out by a later statute which declared, significantly, that the previous action was and always had been legal.

There used to be in New Zealand a body called the Monetary and Economic Council which established under a 1961 act of parliament. The purpose was to establish a group of qualified and independent people to make objective and public reports on economic questions. On 3 February 1978 the prime minister announced that the council was to be disbanded and its role taken over by the New Zealand Planning Council. So a statutory body was wound up by the executive without the consent of parliament – that had to come later.

On another occasion a different provision of the Bill of Rights was breached. Article 9 of the Bill of Rights provides:

That the freedome of speech and debates or proceedings in Parlyament ought not to be impeached or questioned in any Court or place out of Parlyament.

In November 1976 the cabinet ordered that a commission of inquiry investigate what had become known as the Muldoon-Moyle affair, one of the most lamentable occasions in the New Zealand public life. The prime minister suggested in parliament that Mr Colin Moyle had been 'picked up by the police for homosexual activity'. After a great hue and cry the government set up the commission to investigate, among other things, the police file on the matter and whether information on it had been disclosed to any person. Part of the terms of reference called for findings on the accuracy of statements made in the House of Representatives. Because of the Bill of Rights, the terms of reference should have been interpreted as precluding the commission from examining, questioning or discussing what members of the House of Representatives said in the course of debate. But the commission did enter into such an inquiry at the request of the government: it was contrary to the Bill of Rights.

Administrative law

People who are not lawyers know little about the courts' activity in what is called administrative law. Broadly, administrative law deals with legal checks on the exercise of power by ministers, officials and government generally. Government has conferred upon itself wide discretionary powers in many different areas of activity. As we have seen, numerous tribunals exist to decide specialized questions of licensing and registration. When ministers, public servants, local authorities or tribunals act in a manner which is illegal or unfair their decision can be quashed by a court.

Administrative law is a complex area of law which is rapidly changing. In order to explain some of its capacities to act as a check on official action let me give some New Zealand examples.

1. An act of parliament provides only one way to close off a street. Any city council wishing to close off a street must take certain steps and comply with certain requirements for public inspection of the plan for closing the street; notice of the proposals must be given; and provision must be made to allow people to object. Where there are objections, the city council can 'inquire into and dispose of' the objections. A city council entered into a contract with a business concern to provide land for a shopping development. The contract called for the city council to block a certain street. The court issued an order to the council prohibiting it from inquiring into and disposing of objections made to the closing of the street.

114

The action of the council was contrary to the rules of natural justice because a fair-minded person would conclude that the council must to a large extent have pre-determined the issue. The undertaking in the contract in advance of hearing objections to close the street meant that the council had not acted fairly. Because the council had prevented itself from acting fairly, it was not permitted to act at all. (*Bank* v. *Lower Hutt City Council*)

2. A female school teacher, married and living with her husband, was promoted to a position at a school away from the town in which she was then living. A teacher in those circumstances was entitled 'to actual and reasonable expenses of his removal to the other position' under regulations which were in force. The regulations also said 'The Minister shall lay down from time to time the general conditions governing payment of removal expenses...'. The Department of Education followed a practice (which had been laid down by the minister on the department's recommendation) of not paying full removal expenses under the regulations to a married female teacher unless the husband was an invalid or dependent on her financially. In other cases only the wife's own fares for travelling and the cost of shifting her own personal effects and hotel expenses had been paid.

The Supreme Court held that the Department of Education could not lawfully interpret the regulation to discriminate against women in that way and the minister could not validly lay down any such condition. The Court of Appeal upheld the Supreme Court's decision. (*Van Gorkom* v. *Attorney-General*)

3. Regulations provided that money could not be borrowed outside New Zealand except with the consent of the minister of finance. A company which was controlled by a citizen of the United States bought a big block of land and developed it as a tourist resort. To get out of financial difficulties the company wanted to borrow a lot of money overseas. The regulations gave the minister power to refuse consent, grant consent wholly or in part or subject to conditions, as the minister thought fit. The minister of finance at the time, Mr W.E. Rowling, wanted to stop overseas ownership of New Zealand land and said he would not regard with favour any application which did not ensure that the ownership of the land would revert to New Zealand interests. The Court of Appeal held that the purpose of the regulation was to safeguard New Zealand's overseas exchange reserves, credit and economic and financial development. The ownership of land was a distinct and different matter. The minister could not exercise his power under the regulations for the purpose of causing the land to revert to New Zealand hands. That was an irrelevant matter in terms of the regulations. The court said the minister had acted unlawfully. (*Rowling* v. *Takaro Properties Ltd*)

4. A Rent Appeal Board had power to assess equitable rents for houses in accordance with a number of factors laid down in the statute. The statute said: 'Every assessment shall be in writing and shall show the Board's reason for the assessment.' The board made an assessment in which it said it had visited the premises and taken into account some factors the statute said it should take into account: the locality of the house, the standard of accommodation the house provided and its state of repair. The Supreme Court ordered the board to reconsider its decision and give its reasons, not being satisfied with 'a bald statement of the statutory requirements'. (*Clark* v. *Wellington Rent Appeal Board and Smith*)

5. The Social Security Act provided for payment of domestic purposes benefits to solo mothers under certain circumstances. The statute empowered the Social Security Commission, in its discretion, to 'regard as husband and wife, any man and woman who, not being legally married, are in the opinion of the Commission living together on a domestic basis as husband and wife' and to terminate the benefit accordingly. A woman with three children was separated from her husband and living in the former matrimonial home. She met Mr X who assisted her with transport and offered emotional support. After six weeks X left his wife and rented a flat with one bedroom. X and the woman began to shop on a co-operative basis. They exchanged gifts. They shared mutual interests and friends. They sometimes stayed overnight in one another's houses. They had sexual intercourse. They took holidays together. The Social Security Department took the view that they were living together on a domestic basis and stopped the benefit. The Social Security Appeal Authority agreed. The Supreme Court held that construction of the legislation to be erroneous. The Judge said that 'domestic basis' required 'living together under the same roof on a basis of some permanence'. (*Furmage* v. *Social Security Commission*)

The above are all cases where government action was successfully challenged. There are many unsuccessful challenges. For example, in 1975 a member of the Ananda Marga sect came to New Zealand on a permit to remain for one month. Then he applied for and was granted an extension. Before expiry of the extension a minister of the crown signed and issued a revocation of the extension without giving any reason. The minister gave the applicant no right to be heard. The courts refused to interfere.

A number of important limitations exist on the capacity of the courts to quash and review government action. Sometimes, although less often than used to be the case, the government will try to limit the courts' capacity to interfere or review by express statutory language. The courts have shown a tendency not to be put off by these efforts, but there are areas where it will be difficult to get a court to intervene for that reason. There are other areas where the courts judge it unwise for them to intervene.

The courts usually intervene where the authority concerned has acted without legal power, and that may include situations where the authority acts in bad faith or for a wrong purpose. The courts are committed to ensuring that the rules of natural justice are followed. Broadly this means the courts will ensure that administrators act fairly. The rules set the minimum level for fair decision-making. For example, under these rules no-one can be a judge in his own cause; likelihood of bias is prevented. (Case 1 above was an example where these rules were breached.) Contesting parties are entitled to a fair hearing. Where a person stands to be penalized, he must receive fair notice of the charge and an opportunity to answer the case against him.

All these rules have their most obvious application to tribunals, but they are applied elsewhere as well. Obviously they have no application to legislative rules propounded by government. Where government has a discretion to do things the courts sometimes review that discretion; they check that it has been exercised by someone who is authorized to exercise it. They will interfere where the discretion has been abused, as in case 3 above. Courts will inquire, too, whether the pre-conditions laid down for the exercise of the discretion have been satisfied. A recent decision of the Court of Appeal opens up the possibility of securing damages where loss has been suffered from an invalid decision negligently reached. And liability of public authorities generally for negligent performance of their duties and powers is being extended by the courts.

Government itself has begun to recognize the justice of allowing courts to review the fairness and legality of official decisions. In 1968 an administrative division of the Supreme Court was established to hear appeals from administrative tribunals – there are almost thirty statutes which provide for appeals to the administrative division. In 1972 an act simplified the procedures for reviewing government action.

One of the most important obstacles to be overcome in using the courts to challenge government action lies in that area of the law known as standing. Standing, which has developed a formidable body of case-law, is concerned with judging whether the applicant before the court has sufficient personal stake in the decision he is challenging to challenge it. Standing can be used by the government as a shield, to divert attention from an alleged illegality to an inquiry into how an applicant was specifically affected by the decision. A recent report of the New Zealand Public and Administrative Law Reform Committee proposes cutting away the technicality and providing a simple test. Under this proposal the court may 'refuse relief to the applicant if in the

Court's opinion he does not have a sufficient interest in the matter to which the application relates'. (*Report on Standing in Administrative Law*, p.33) It is to be hoped that the amendment is made quickly.

Regulations and by-laws

The cases discussed earlier in this chapter concerned actions of government which were held to be illegal for one reason or another. It was the courts' duty to ensure that:

- there is a legal rule under which government has acted (see the discussion in chapter 1)
- the rule has been correctly interpreted and applied
- the action is not contrary to the rules of natural justice

In none of the cases we have dealt with so far have the courts questioned the validity of the enacted rule, but there are occasions on which they do. For the purposes of considering whether a bill of rights with judicial review should be part of New Zealand law, it is particularly important to understand the manner in which the judges exercise that right.

New Zealand courts cannot strike down statutes enacted by parliament as invalid. But the power they have in interpreting the words of a statute and applying them to cases is considerable: a statute means what the courts say it means, not what the executive says it means. But parliament's law is supreme and the judges must apply it. Regulations are rules made by the governor-general in executive council on the recommendations of ministers. Regulations are law, but they must be made under the authority of an act of parliament. The courts examine regulations to ensure they are within the scope of power granted by parliament to make the regulations. In carrying out that duty the courts can invalidate regulations which have been made. Two examples will demonstrate the process and the restraint it imposes upon the executive.

1. The Toheroa Regulations 1955 provided that: 'No person shall open toheroa in any place below high-water mark.' The purpose of the regulation was apparently to prevent pollution of the toheroa beds. It might be observed, however, that the wording of the regulation went a very long way indeed: the opening of toheroa on board ship would be prevented. The regulations were made under the authority of the Fisheries Act 1908. Under the act power was given to the governor-general to make regulations for the following purposes among others ('fish' includes 'shellfish'):

- generally to regulate sea fishing in New Zealand
- to prohibit or regulate the possession of any fish
- to prohibit the deposit on any oyster bed of any substance
- to set apart waters or adjacent areas for the propagation of fish
- any other purpose for which regulations are contemplated or required by the act

The court decided the regulations were outside the power conferred by the act and were void. Nowhere did the act give express power to make regulations governing the opening of shellfish. None of the provisions could be interpreted as granting such a power.

2. The Education (School Age) Regulation 1943 made under the Education Act 1914 gave power to an education board to transfer pupils or to refuse to enrol pupils 'for the purpose of ensuring that the best use is made of all accommodation and educational facilities available in school . . .'. (*Reade* v. *Smith*, p. 996) Vernon Smith, a boy aged twelve, was enrolled in Auckland School A in 1954. In February 1955 he was transferred to School B by the board, as a result of zoning decisions. In February 1956 he was transferred to School C. In August 1958 he was transferred to School D. The boy's father refused to send him to the last school, but the boy was refused tuition at his old school and his father was charged under the provisions of the Education Act governing truancy. The prosecution failed because the Supreme Court held the regulations were invalid. The act provided that the governor-general was authorized to make regulations 'for any purpose for which regulations are by this Act authorized or required to be made, and generally for any purposes which he thinks necessary in order to secure the due administration of this Act'. The court refused to be put off by that language. The court would always inquire into any question of law the governor-general may be required to decide, and also the court would decide whether the governor-general would reasonably have formed any opinion, whether law or fact. Mr Justice Turner, therefore, examined the purposes which could have been considered by the governor-general as necessary to secure the due administration of the act and found nothing to justify the regulation. Setting a maximum number beyond which new enrolments might not be accepted was all that was necessary. Another provision in the Education Act gave the governor-general power to 'make such Regulations as he thinks necessary or expedient for avoiding doubt or difficulty which may appear to him to arise in the administration of the principal Act by reason of any omission or inconsistency therein, and all Regulations shall have the force of law, anything to the contrary in the principal Act notwithstanding'. That provision appeared to do great evil: to allow the executive to make regulations contrary to provisions in a statute. But still Mr Justice Turner was unmoved. He construed it strictly, and there was no doubt or difficulty, he said.

The case is a classical example of how far a court will go, in a case where justice requires it, to strike down a regulation which is unfair and oppressive, even though the power given to make regulations is a very wide one. The power is drafted widely to try to prevent the courts reviewing regulations. Sometimes the courts will give in without a struggle. For example, regulations dealing with emergency situations tend not to be interfered with easily. And the number of occasions where a regulation is outside the power given to make it are few. Where a specific power is granted to make a regulation on a specific topic, and the regulation is within the power, the court is powerless to strike it down.

The courts can strike down a by-law made by a local authority on the ground that it is unreasonable. Just one example will suffice to illustrate how this works. In 1930 the Waipawa County Council made a by-law which provided that hawkers trading within the county should pay a licence fee of £5 for every half year (that would be a substantial amount in today's money – probably an average person's earnings for a week). It was said in evidence by the county clerk that the purpose of the by-law was to restrict hawkers and pedlars as much as possible. The court held the by-law void for unreasonableness, so that a person prosecuted under it could not be convicted.

Government reversal of court decisions

A fundamental limitation on the power of the courts to check executive decisions results from the government's control over the legislative machinery of government. The government can change any regulation at will. And it can amend statutes with only a little more trouble. It is common in New Zealand for governments to react swiftly and decisively against judicial decisions which are unacceptable to them. For example, in case 5 on p. 116 an amending act was passed in 1978 deleting the words 'living together on a domestic basis as husband and wife' and substituting a new section giving the social security authorities power to 'regard as husband and wife any man and woman, who, not being legally married, have entered into a relationship in the nature of marriage . . .' (*Social Security Amendment Act 1978*, s. 17) That seems to be an attempt to reverse the Supreme Court decision, although it remains to be seen whether the courts will say it has accomplished the purpose.

The Department of Social Welfare figured in another case which deserves to be dealt with at some length. I am indebted to an article by Dr G. P. Barton for the details. Decisions on many social welfare matters are made by the Social Security Commission, comprising high-ranking officers of the department. The commission is under the statute subject to 'the general direction and control' of the minister. One of the social security benefits is the family benefit, $3.00 per week for each child free from any income or means test. The family benefit can be 'capitalized' in certain circumstances to help the parents of a child to buy a house as a home in which the child can live. An outline of the developments in the case follows.

1. In November 1975 the minister of social welfare issued a directive setting out the basis upon which applications for family benefit capitalization should be dealt with. The directive imposed dollar limits upon income and assets beyond which applications should not be granted.

2. Mrs K. M. Macfarlane applied to the department to be classified as eligible for capitalization to build a home on the section she and her husband owned. The application was declined because the income of Mr Macfarlane exceeded a figure which was set as the maximum in the minister's forthcoming directive.

3. Mrs Macfarlane applied for a review of the decision, but the original decision was adhered to.

4. Mrs Macfarlane took legal advice and made an appeal to the Social Security Appeal Authority. Relying on a provision in the relevant statute laid down as one of the criteria for making a decision, 'The applicant or the spouse could not reasonably be expected to arrange finance from any other source . . .', the Appeal Authority allowed the appeal. That seemed to suggest that the minister's directive was not binding. The decision was made on 3 March 1976.

5. The Social Security Commission appealed to the Supreme Court. Mr Justice White dismissed the appeal in a decision on 14 December 1977. He held that where a statute contained detailed provisions as to its application those provisions could not be over-ridden by directives from the minister.

6. When the judge's decision was announced, the Social Security Amendment Bill (No. 2) 1977 was before parliament. It made alterations to various benefits, but did not deal in any way with the issues which had been before the court.

7. At 10.36 p.m. on the day following the court decision the minister of social welfare moved to insert new clauses in the bill to reverse the effects of the judge's decision. Under the terms of the amendment the commission would be legally bound to comply with any special or general directions given by the minister in writing. The next day, on the final sitting day of the session, the house agreed to insert the minister's amendment in the bill. There appears to have been no explanation of the purpose of the amendment, no reference to the decision of the court, no discussion and no debate.

8. The bill received the royal assent on 23 December 1977 and became law on that day.

In discussing the events set out above, Dr G. P. Barton concludes:

Thus we have come full circle. Ministerial control of the Commission in matters of detail and Ministerial interference with the exercise of discretionary power were foiled by the rule of law. Ministerial control and Ministerial interference are now legitimated by rule by law. It is not a pretty sight.
(*Victoria University of Wellington Law Review*, vol. 9, p. 393)

Indeed it is not and it is not one which was in any way necessary. It illustrates how a determined executive can use its domination of parliament to reverse the effect of just decisions of the courts with no proper consideration.

Conclusion on the courts

The existing capacity of the judges to protect people against excessive and arbitrary power exercised by government depends upon important fundamental concepts. The courts interpret statutes and regulations in the event of dispute. Although the executive branch of government has scope for much interpretation in order to run government on a day to day basis, the authoritative and binding interpretations come from the judiciary. It is the province of the judges to say what the law is in any given case. We have seen examples where the courts, in providing authoritative interpretation, have curbed the executive. Sometimes the response has been to legislate away the court's interpretation, a dubious practice. The courts, however, do not give in without a struggle.

Apart from the power of statutory interpretation, the courts have the ability to give judgments against the government; occasionally in constitutional block-busting cases like *Fitzgerald* v. *Muldoon*, but more usually in applying the growing remedies in the field of administrative law, examples of which have been given. The increasingly bold manner in which these powers are being exercised suggests that our judges are not blind to the growth of executive power in New Zealand and that they are prepared to act when appropriate cases come before them.

It might be remembered that our judges in New Zealand are often employed in a policy role too. Quite frequently they are called upon to chair royal commissions to make recommendations for changes in policy. Sir Thaddeus McCarthy, both while he was a judge and since he retired, has chaired a number of important royal commissions. Sir Owen Woodhouse chaired the Royal Commission on Personal Injury, which broke fresh ground and led to the Accident Compensation Act. Mr Justice Beattie recently chaired the Royal Commission on the Courts. So our judges have demonstrated a worthwhile capacity to provide ideas of measured innovation.

The recent report of the Royal Commission on the Courts is important in another respect. It makes some cautious recommendations for change in the structure of our courts, but the basic aim of the recommendations appears to be to strengthen the support given the courts so that they can achieve their tasks more quickly and efficiently. There is to be a new District Court (including a Family Court) with increased power. There are recommendations for improving procedures and facilitating access by the citizens to the courts.

The courts have a vital role to play in prodding government to be fair and checking it when it is not. To the extent we have trusted the courts in the past they have not let us down. The need for an expansion of that role seems called for. We should increase their capacity to review administrative decisions of government and provide new remedies for them to use.

The ombudsmen

In 1962 New Zealand made an important constitutional innovation: it established the office of ombudsman. The idea was based on an institution which had existed in Sweden since 1809 and was later adopted in other Scandinavian countries. In a bold move New Zealand picked up the idea, adapted and implemented it – the first English-speaking country to do so. The basic purpose of the ombudsman in New Zealand has been to provide an individual who is aggrieved with decisions of government with an avenue of redress. The ombudsman's role has been described as that of 'the formulator of administrative equity by the power of persuasion'. (Quoted in the 1978 *Report of the Ombudsman*, p. 17)

By 1978 there were three ombudsmen. They are officers of parliament and are appointed for five-year terms; appointments are made on the recommendation of the House of Representatives. They are empowered to investigate 'any decision or recommendation made, or any act done or omitted . . . relating to a matter of administration' affecting a person individually. The relevant act sets out the departments and organizations whose decisions can be investigated, a list which includes forty-four government departments as well as nearly fifty quangos. By amendments made in 1975 the ombudsmen are now empowered to investigate decisions made by local government, such as city and county councils and many others. Investigations can be made by ombudsmen either after a complaint in writing made by a member of the public or on their own motion. They can also carry out special investigations which the prime minister considers should be instigated. The act also lists a number of matters the ombudsmen cannot investigate: for example, where there is a right of review by a court on the merits of a decision.

The ombudsmen have no power to alter decisions. They simply investigate and report upon them. Nonetheless these investigations, the recommendations they make and the publicity given to them exert a considerable influence in righting injustices which have occurred in administration and changing the way in which officials approach some tasks. The ombudsmen may decide that a decision was unfair on a number of grounds – that it was:

- contrary to law
- unreasonable, unjust, oppressive or improperly discriminatory
- made under an act, regulation or by-law that was unreasonable, unjust, oppressive or discriminatory
- based on mistake of fact or law
- simply wrong
- made in the exercise of a discretionary power used for an improper or irrelevant purpose.

Where the ombudsman reaches an unfavourable view of a decision he can say:
- the matter should be further considered by the appropriate authority
- the omission should be rectified
- the decision should be cancelled or varied
- the practice on which the decision was based should be altered
- the act, regulation or by-law on which the decision was based should be reconsidered
- reasons should have been given for the decision
- other steps should be taken

The ombudsman must report his opinion and reasons for it to the appropriate department or organization. If no adequate action is taken the ombudsman can report the matter to the prime minister and thereafter report to parliament as he thinks fit. The complainant must also be informed of the result of any investigation.

Every year the report of the ombudsmen tabled in parliament contains accounts of the cases investigated, the recommendations they made and the results achieved. Of the 1,031 complaints fully investigated by the ombudsmen in the year ended 31 March 1978, 381 were sustained. In the remaining 650 cases the ombudsmen did not think the official action could be seriously criticized. I give one short simple example to show how the ombudsmen work. (The case is contained in the 1978 annual report, p. 53.)

Accident Compensation Commission

Case No. W12796

A firm of solicitors wrote to me about the manner in which the Accident Compensation Commission had handled claims made by two of their clients, a mother and daughter.

The solicitors alleged that the Commission had delayed unreasonably in reaching a decision on one of the claims and had failed to advise them of the reason for this delay. The solicitors also complained that the commission had failed to respond to correspondence concerning their clients' claims. As a consequence the solicitors alleged that their clients had incurred unnecessary additional legal fees in pursuing their claims.

In his report the chairman of the Commission acknowledged that the claims had not been handled as well as they should have been. He stated that the Commission had instructed its staff to provide an interim acknowledgment of correspondence within 3 days of receipt and a full reply within 3 weeks. If it was not possible to give a full reply, the instructions were that the inquirer must be told the reasons for the delay and kept informed of the progress of the inquiry. This practice had not been followed in respect of the claims in question and I therefore regarded the complaints as sustained.

At my request, the solicitors estimated the additional costs directly related to these delays and failures. I advised the Chairman of the Commission that in my view it was inequitable that the claimants should have to meet these additional costs which resulted from omissions for which the Commission had accepted

124

responsibility. I said that in my view these costs should be met by the Commission. In his reply the Chairman informed me that the claim for legal costs would be considered by the Compensation Division and that the decision on it would be subject to the normal review and appeal provisions of the Accident Compensation Act 1972.

I advised the solicitors of my findings and they informed me that as a result of my intervention their clients' claims were nearing finality and they were grateful for my assistance.

The ombudsmen are a worthy addition to our government, redressing the balance somewhat in favour of the citizen. Their method of looking at decisions is quite different from that used by the courts and forms a useful addition to judicial review of administrative action. The ombudsmen have demonstrated, following the model set by the first ombudsman, Sir Guy Powles, that they can right wrongs and act as a check upon the excesses of the bureaucracy. The office has undoubtedly been a success within the limits of the conception, but the idea has probably come close to its limits as a means for checking government. On the big questions of public policy concerning the exercise of executive and legislative power, the ombudsmen cannot be expected to be an effective check; they are individual grievance men – with a valuable but different function.

10

A written constitution and/or a bill of rights?

Ever since the abolition of the upper house of the New Zealand parliament in 1950, there have been spasmodic demands for a written constitution in New Zealand. During the fifties and sixties the Constitutional Society for the Promotion of Economic Freedom and Justice in New Zealand (Inc.) devoted considerable efforts to promoting a written constitution for New Zealand. The society also advocated the re-introduction of a second chamber for parliament and a bill of rights within a written constitution. In a 1961 petition to parliament the Constitutional Society advocated all three in a draft document.

A bill of rights could be introduced quite independently of a written constitution or it could be combined with a written constitution. By a bill of rights is simply meant a statement of fundamental principles which constitute the supreme law and to which all other laws are subject; a different type of document from the English Bill of Rights 1688 mentioned in chapter 9. Proposals for a written constitution and a bill of rights are separate suggestions, each with different implications, although there is some overlap between them.

A written constitution

A written constitution, without a bill of rights, would bring together the various elements of our existing arrangements. Some existing elements are in acts of parliament; others are not written down in any law. Indeed, some of the most important points in our constitution depend upon customs known as conventions. In 1977 Dr D. E. Paterson prepared a draft written constitution for consideration by the New Zealand Section of the International Commission of Jurists. Dr Paterson's draft illustrates the sort of matters a written constitution would cover.

- the territory of New Zealand – the boundaries
- the sovereign, including the royal style and titles and setting out the powers, privileges and obligations of the sovereign. In particular the

126

'reserve' powers of the sovereign are defined, particularly the occasions when the sovereign is not obliged to act on the advice of the ministers
- the role and functions of the governor-general are defined and the instances in which the governor-general could, in exceptional situations, act other than in accordance with the advice of the executive council are set out as above
- where the governor-general cannot act, provision is made for an administrator to act as a substitute; provision is also made for the office of deputy governor-general
- the composition of the executive council is defined and the functions of that body set out
- the office of prime minister is dealt with, the method of appointment and the broad constitutional functions of the office
- cabinet composition and the powers and duties of ministers of the crown are set out. Ministers shall 'determine and formulate policy, and secure the implementation of that policy . . .'
- departments of state, public corporations, commissions and councils, the armed forces and the police force are briefly described
- the most basic rules governing elections are put in the constitution – secret ballot, drawing up of electorates by the Representation Commission, the Maori seats and the qualifications and disqualifications for being a member of parliament
- the functions of parliament are briefly mentioned
- the court structure is set out
- the basic functions of tribunals and the ombudsmen are defined
- the constitution is expressed to be the supreme law of New Zealand and all other law must be subject to it and void if there is any inconsistency
- amendments can be made by two methods – by a majority of two-thirds of all members of the House of Representatives or by an act of parliament passed by a simple majority of members of parliament and endorsed by a simple majority of electors.

Opinions differ on the appropriate content of a written constitution. Dr Paterson's aim seems to have been to put down exactly in writing the best understanding of our existing arrangements; no great changes are contemplated. The proposed functions of the branches of government are almost identical to what they are now. Perhaps the biggest change is to try to clean up what is known as the 'reserve' powers – the difficulties of which are discussed in chapter 2. Notwithstanding the fact that a written constitution may represent little alteration from current reality, it represents a big break from our existing constitutional law.

At present we have no supreme law. Parliament can pass any law without being subject to any higher law enshrined in a constitution. (There are some provisions in the Electoral Act which require a majority of 75 per cent of all the members of the House of Representatives or majority vote in a poll of electors.) To set out the functions of the prime minister and ministers would make a great change to our constitution.

By placing the functions and powers of the various parts of government in a constitutional document the capacity for evolution would be reduced. Our constitution has evolved by usage. Such evolution would be restricted in the future by the need to conform to the written words of the constitution. I do not want to overstate the effect of such an inhibition; the type of written constitution under discussion is fairly loose and flexible.

There are some other arguments against a written constitution. Once the basic powers of the branches of government are written down, disputes could arise over whether each branch has acted within its proper sphere. Those disputes could result in litigation. The opportunity for such disputes does not seem very great, when no bill of rights accompanies the written constitution, but it must be expected that there would be some. In that sense, the courts would play a greater role in determining our constitutional arrangements than they do now. That may be no bad thing. The courts would simply be deciding what the supreme law in the constitution means, but it would involve them in a new function and it is as well to recognize the fact.

Codifying the fundamentals of a parliamentary democracy might appear to be a protection against an easy road to dictatorship. Certainly it seems likely such a document may prevent us slipping from one pattern of government to another but its capacity ought not to be exaggerated. Such a document would not prevent our democracy breaking down if conditions were propitious for its collapse. And the courts could not save us if we were determined to travel to the edges of anarchy.

Another difficulty with a written constitution arises from the argument that it cannot be made into supreme law. It is said that parliament cannot bind its successors by deciding that any particular law should require more than a simple majority to alter it. Here 'entrenched' clauses of the New Zealand Electoral Act become relevant.

Section 189 of the Electoral Act provides that the sections of the act setting the duration of the House of Representatives at three years, the Representation Commission, the method of voting, the voting age and some other important provisions cannot be altered unless 75 per cent of all members of the House of Representatives vote for the change or a majority vote for the change in a poll of electors. But section 189 itself is not subject to the same requirement. That means, as a matter of law, that parliament could change the basic provisions in the Electoral Act by repealing section 189 by a simple majority. The 'entrenched' provisions have a sort of moral sanctity, but they enjoy no legal immunity from change by parliament more than any other law. Some constitutional

128

lawyers maintain that any effort to entrench the 'entrenched' provisions themselves would not be effective. They say it would not be possible to make section 189 itself subject to a 75 per cent majority before it could be changed.

If a written constitution were passed as an act of the New Zealand parliament, containing provisions requiring special procedures to be followed for amendment, the same problems would arise. Could such a Constitution Act be made more difficult to alter than an ordinary act of parliament? If one parliament adopts a statute called the Constitution Act which stipulates it cannot be changed except with the concurrence of two-thirds of the members of parliament (or by referendum or some other procedure) can a later parliament repeal the earlier measure without following the procedure? Some argue that where the supremacy of parliament and the supremacy of the law conflict, then the law must be regarded as supreme where it provides conditions which must be fulfilled to make a law. I think a better view is that parliament as organized at a particular time can lay down particular procedures for the method of amendments of certain acts. And I believe the courts would recognize those restrictions and require that they be observed. That means New Zealand has the ability to transform the constitution into a written one and insulate the new constitution from amendment by a simple majority in parliament.

There are more elaborate ways New Zealand might establish a written constitution. We could ask the parliament in the United Kingdom to pass a statute which embodies our constitution. That parliament would do so if asked by the New Zealand parliament. The Australians received their constitution that way. But times have changed since 1900 and the legal organization of the Commonwealth is no longer that of the British Empire. If we want a written constitution we ought to be able to do it ourselves.

We might conceivably elect, under a statute passed in New Zealand, members to a constitutional assembly. They could deliberate upon the content of any constitution and settle a document which would then be put to the public in a referendum. It would be simpler to enact the constitution as an ordinary act of parliament, which could make provision for electors to register their views in order for the constitution to become law. Or it would be possible to enact the constitution as an ordinary statute which contains special provision for amendment without any need for referendum.

The point to emphasize is this: it is possible for New Zealand to adopt a written constitution that constitutes a supreme law more difficult to change than ordinary laws. For many years the erroneous view has been propounded that such is not possible in New Zealand. Of the procedures available, the following seems best to me. A royal commission should be appointed to consider whether New Zealand should adopt a written constitution. If its view were that a written constitution should be adopted the commission should prepare a draft constitution. The proposed constitution could be discussed. The constitution itself would provide for a method of amendment, probably including a vote by the public. The document should be adopted by the same procedure. A royal commission inquiry is not legally necessary, but would provide greater political authority for the document.

A bill of rights?

Attaching a bill of rights to a written constitution adds another dimension to the issue. Depending on the form adopted it could involve more fundamental redistribution of power among the branches of government. It involves a decision that the executive and parliament cannot be trusted to preserve certain fundamental freedoms and that other institutions must be charged with the task. Of all the proposals for change discussed in this book, a bill of rights would involve the most radical alterations to our existing constitution.

Serious proposals for a bill of rights for New Zealand first appeared in the 1960 general policy of the National Party where it was stated:

A National Government will pass a Bill of Rights similar to that recently adopted by the Canadian Parliament.

In 1963 a bill of rights was introduced into parliament. It was designed to give statutory recognition to the fundamental rights and freedoms that existed in New Zealand. The form of the proposed legislation owed much to Canadian legislation of 1960. The Canadian model requires that where a provision in the bill of rights is to be over-ridden, the act over-ruling it must say so explicitly. But there is no great protection in that although there would be political heat applied when the government wants to over-ride the bill of rights. In the 1963 general policy the National Party said:

The National Government, in fulfilment of its policy, introduced a Bill of Rights into Parliament and this together with a petition praying for a written constitution and a second chamber has been referred to a Recess Parliamentary Committee representative of both parties. The National Government will give earnest consideration to the recommendations of this committee.

A considerable body of evidence was given to the select committee, much of it opposed a bill of rights on the Canadian model or a bill of rights in any stronger form. The committee recommended that the bill not proceed and it did not. Those arguments took place in New Zealand when the economic and political climate was very different from that now prevailing in the country. The case for a bill of rights requires re-examination in the light of current conditions. In 1968 I published an essay which opposed the introduction of a bill of rights for New Zealand. Ten years later I feel differently.

There are a number of forms that such a bill could take. Clearly it would be possible to pass a statute which declares certain broad principles as values in which the New Zealand community believes. The 1963 proposal made no attempt to create a higher law against which all else had to be measured. It was to have been enacted as an ordinary statute and could have been as easily repealed. It is possible to go a little further and instruct the courts to construe other legislation to conform with the bill of rights unless the latter is expressly over-ridden.

To enact a bill of rights with teeth entails going further. The argument is that certain freedoms – of thought and expression, religion, free association, the absence of discrimination based on race, national origin, sex or belief – are fundamental to a free society. Through incorporation into the basic law, these could be withdrawn from the realm of political controversy. They would be higher values embodied in a higher law to which all other law would conform.

There is an intermediate stage between mere declarations of principle and giving a bill of rights real force. Such an approach is to be seen in the 1977 legislation setting up a Human Rights Commission. That act provides various protections and remedies against discrimination in employment on grounds of sex, marital status, religious or ethical belief, and against discrimination in other matters such as the provision of goods and services, housing, education, advertizing and victimization. One of the functions of the Human Rights Commission is to provide a human rights audit on proposed legislation. The commission is empowered to report to the prime minister on 'the implications of any proposed legislation (including subordinate legislation) or proposed policy of the government which the Commission considers may affect human rights'. (*Human Rights Commission Act 1977*, s.6) Such a provision stops far short of actually invalidating legislation or administrative action which is contrary to human rights.

For a bill of rights to be effective, a body other than that enacting the laws must measure the laws against the statement of principle in the bill of rights. Such a step involves a judgment that parliament is occasionally not to be trusted; that parliament is an institution which may be unsympathetic to the need to protect the democratic ground rules; that it may allow officialdom to ride roughshod over the rights of individuals. If that judgment is made it requires some limitation upon the capacity to legislate. Some body other than parliament or the executive must have the power to say when parliament has infringed the bill of rights. The most obvious way to do this is through the courts. The Supreme Court could be used. Conceivably some sort of second chamber might carry out the task. But by far the most preferable forum in my view would be the Supreme Court. The courts see the results of legislation worked out in individual circumstances. And the impact of a law often is not clearly appreciated until it has been applied in particular circumstances.

A number of powerful arguments can be marshalled against the introduction of a bill of rights which gives the courts power to strike down legislation repugnant to the fundamental principles enshrined in it.

The arguments are that a bill of rights would:
- create uncertainty in the law. It may not be easy to predict which pieces of legislation would be struck down
- cause an increased volume of litigation. Efforts to have laws declared unconstitutional would involve expensive and long drawn out litigation
- catapult New Zealand judges into a political role for which they do not have much background
- threaten the stability and respect of our judicial system because judges would be involved in the interpretation of vague and unmanageable principles
- reduce the flexibility of our system
- introduce an anti-democratic element into our constitution because although judges are not elected they would be interfering with what the elected representatives of the people have passed into law
- give judges the capacity to do evil by judicial review of a bill of rights equal to their capacity to do good.

Arguments can also be made in favour of the introduction of a bill of rights. A bill of rights in New Zealand would:
- indicate that New Zealand no longer leaves the protection of fundamental freedoms to politicians
- ensure fundamental values are protected
- restrain the abuse of power by the executive and parliament
- restrain the abuse of power by other organizations, such as businesses, trade unions and other bodies
- provide an important source of education about the importance of fundamental freedoms in democratic society
- allow a remedy to individuals who have suffered under a law which breaches fundamental rights
- give individuals a greater sense of commitment to their society by providing a set of guaranteed minimum standards to which public decision-making must conform
- associate New Zealand with a growing international movement for the protection of human rights
- give the opportunity to improve our commitment to human rights and fundamental liberties.

To evaluate the strength of the arguments it would be as well to specify what is involved. A set of fundamental principles of the type which may be involved in a bill of rights in New Zealand is contained in the European Convention for the Protection of Human Rights and Fundamental Freedoms, an international agreement entered into by various European governments in 1950. It has served as an influential model for the statements of basic principles which have been introduced in the constitutions of countries in the Commonwealth which have become independent in recent years. Fiji, for example, has a constitution which guarantees fundamental freedoms as part of the supreme law. The European Convention for the Protection of Human Rights and Fundamental Freedoms guarantees the following freedoms (in the convention they are stated in considerable detail and with many qualifications not included here):

- everyone's right to life shall be protected
- no-one shall be subjected to torture or to inhuman or degrading punishment or treatment
- no-one shall be held in slavery or required to perform forced or compulsory labour
- everyone has the right to liberty and security of person and can be deprived of liberty only in accordance with law
- everyone is entitled to a fair trial and public hearing within a reasonable time by an independent and impartial tribunal established by law. There is a presumption of innocence until the person has been proved guilty according to law
- no-one shall be held guilty of any criminal offence if it was not an offence at the time it was committed
- everyone has the right to respect for his private and family life, his home and correspondence
- everyone has the right to freedom of thought, conscience and religion
- everyone has the right to freedom of expression, to hold opinions, to receive and impart information
- everyone has the right to freedom of peaceful assembly and to freedom of association including the right to form and to join trade unions for the protection of his interests
- men and women of marriagable age have the right to marry
- people whose rights and freedoms are violated shall have an effective remedy
- rights and freedoms shall be secured without discrimination on any ground such as sex, race, colour, language, religion, political or other opinion, national or social origin, association with a national minority, property, birth or other status.

A more elaborate formulation of human rights is contained in the International Covenants on Economic, Social and Cultural Rights and Civil and Political Rights. These covenants, adopted by the United Nations, have now been ratified by New Zealand, which means we are bound under international law to observe their terms. Ratification of the covenants turns the spotlight on human rights in New Zealand and provides a useful set of principles against which to measure our laws. They could form the basis of a bill of rights New Zealand could adopt.

The implications of such a set of principles suddenly becoming law in New Zealand overnight are serious. Much existing legislation would have to be tested against the principles and a fair quantity of it would be struck down. The ordinary civil law of defamation would have to be weighed against the freedom of expression provision. In the United States, for example, such laws have been struck down as being repugnant to the freedom of expression principle in the bill of rights. The same point arises in relation to several hundred other provisions in various acts of parliament.

Indeed if we are to understand the impact on our society of such a change it is to the United States experience we should turn. Judicial review of a bill of rights is a characteristically American contribution to the science of government. The Americans have a set of fundamental principles in their bill of rights which is similar in many respects to the European convention. For nearly two hundred years American courts have been involved in measuring legislation against the principles. The notable feature of that experience is its complexity and subtlety. It becomes evident at once that the way a bill of rights is interpreted depends upon who makes the interpretation. The specific language of the bill of rights answers few particular questions. And fashions of interpretation in the United States Supreme Court have changed between one period of history and another. The court does not strike down many statutes compared with the number enacted and it has available a series of techniques for avoiding difficult decisions. As one American Supreme Court judge once said: 'The most important thing we do is not doing.' (Quoted by Bickel in *The Least Dangerous Branch,* p.71)

Another salient feature of the American experience is the time it has taken for the impact of the bill of rights to be felt. For example, it was 1919 before the Supreme Court examined a law under the freedom of expression provision. It is essential to understand that there remains in the United States profound doubt as to the proper scope of judicial review of the bill of rights. Considerable judicial restraint has been exercised and that would appear to be essential for the survival of the institution of judicial review. The American experience is buttressed by an examination of the experience in those Commonwealth countries which have adopted bills of rights. The judiciary has been most cautious in applying the general provisions to specific legislation.

It is as well to appreciate the limitations on the capacity of a bill of rights with judicial review to order society and contain social action. Mr Justice Jackson of the Supreme Court of the United States wrote:

... I know of no modern instance in which any judiciary has saved a whole people from the great currents of intolerance, passion, usurpation, and tyranny which have threatened liberty and free institutions ... No court can support a reactionary regime and no court can innovate or implement a new one. I doubt that any court, whatever its powers, could have saved Louis XVI or Marie

Antoinette. None could have avoided the French Revolution, none could have stopped its excesses, and none could have prevented its culmination in the dictatorship of Napoleon.

(*The Supreme Court in the American System of Government*, p.81)

Some examples of American decisions will be given so that New Zealanders can better appreciate what a bill of rights may involve for us. (These examples are cited in G. Gunther, *Cases and Materials on Constitutional Law*.)

1. The Supreme Court held in 1965 that a state statute cannot make the use of contraceptives by married persons a crime and cannot punish someone who provides married persons with contraceptives and with information concerning their use. The state's law was struck down because it invaded the 'zone of privacy created by several fundamental constitutional guarantees'.

2. In 1973 the Supreme Court decided that the constitutional right to privacy was 'broad enough to encompass a woman's decision whether or not to terminate her pregnancy'. During the first trimester of pregnancy the state law may require only that the abortion be performed by a licensed physician. No further regulations can be justified in that period, because the decision to end a pregnancy is fundamental and only a compelling state interest can justify state regulations impinging on that right. Once the foetus is 'viable' in the sense that it could survive outside the uterus the state interest in preserving the foetus becomes compelling and laws can be passed protecting it.

3. In 1965 two high school students wore black armbands to school to publicize their objections to the Vietnam war and their support for a truce. They were asked to remove the armbands and refused. The school authorities sent the students home and suspended them until such time as they would return without armbands. The Supreme Court held that the action of the school authorities was an unconstitutional interference with the right of freedom of expression. Students in schools have fundamental rights, the court said.

4. Religious teachers held classes on public school premises for those students whose parents had signed request cards. The Supreme Court held that such instruction in the circumstances combined church and state in an unacceptable combination and was unconstitutional.

5. State Law provided that it was the right of any person to decline to sell, lease or rent real property 'to such person or persons as he, in his absolute discretion, chooses'. The Supreme Court held that the provision authorized racial discrimination in the housing market and was unconstitutional.

6. Several states had statutory provisions which denied welfare assistance to residents who had not resided in the state for at least one year immediately preceding their applications for welfare. The Supreme Court said the effect of such laws was to create two classes of needy

resident families indistinguishable from each other, except that one was composed of residents who had resided a year or more and the second of those who had resided less than a year in the state. It held that the classification in the state laws constituted an invidious discrimination denying citizens the equal protection of the laws and was unconstitutional.

One question which has to be asked in the New Zealand context is: how many fundamental principles are New Zealanders likely to agree upon? I expect that there would be wide areas of disagreement, particularly on the application of the principles to specific cases. New Zealanders may agree, for example, that they believe in freedom of expression, but have deep disagreement on how much censorship of movies or pornographic books should be exercised A bill of rights would prevent the political process being the final arbiter on these questions. It is vital to the success of a bill of rights that there is widespread agreement on the content of the principles, real consensus and understanding, not restricted to abstract principle. Such a consensus would be hard to achieve in New Zealand. The abortion issue provides a ready example of how difficult that can be. New Zealanders would find it difficult to accept that ultimate decisions on such an issue would be made not by parliament but by a court. Specific application of principles could not be worked out in advance, so people would not know, to a large extent, what they were getting before a bill of rights was adopted. That would not help people to arrive at a consensus.

Can parliament be trusted?

If New Zealanders understand the costs involved in having a bill of rights, appreciate its limitations and do not expect too much from it, then there is no reason why they should not have one. The question is whether the risks of not having a bill of rights outweigh those accompanying one. That, in turn, depends upon an evaluation of the legislative record of New Zealand parliaments and executive action to define civil liberties and protect them. Under our existing structure, parliament attempts to balance the conflicting interests and draws the line; then our courts try, by reference to basic constitutional principles, to carry out parliament's intention. As has been made clear earlier, however, in fact the legislative function in New Zealand tends to be carried out by the executive branch of government. That fact certainly adds weight to the case in favour of a bill of rights.

There has been in New Zealand a tendency to take our human rights and civil liberties too much for granted. Indeed it is not clear that as a society New Zealand is heavily committed to civil liberties. We put most of our faith in public opinion; but on occasions public opinion, or the will of the majority, is prepared to tolerate considerable interference with basic freedoms. In New Zealand commitments to pragmatism and equality outweigh those to liberty and restraint. Principle is usually ignored. But we do have some organizations attempting to alert public opinion to civil liberties issues. New Zealand has a Council of Civil Liberties, formed in 1951, which carries out valuable watchdog functions. In the words of the council's chairman, Mr W.J. Scott, it carries out the following activities:

It keeps an eye on coming legislation, and where a Bill involves the curtailment of any existing liberty, it makes carefully considered submissions to the Parliamentary Select Committee considering the Bill. These submissions are not always in opposition to the proposed curtailment of liberty; . . .

It issues statements for publication in the media whenever any important matter concerning civil liberty arises in the community, such as the 1976 random checks on overstayers. . . .

As part of its task of keeping people informed of their rights under the law, the Council from time to time publishes articles, bulletins, reports. . . .

To keep members informed of what is going on, the Executive Committee publishes a regular Newsletter. . . .

It cooperates with other bodies concerned with human rights in organizing public opposition to moves to restrict freedom and deprive citizens of specific rights – for example, with Amnesty Aroha on the overstayers' issue, 1976, and on the Security Intelligence Service Amendment Bill 1977.

It handles complaints made by individual citizens against one or other of the authorities – the police, other state departments, local bodies, employers etc.

(Civil Liberty, no.4, p.4)

In 1978 a further institution of substance was added – the Human Rights Commission. It is equipped to investigate a wide range of complaints about breaches of human rights, especially discrimination in employment and organizations connected with employment. The discriminations covered may be on grounds of sex, marital status, race, religious or ethical beliefs. Discrimination involving access by the public to places, vehicles and facilities are covered. There are provisions making unlawful discrimination in the supply of goods, facilities or services to the public or any section of the public. Special provisions cover discrimination in housing and the sale of real estate.

The functions of the commission are to:
• promote by education and publicity, respect for and observance of human rights
• encourage and co-ordinate programmes and activities in the field of human rights
• receive and invite representations from members of the public on any matter affecting human rights
• make public statements in relation to any matter affecting human rights
• report on progress being made towards amendment or repeal of laws which involve discrimination and the elimination of discriminatory laws and practices

137

- investigate and report on the need for action to protect the privacy of the individual
- exercise powers and functions under the Race Relations Act
- report to the prime minister on matters affecting human rights.

Civil proceedings can be brought before the Equal Opportunities Tribunal when the commission, following mediation, has failed to get agreement. Damages can be awarded in certain circumstances.

The commissioners and the tribunal are appointed by the government. Their independence from the government is less than that of a judge as their terms are limited to five years. The powers in the Human Rights Commission Act stop short of giving anyone the power to invalidate legislation which is offensive to any fundamental principles.

It is too soon to evaluate how effective the Human Rights Commission Act will be in promoting its objectives. It must be admitted, however, that the act provides a range of protections for human rights not previously available in New Zealand. Any decision to go further by enactment of a bill of rights with judicial review would involve a judgment that the protections afforded by the 1977 legislation are not sufficient. I will now outline some examples of recent legislative and administrative activity upon which such a case could be based.

1. The Security Intelligence Service Amendment Act 1977 placed considerable additional power in the hands of the executive and does not provide real safeguards against abuse. The act gives the security service the right to open mail, steal property, tap telephones, eavesdrop – things which would be illegal if done by the ordinary citizen. Where interception warrants are required they are issued by the minister in charge of the service, hardly a comforting thought. It would have been much better to have provided that such warrants should be issued by a Supreme Court judge. We could feel sure then that political surveillance was not being conducted by the party in power. The act effectively blocks a court from inquiring into the legality of any interception and makes the warrant of the attorney-general conclusive evidence as to all matters certified in it. The number of warrants issued and the average length of time they are in force over a year must be reported to parliament, but nothing more. Matters which may be investigated under the act include 'terrorism' which is very broadly defined. The powers conferred upon the executive by the act are not those anyone should be entitled to exercise in a free society without some sort of check. And yet there is no check of substance upon them.

2. The claim that a New Zealander's home is his castle rings hollow when faced with the arsenal of statutory powers which authorize entry. A report by the ombudsman in 1976 found that officers of government or local authorities have a right of entry on to private property under at least 150 statutes. Sir Guy Powles observed: ' . . . it appears that there has been an average of four or five Acts passed each year by Parliament

which contain such an authorisation.' (1976 *Report of the Ombudsmen*, p.11) Most of the entries permitted would not be permitted by common law. And the ombudsman found that most of the statutory provisions which authorized entry without consent and judicial approval did so in situations which could not be considered emergency situations. The list of statutes allowing such entry contains some strange relics: the Swamp Drainage Act 1915, Timber Floating Act 1954, and the Military Manoeuvres Act 1915. Although some of these powers are necessary, it seems incontestable that the New Zealand parliament has bestowed such important powers too liberally and without sufficient weighing of the competing interests involved. It is another example of legislation by the executive branch of government for the benefit of the executive branch. It was encouraging to see in 1976 that protest caused an entry provision in the Electricity Amendment Act to be narrowed. A bill of rights with judicial review could restrict the occasions upon which such powers could be granted in legislation.

3. In 1977 a union was holding an election. The rules of the union provided that no-one who had been convicted of a theft should be eligible to be nominated for any position on the union. The incumbent president faced a challenge. The president approached a police constable he knew to find out if the opponent and allied candidates for other positions had any convictions. The police constable ran a check on the Wanganui computer, contrary to police regulations and general instructions. It was found that none of the people had a record and the fact was disclosed to the inquirer. The Wanganui computer centre is an extensive repository of important government records on law enforcement. The computer has scores of terminals around New Zealand through which access to the information can be had. Under legislation a privacy commissioner has been established to investigate complaints about the computer facility. The new candidate for president in the union election complained. The commissioner found that the police were not very co-operative with his inquiry. The commissioner's report, and some of the circumstances surrounding the use of the computer centre so far, suggest that more protection is needed against this vast storehouse of information the government holds about its citizens. A bill of rights may assist in the provision of safeguards.

4. In 1976 there was a clamp-down instituted by the government on persons in New Zealand who have remained after the expiry of their immigration permits. The 'overstayers' controversy involved random police checks on the streets of Auckland of people who looked like immigrants from the Pacific Islands. The police stopped people and questioned them about their names and nationality without having good cause to suspect they had committed any offence. The law requires such suspicion before the police can stop a person. It was reported that some people were told by the police that they did not look like New Zealanders

and should carry passports. The police appear not to have followed the law in the overstayers case. A bill of rights would provide further protection against the abuse of police powers in appropriate cases.

5. In the area of freedom of expression New Zealanders tolerate more restrictions than many countries. Blasphemous libel, criminal libel and the law of sedition place restrictions on our utterances which could be unconstitutional in the United States. So does the ordinary civil law of defamation. Our obscenity laws and film censorship are strict by some overseas standards. Much of the New Zealand law relating to contempt of court would be unconstitutional if it were the law in the United States.

Only a few examples have been chosen to illustrate the type of threat that unbridled government power presents to the citizen. As technology becomes more complex and sophisticated so the threat increases. The New Zealander has no rights secure against violation by legislation. Wide powers of search, seizure and arrest are given under a wide variety of statutes – the Crimes Act, the Transport Act, the Misuse of Drugs Act, the Gaming Act, the Sale of Liquor Act. The issue to be determined is whether the legislature, under the domination of the executive can be trusted to draw the line in the right place.

If New Zealand had a bill of rights with judicial review the line would be drawn by the courts. Interference could not be expected as a matter of course. The legislation or administrative action under challenge would have to be shown to violate one of the principles stated in the bill of rights. The introduction of such a system would not mean that utopia could be produced overnight. It would take years of effort, the development of case law, and patient plodding towards the goal of greater concern in our law for fundamental principles and basic freedoms.

From the examples mentioned it is obvious enough that a bill of rights is merely one way of resolving the problems posed. Many would argue that initiatives like the Human Rights Commission Act provide a better way of dealing with the problem in the constitutional environment of New Zealand. The ultimate question is whether the limitations upon governmental power in New Zealand reach an acceptable balance without a bill of rights with judicial review. It is not an easy question to answer, but I am no longer confident that the existing restraints are sufficient. So the royal commission recommended earlier in the chapter should be charged to investigate the issue of a bill of rights for New Zealand. It is interesting to note that the Values Party and the Social Credit Political League both proposed a bill of rights for New Zealand in the 1978 election campaign.

11
A second house of parliament?

The idea of a second chamber

Many legislatures have two chambers. The New Zealand parliament has had only one since 1 January 1951. There has been a trend toward unicameral legislatures (those which have only one house) since then. Finland, Denmark and Sweden have only one house, as do many of the newly independent countries. But the two-house legislature has been characteristic of the Westminster model of government, which is the prevailing pattern in the United States, Canada and Australia as well as in the United Kingdom.

In many instances where parliaments have two chambers, one chamber enjoys more power and prestige than the other. It is well known that the second chamber in the United Kingdom parliament, the House of Lords, has for many years been limited in its capacity. The House of Commons can pass a money bill over opposition in the Lords after delay of a month and any other bill after a maximum delay of twelve months from the time when the bill was first given a second reading by the House of Commons. The United States Senate, on the other hand, has legislative capacity almost identical with that of the House of Representatives. Under the constitution, bills for the raising of revenue and, by custom, tax and appropriation bills originate in the house; but they all must pass the Senate. And the Senate is the most powerful and prestigious of the two houses of Congress. The Australian Senate, too, enjoys more power than the House of Lords. Like the modern United States Senate, it is now directly elected.

Senates, in both Australia and the United States, owe something to the fact that both countries are organized along federal lines. The rights of the states are seen as represented in both institutions. In both countries each state has equal Senate representation regardless of that state's population.

What can two houses do that one cannot? The obvious answer is that a second house can do all the things a single house can do, but do them again. So far as the consideration of legislation is concerned, real advantage could flow from a second appraisal. More flaws could be detected before bills were passed; more attention could be given to drafting problems; legislation could be passed more slowly. An upper house, then, constitutes a brake on the activities of the lower house. It slows things down, it gives opportunity for sober second thought. Sometimes quite strong claims have been made about the protections afforded by a second chamber. The most ardent advocate of a second chamber in New Zealand in modern times was the late D. J. Riddiford, who some years after the period of his advocacy, became a National member of parliament and later a minister of the crown. In 1951 he favoured a second chamber as:

. . . a necessary safeguard against a single assembly seizing excessive power, and against the further danger of an ambitious politician, through his dominance over his party, virtually becoming a dictator. Lust for power being a fundamental human passion, the menace of despotism is always present.

(*Political Science*, vol. 3, p. 23)

In order to satisfy such a watchdog role a second house would need power enabling it to return, if not reject, proposals which had gone through the other house.

Consider, however, the way in which modern party politics complicates the approach. If one party controlled both houses, the ability of the second house to exert any check upon the first would be negligible. Party discipline in New Zealand in modern times has been so strict that it would be idle to believe that members of the government party in the second house would not support the government as much as they do now in the House of Representatives. If, on the other hand, one party controlled the first house and another the second, the capacity of the government to pass any of its proposals would be in jeopardy. In that situation a second house would be bent on a programme of political destruction, not of checking excesses or revising the work of the other house. The frustration and bitterness such a situation can engender was well illustrated by the Whitlam administration in Australia which at no time enjoyed a majority in the Senate.

A fully effective second chamber, then, could defeat altogether the actions of the first. A stalemate could ensue, thus defeating the first aim of government, which is to govern. So we have a dilemma. How can a second chamber be designed which can perform useful functions in checking and revising the work of the other chamber but not be so potent as to obstruct it. Of course some would say that less legislative output is the very purpose of the exercise. The matter is further complicated in our system because the ministers, the chief executives, are part of the legislature. In a system where there are two houses, to which house should they be answerable? The Australians solved the problem by providing that a government shall hold office so long as it commands a majority in the House of Representatives. Once the fact of cabinet government is admitted, however, some differentiation in powers between two houses of parliament seems inevitable, if government is to be conducted at all.

The New Zealand experience

The New Zealand Constitution Act 1852 provided for a Legislative Council. The number of members varied from time to time during its history – it rose as high as fifty-three in 1885–6; in the years prior to its abolition it was thirty-six or forty. All members were appointed, not elected: until 1891 they were appointed for life; afterwards they were appointed to a term of seven years with eligibility for re-appointment. Women did not become eligible for appointment until 1941.

Throughout its history many calls for reform of the Legislative Council were made. The most important effort was that of Sir Francis Bell, a member of the Council and a minister for many years. He drafted a bill which was actually passed in 1914. It provided for the Legislative Council to be elected from four electorates into which New Zealand would be divided for the purpose. There were to be forty members, each having a term twice as long as members of the House of Representatives. In relation to money bills, the new body was to have a delaying power of one month. Other bills it would be able to reject. In the event of disagreement a joint sitting of both houses would be convened. If the bill was still not passed by a majority of those sitting, both houses would be dissolved and there would be elections. Election to the Legislative Council was to be on the basis of proportional representation similar to the system for the Australian Senate. Sir Francis Bell's act was to come into operation on 1 January 1916. The Liberal Party insisted upon postponement of the act when they entered the war time coalition government. In the event, the act was never brought into effect, apparently because people who had initially supported the idea became nervous about proportional representation.

In 1951 the attorney-general of the day, T. C. Webb, said publicly:

I do not think I am doing Sir Francis Bell an injustice when I say that his principal object in pressing for an elected Upper House was to prevent a Labour Government from gaining control – that is, to prevent what in point of fact happened.

(*New Zealand Law Journal*, vol. 27, p. 107)

The person who has researched the activities of the Legislative Council most thoroughly, Professor Keith Jackson of the University of Canterbury, has pointed to a weak performance by the Council over a period of many years:

The decline in the Legislative Council's role can be seen at its clearest in the sphere of legislation. The most important work of the Council throughout its existence was to be found in its role as a revising Chamber. In 96 years of existence, 34 per cent of the Bills from the House of Representatives which passed through the Council were amended. There was, however, an uneven distribution of activity, for between 1854 and 1890 some 50 per cent of legislation submitted was amended, compared with 26 per cent from 1891 to 1950.

(*Parliamentarian*, vol. 54, p. 19)

When the Legislative Council was finally abolished many people thought it was only a recognition of reality. The main architect of the Council's destruction, S. G. Holland, told the House of Representatives in 1950:

The Council as at present constituted, is a costly farce. It no longer initiates legislation. It no longer revises legislation. None of us can say that the Council has amended legislation in our time . . .

(*New Zealand Parliamentary Debates*, vol. 289, p. 540)

The National Party was pledged to 'examine the possible alternatives to provide for some form of safeguard against hasty, unwise or ill-considered legislation'. The promise was made in 1949 and New Zealand still awaits a means to prevent the evil. There seems to have been a general expectation at the time of abolition that some form of second chamber was needed; the problem lay in choosing the form. In 1952 a select committee, the Constitutional Reform Committee, reported to the House of Representatives. In fact this was a joint committee of members from the House of Representatives *and* the Legislative Council. The Labour opposition, however, refused to participate. The Constitutional Reform Committee recommended that:

- there should be a second chamber called a Senate, its only power being to delay legislation
- the Senate would consist of thirty-two appointed members
- the political parties in the House of Representatives were to be represented in the Senate by numbers that were to bear the same ratio as their strength in the House
- the prime minister and leader of the opposition would nominate the members

These proposals were not well received, and failed to gain any support from the government or indeed any other quarter. Mr Maurice Joel, lecturer in constitutional law at the University of Otago wrote:

It is quite clear that the predominant idea in the minds of the makers of the Report was to produce a design for a Senate which was politically so completely devoid of power as to be unobjectionable to any party on the grounds of its possibly limiting the present absolute power of the Lower House. In this aim the Report has surely succeeded most admirably. In all the history of man there can rarely have been proposed an institution so utterly powerless.

(*New Zealand Law Journal*, vol. 28, p. 217)

The Legislative Council had long been regarded as a repository for political patronage; a place where political hacks could be rewarded and put out to pasture. Since the 1952 report less has been heard of the need for a second chamber in New Zealand. R. M. Algie, who chaired one of the 1952 committees wrote in the *Parliamentarian* in 1961: 'I still feel we should use our best endeavours to find an alternative for the Second Chamber that was swept away in 1950.' (vol. 42, p. 203) In a 1961 petition, the Constitutional Society proposed a senate of twenty elected senators (one each to be elected by the voters in four electorates) and an additional sixteen 'who shall be persons who shall have rendered distinguished service to New Zealand, or whose training or experience are such as are likely to be of special value in the conduct of the business of the Senate'. (*Report of Public Petitions Committee*, 1961, p. 13) These latter senators were to be appointed by the leaders of the political parties in the House of Representatives in proportion to the number of seats held in the house. There were provisions, similar to those in Sir Francis Bell's act, for the procedure to be adopted in the event of disagreement between the two houses.

Again, nothing happened. Both the idea and the substance of the second chamber in New Zealand has been dogged by the undemocratic features of the proposals. There were overtones of a landed aristocracy redolent of the House of Lords which, in some quarters, supported the concept. The notion that some distinguished people who were not elected should serve was a persistent one. Neither of these ideas was or is acceptable in the egalitarian climate of New Zealand. That means the only possibility is a fully elected body. If it is elected, and political parties are active in its election, the manner in which the second chamber can be different from the House of Representatives becomes a serious issue.

A number of specific tasks do exist, however, which could be performed by a second chamber in the New Zealand parliament:

- scrutiny of regulations as discussed in chapter 8
- delay of legislation passed by the House of Representatives for the purpose of reconsidering it with emphasis on drafting, clarity and presentation of the law
- thorough reviews of government administration by select committee inquiry including a review of annual reports of government departments
- examination and review of quangos
- oversight of matters such as civil liberties and human rights.

The tasks need to be carried out and have been sufficiently neglected by the House of Representatives to warrant emphasis. The question must be faced, however, as to whether they are tasks which justify the creation of a second house. They are jobs which could just as effectively be carried out by an enlarged House of Representatives where business was organized on a different footing from now. The effect of delay in the passage of legislation is incontestably beneficial, but a second chamber is not needed to do that. With thorough-going reform of the House of

Representatives most of the advantages of a second chamber could be secured without actually having one. If there were sufficient political will to contemplate the re-introduction of a second chamber, there should be enough to reform the House of Representatives.

The question of political will is an important one in all parts of constitutional reform. No written constitution, bill of rights or second chamber can be introduced unless public opinion sees a definite need for such institutions. The public demand will need to be clear as such changes do not appeal to politicians, especially those who happen to make up the government at any time. Any of the changes involve a reduction in the power of government. The record of governments voluntarily relinquishing power is not one to inspire confidence that change will occur unless politicians feel politically at risk. It is not easy to turn questions of constitutional reform into a sufficiently salient public issue to have the impact necessary to secure the change. People do not know much about how government works, and they know even less about how it could be altered.

Discussion of a second chamber forces some consideration of the electoral law. If an elected second chamber is going to differ from the House of Representatives it will need to be elected by a different formula. A second chamber designed to check and control the House of Representatives would need more independence from party control than the lower house. A system of proportional representation could produce a chamber with a wider range of political views than the first-past-the-post system of voting in the House of Representatives.

Again the question must be faced: if a different method of election will produce representation for more shades of the political spectrum, why not allow that to occur in the House of Representatives rather than create a new forum in which that particular virtue can be exhibited? In New Zealand, therefore, any discussion about re-introduction of a second chamber drives the observer to consider the methods for electing members of parliament.

12
Electoral law

In a democratic country like New Zealand there can be no doubt about whether the majority should rule. The question is what kind of majority should rule. People who vote exercise a choice. It is expected that the people who are elected will make decisions, a point that needs considerable refinement in the context of the New Zealand system of government. The system recognizes that it is not possible for all citizens to be involved in all public decisions. The whole of our system of government can be understood as a way of channelling communication between the voters and the decision-makers. And the fact that voters vote exercises a check on the decisions of their representatives. Only by competitive election can the identity of the main decision-makers be changed.

In New Zealand, voting takes place after a public fight between contesting adversaries which are known as political parties. The parties ostensibly present contrasting views on issues; voters then decide which set of preferences they want. The method encourages fierce competition which is often irresponsible in the claims that are made. It guarantees oversimplification of issues, it promotes distortion and lies. The outcome of the contest is that one party will control the power of government in the country. Results are decisive. Either a party controls all the power of government or none of it. At times in the past New Zealand has had coalitions of political parties forming a government and that could recur in the future. But the dominant pattern of modern New Zealand is single party government. Between 1957 and 1960 the Labour government enjoyed a majority over the National opposition in parliament of only one. But Labour ran the government and National had no part in it. On 1978 election night figures Labour polled more votes than National but National had more seats. Our system is 'winner takes all'. The existence of the two party system in New Zealand, and the contest between the parties, has been the dominating feature in determining the nature of our government for the last forty years.

Political parties select the candidates for election. It is from among those candidates who are elected to parliament that the chief executives are selected. Candidates who are independent of any political party have not sat in the New Zealand House of Representatives since 1946. Parties determine much of the policy which will be embodied in decisions. They provide the link between popular consent and representative government. They are active in rousing the inactive portion of the population to think about public issues and take part in elections. There are now signs in New Zealand that domination of the system by two parties alone will not continue. One way to reduce the importance of the party system is the use of referenda.

Referenda

From time to time important public issues in New Zealand are decided by referendum. Questions upon which the procedure has been used over the years in New Zealand include:
- control of alcoholic liquor
- licensing hours
- whether the term of parliament should be extended to four years
- conscription during peace
- the control of betting on horse races

Referenda can be in two forms. The results can be made to have a legally binding effect, as in the liquor referendum held every three years in New Zealand. If prohibition were carried, for example, the statute under which the referendum is held provides for what happens in that event. Or a referendum could be advisory, not producing any change in the law but its results being a guide for politicians.

A related method of decision-making is the free vote in parliament. Under that system, which has been used in recent years for liquor legislation, the capital punishment issue and abortion legislation, members of parliament do not vote in accordance with a party line but according to their own consciences. The tangles into which parliament often gets itself over these issues, particularly abortion, is a result partly of the unaccustomed role for parliamentarians having a free vote and not having a means of working out new groupings, and partly of the passionate views of the community on these topics.

Frustration with the working of New Zealand politics has led to suggestions that more use be made of free votes in parliament and of referenda. In other parts of the world, notably Switzerland, many important questions are required to go to a referendum. In many American states, referenda on important issues of public concern are frequent.

Although the introduction of more referenda to decide public issues has attractions, it would involve changes in our decision-making system. Its use could encourage decision-makers to not make decisions and to wash their hands of the consequences. Ministers could say, with justice, that they could not be held accountable for policy decisions made by referendum. The irony is that by moving towards a pattern of frequent referenda, the public may believe it would receive government which was more accountable to it, when in reality it would be less so.

Decision on which issues to put to a referendum poses problems. The formulation of a particular issue to put to a referendum can cause great confusion. Questions must be put so that people understand them, so refinements cannot be incorporated if the issue is to remain comprehensible. Referenda are expensive to conduct. If an indication of public opinion on an issue is wanted public opinion polls may be just as good. Nonetheless, referenda really are democratic. They do give every one a chance to have his or her voice heard. And they must reduce the level of public dissatisfaction with some types of decision. They are fairer than a free vote in parliament.

Use of referenda is common in the United States. The most dramatic provisions are contained in the constitution of the state of California. That constitution states that 'the people reserve to themselves the power to propose laws and amendments to the Constitution, and to adopt or reject the same, at the polls independent of the Legislature, and also reserve the power, at their own option, to so adopt or reject any act, or section or part of any act, passed by the Legislature.' (Article 4, s.1) Elaborate provisions give effect to that principle in three main ways:
- where a petition signed by a number of electors equal to 8 per cent of all the votes cast in the elections for governor is presented asking for an initiative measure to be put to the electors, then the proposition must be put at the next election. The petition must contain the proposed law in full.
- a petition can also be presented to the legislature where it is signed by 5 per cent of the electors as defined above and whether it is accepted or rejected by the legislature, the law proposed must be submitted to the people
- acts passed by the legislature do not come into force for ninety days after the adjournment of the session and if 5 per cent of the electors as defined above so petition, any act or part of an act passed by the legislature must be submitted to a referendum

All measures to be submitted to a vote of the electors, together with properly prepared arguments for and against each measure, must be mailed to each elector before they are voted on. Laws made by local government are subject to the same method of control by the relevant electors in California.

New Zealanders may reduce the grip of executive government and be more satisfied with public decision if a general statute were passed allowing for referenda to be held on important public questions where 100,000 qualified electors so petitioned. The Social Credit Political League made a similar suggestion in its 1978 election manifesto.

How the electoral system works

The present electoral system is the essence of simplicity. New Zealand elections work on a first-past-the-post system. In each electorate each eligible voter has one vote. The voter casts that vote for the candidate of his or her choice. The candidate with most votes wins. If there are only two candidates the winner needs more than 50 per cent of the votes cast to win. But now there are often four or more candidates. The candidate with most votes may not have as many votes as all his opponents combined although the candidate with most votes still wins. So a result can be reached where the elected candidate has a minority of the valid votes cast, say 40 per cent, while three other candidates received 60 per cent between them, none of the three receiving as many votes as the elected candidate.

The number of seats in the New Zealand House of Representatives is determined by the Electoral Act 1956, which has been amended on a number of occasions. At every census the chief electoral officer arranges to have forms for registration of electors delivered to every occupier or person in charge of a dwelling. Every adult living in the dwelling is obliged to complete the form and return it. And after the census, which is held every five years, new electorate boundaries are drawn up.

The boundaries are settled by the Representation Commission. It comprises:

- the surveyor-general
- the government statistician
- the chief electoral officer
- the director-general of the Post Office
- chairman of the Local Government Commission (who does not vote)
- a nominee of the government
- a nominee of the opposition
- an eighth member appointed to be chairman and chosen by the other seven or a majority of them.

It should be observed that the Representation Commission contains a majority of politically neutral public servants. The commission has demonstrated over a long period a complete lack of partiality to any political party. And the act gives politicians no ability to interfere with the apportionment arrived at by the commission.

Electorates are drawn on the basis of total population. Consideration is given to existing electoral boundaries, community of interest, to facilities of communication and topographical features. The Electoral Act 1956 states: 'The Commission may for any district make an allowance by way of addition or subtraction . . . to an extent not exceeding 5 per cent.' (s. 17) Although the electorates are drawn up on the basis of total population, they vary quite markedly in the number of actual voters on the roll. Total population and numbers of eligible voters do not coincide very closely. In 1978, according to Dr S. I. Levine, a political scientist, the smallest electorate had 18,640 on the roll and the largest 31,060. That difference of over 14,000 suggests that New Zealand's system of apportionment is not achieving the ideal: one person, one vote. But by the standards of many overseas democracies the tolerances for the total population are low and result in drastic redrawing of boundaries after every census. The dedication in the current New Zealand electoral system to equality of total population produces in a country with difficult terrain considerable disruptions for politicians, political parties and communities.

The number of seats in parliament is determined by a formula. The European population of the South Island is divided by twenty-five and the number so obtained is the quota for the South Island. That quota is also used to determine the number of seats in the North Island. The North Island European population is divided by the South Island quota to arrive at the number of European seats. Then the quota for the North Island is arrived at by the dividing of European population of the North Island by the number of seats arrived at in the earlier calculation. That method of drawing boundaries has a number of results. The South Island can never have less than twenty-five parliamentary seats, even if its population declines relative to that of the North Island. Yet a vote in the South Island is not worth more than one in the North. The North Island simply receives more seats in parliament as its population increases. Under the above procedures the parliament elected in 1978 has ninety-two members.

Maori seats are set at four. The total Maori population is the number of Maoris or persons of Maori descent who have elected to be considered as Maoris, who have chosen to be registered as electors of Maori electoral districts. Maoris can register on the roll for general electoral districts if they wish. Maoris can also stand as candidates for those seats. Two Maoris represented general electorates between 1975 and 1978.

The question of continued separate representation for Maoris is a vexed one about which a great deal could be said. It may prove possible to abolish the Maori seats if the trend towards Maoris opting to go onto the ordinary rolls continues. The average number of people who voted in the Maori seats in 1972 was 10,497 compared with 16,375 in general electorates, and the same trend was evident in 1975.

The percentage of eligible voters who actually vote is high in New Zealand, although it has been falling in recent elections, as shown in Table 9. In New Zealand it is not compulsory to vote although registration is legally required.

Table 9   Voting figures for eligible voters, 1969–75

Election year	Percentage of eligible voters who voted
1969	89.88
1972	89.05
1975	83.12

The effect of the first-past-the-post system in New Zealand can be seen by a comparison between votes cast in favour of political parties and seats secured in parliament, as shown in Tables 10 to 14.

Table 10   1966 election: votes cast compared with seats gained in parliament

Party	% of votes recorded	% of seats
Labour	41.44	43.75
National	43.64	55
Social Credit	14.48	1.25
Others	.44	0

Table 11   1969 election: votes cast compared with seats gained in parliament

Party	% of votes recorded	% of seats
Labour	44.18	46.42
National	45.22	53.58
Social Credit	9.07	0
Others	1.53	0

Table 12   1972 election: votes cast compared with seats gained in parliament

Party	% of votes recorded	% of seats
Labour	48.37	63.2
National	41.5	36.8
Social Credit	6.65	0
Values	1.96	0
Others	1.52	0

Table 13   1975 election: votes cast compared with seats gained in parliament

Party	% of votes recorded	% of seats
Labour	39.7	36.8
National	47.44	63.2
Social Credit	7.43	0
Values	5.19	0
Others	.23	0

Table 14 1978 election: votes cast compared with seats gained in parliament*

Party	% of votes recorded	% of seats
Labour	40.4	44.57
National	39.8	54.35
Social Credit	16.1	1.08
Values	2.4	0
Others	1.3	0

*Provisional

A number of points emerge from the figures. The support for minor parties, other than National and Labour, has fluctuated between 10 and 19 per cent over the period 1966–78, but in all that time only two parliamentary seats were secured by a third party at a general election – Social Credit in 1966 and in 1978 (Mr Beetham was first elected to parliament in 1978 at a by-election). The effect of the first-past-the-post system clearly makes political life hard for third parties. The minority of people who support such parties do not have their views directly represented in parliament.

The next point is that first-past-the-post in New Zealand exaggerates the preferences of electors when translated into parliamentary seats. In 1972 and 1975 the difference in voter support for National and Labour was 6.8 per cent and 7.7 per cent respectively. Yet those differences produced on both occasions a disparity of more than 26 per cent in parliamentary seats gained. Quite small changes in the level of relative support can produce a landslide in parliamentary seats. On the other hand, in 1978 both major parties were supported by the voters nearly equally, but there was a disparity of 10 per cent in seats secured.

It is clear from the figures that New Zealand governments were returned in all the elections examined with the support of less than 50 per cent of the people who voted. When the people who did not vote at all are taken into account, it becomes evident that the level of support for a government is even further reduced.

The conclusion that must be drawn from the recent New Zealand experience is that the method of election supports the two-party system more than the views of the voters would suggest that they support it. The biggest obstacle to the reform of the electoral system lies in the resistance to the idea from both major parties, who clearly benefit most from the first-past-the-post system.

Possible changes

There are a number of methods by which the voting system could be altered to make it a more accurate instrument for converting the preference of voters into parliamentary representation. The possibilities will be discussed in as simple terms as possible.

The main possibilities are as follows:

1. *Plural voting* The candidate with the most votes wins whether or not he obtained a majority of the votes cast. This is the present New Zealand system.

2. *Preferential voting* The voter has an opportunity to express a second choice. If no candidates have a majority on the first count, preferences of voters are examined to determine who is elected. Elections for the Australian House of Representatives are conducted by this method.

3. *Proportional representation* Seats are allocated to parties in proportion to each party's share of the vote.

Different possibilities are available under each of these methods and combinations of methods can be endless and complicated. The simplest way in which they work can be illustrated as follows.

1. Voter indicates candidate of his choice. Candidate with highest number of votes wins.

2. Voter ranks candidates in order of his preference: 1, 2, 3 etc. If no candidate achieves 50 per cent of first preference, the candidate with fewest first preference votes is eliminated and his supporters' second preferences are distributed. That process continues until one candidate has an absolute majority.

3. Voters are presented with lists of candidates of all parties. Say, as in the Australian Senate, there are ten positions. Voters list all candidates in order of preference, but the rules for counting the votes is by way of proportional representation. The result is that parties are represented in the Australian Senate in proportion to the votes cast for their candidates. If a minority party received about 10 per cent of the vote it would receive one seat in the Senate.

It is possible to have a combination of the above methods. Perhaps the best known example of that is in West Germany, where half the legislature is elected on a first-past-the-post method and half by proportional representation according to strength of support for political parties. For a party to qualify for allocation of seats in West Germany it must first gain at least 5 per cent of the total vote.

Each of the broad systems sketched above has its advantages and disadvantages. Our present system means that minorities are under-represented in parliament. The composition of the house does not reflect closely the voting figures in the country as a whole. As we have seen, it is possible to enjoy a majority of the seats in parliament with the support of many less than half of the eligible voters.

The preferential system, while only a little more complex than first-past-the-post, still discriminates against minorities; there is a strong element of chance in its working.

Proportional representation has the disadvantage of being complex. It requires electorates which return several members, thus destroying the representational quality between the member and his electorate that we have now. But the system gives most choice to voters and lessens the grip of the two party system on elections. It may also produce a less clear election outcome. Small parties may be in a position of holding the balance of power; such a possibility exists under our present system but is much less likely to occur. The composition of the party lists gives considerable power to political parties. But the prime virtue of proportional representation is that the composition of the parliament would reflect voting patterns.

Drs R.M. Alley and A.D. Robinson, political scientists from the Victoria University of Wellington, designed proposals for the enlargement of the House of Representatives. Their ideas were also presented to the Parliamentary Select Committee on Electoral Reform which sat in 1974. In their submissions a change was advocated to overcome some of the difficulties of the electoral system outlined above.

We propose that a supplementary set of multi-member electorates should be added to the present system of single-member electorates. Multi-member electorates are not new to New Zealand; they were used along with single-member electorates in most elections last century. In this proposal the additional members required for the House would be elected on the basis of the votes received by party lists in three regions, Southern, Central and Northern, with seats allocated among the parties in accordance with the votes received in each region. The Southern region would comprise the whole of the South Island, the Central region the southern half of the North Island, and the Northern region the northern half of the North Island. Single-member electorates would be stabilised at their existing number of 87 and 45 new seats would be allocated among the three regions.

(Submissions on Electoral Reform, pp.10-11)

Under the system each voter would exercise two votes. One for the local candidate standing in the single member electorate and the other for a regional party list. The seats in the multi-member electorates would be allocated on the 'highest average' system in which the seats are allocated one by one and each goes to that party which would have the highest average number of votes per seat if it received that seat. The authors of the proposal made the following claims for it.

- Parliament would have more members to assist in the exercise of its functions. The major parties can provide for the election of Maoris, of women and of other minorities not adequately represented through the present system of single member electorates.
- The safe seats provided by the party lists, accompanied by new regional or national selection procedures, would encourage and enable more highly talented people to enter politics as a career. Moreover, the services of talented sitting members could be retained,

or of ex-members regained, through the appropriate use of party lists.

- The greater stability of the boundaries of single member electorates brought about by absorbing new seats into the multi-member electorates would reduce the precariousness of parliamentary careers and enable more members to build up strong local support than they have been able to in recent years.
- The entitlement of electors to cast two votes would help talented local members to survive by means of split voting.
- Regional interests as well as local interests would be represented in parliament.
- The future of the Maori seats could be looked at in a new light once Maoris are elected in the new multi-member electorates.
- The parties would have a more active internal political life. Firstly, there would be the new task of selecting candidates for the three regional electorates. Secondly, there would be extra encouragement for party officials and party supporters at branch and electorate level in safe or hopeless seats as all potential voters for their party, whatever their area, would be able to have an impact on the results.
- For electors, voting would be a more interesting and satisfying act. It would offer the possibility of a wider range of choice in voting, including voting solidly for a party or dividing one's votes to take into account strong feelings about the local candidates.
- Voters would feel more effective in areas that are now regarded as one party strongholds. Not only would the votes for party lists be seen to add up to the selection of regional representatives, but also they would be seen to attract the attention of politicians rather more than has been the case to areas not regarded as marginal seats.

It might be added that the system would give greater opportunity than the existing system for third parties to be represented in the House of Representatives.

Conclusion

Any changes in the electoral system designed to give or assist minority representation would tend to break up the two party domination in parliament. Some suggest the effect would be to weaken government. I prefer to suggest it would reduce the domination of the executive. Our present electoral system tends to guarantee domination by the executive, but New Zealand needs all points of view represented in its public decision-making. Electoral reform offers the chance to reduce the stranglehold of the two party system and the adversary style of politics it has engendered. In the form recommended by Drs Alley and Robinson, however, rapid changes in the style of government would not come over night. It is very unlikely under the particular mix suggested that minority parties would ever have a disproportionate influence over the will of the majority. The proposal would not produce the prospect of continuous coalition government in New Zealand, but it may produce a moderating influence on the major parties. If it did that it would have been of benefit.

I suggest that single member electorates be limited to eighty, and that forty other members be elected by the method outlined above.

13
Access to official information

Information gives power to those who have it and deprives those who do not. The near monopoly on information enjoyed by government is an important source of executive power in New Zealand. An increase in the amount of government information available to parliament and the public should assist in the checking and scrutinizing of decisions reached by the executive branch of government. As a famous American judge, Mr Justice Brandeis, once said: 'Publicity is justly commended as a remedy for social and industrial disease. Sunlight is said to be the best disinfectant and electric light the most efficient policeman.' Government in New Zealand is organized on the opposite principle. The presumption is in favour of secrecy and that preference is backed by extraordinarily severe laws.

Secrecy in New Zealand
The heavy artillery protecting official information appears in the Official Secrets Act 1951, a piece of legislation which also contains provisions about spying and harbouring spies, unlawful use of uniforms and interfering with persons on guard at prohibited places. The act contains an ugly provision which casts the burden of proving innocence on the accused if 'from the circumstances of the case, or the conduct of the accused person, or his known character as proved, it appears that his purpose was a purpose prejudicial to the safety or interests of the State . . .'. (s.7)

Under the Official Secrets Act any person who has any official information entrusted to him commits an offence if he:
- communicates the information to any unauthorized person (any person receiving the information also commits an offence)
- uses the information for any purpose prejudicial to the safety or interests of the state
- retains the information when he has no right to retain it
- fails to take reasonable care of the information

158

Our legislation follows the British legislation passed in great haste in 1911; it must be amended. The act gives the New Zealand government absolute power over the information it gathers, and it may be information of the most trivial kind. Disclosure is under the control of the executive branch. We have added a number of other laws which prevent disclosure: The State Services Act 1962 states that a public servant who 'directly or indirectly discloses or for private purposes uses any information' acquired in the course of duty breaks the law. (s.56) Further restrictions appear in the Public Service Regulations. Furthermore, the law relating to many specialized activities contains provisions restricting the use of information: for example, census, statistics, taxation, factories and hospital records. The Wanganui Computer Centre Act contains controls on the use of information stored in that facility.

Some restrictions on the use of official information are necessary. People would be outraged if anyone could have access to their hospital records, the details of their income or their trade secrets. Government holds an enormous amount of information about all citizens on a great variety of topics. It would be unacceptable for all the information to be disclosed without restriction. Quite apart from arguments relating to the security of the state, privacy and human considerations demand that not everything be made available.

The grades of classification for official documents in New Zealand are as follows.

1. *Top Secret*: documents relating to negotiations for alliances, defence strategy, methods used by New Zealand intelligence and counter-intelligence services and major government financial proposals, premature disclosures of which could damage the economy.

2. *Secret*: economic proposals of which disclosure before they come into effect would prejudice their operation, directives to New Zealand representatives overseas regarding negotiations with other countries and defence matters.

3. *Confidential*: the most commonly used classification, which covers material the disclosure of which 'would be prejudicial to the interests or prestige of the nation'.

4. *Restricted*: routine government documents intended for government use only.

Cabinet ministers are under severe restrictions as to what they can reveal about information coming into their hands. An executive councillor (which all cabinet ministers are) must swear that he will not directly or indirectly reveal such matters as shall be debated in council and committed to secrecy. The oath continues to bind ministers even after they have ceased to be ministers. Whether the oath has any

159

application to matters discussed in cabinet must be regarded as legally dubious, however. But cabinet ministers in New Zealand are under instructions:

- not to disclose the course of discussions and the views of individual ministers on a particular matter in cabinet
- that if a minister wants to publicly disassociate himself with a decision of cabinet he must resign first
- that the contents of cabinet papers should be disclosed only in the most exceptional circumstances with the prior consent of the prime minister
- in supporting a cabinet decision in public, ministers are free to draw on knowledge gained in cabinet discussion
- that all requests to produce cabinet papers or give evidence in court must be referred to the prime minister, thence to the attorney-general to take advice on whether the crown should resist the claim. Requests by the ombudsmen are treated in a similar way.

Cabinet is the key decision-making body in the New Zealand government. It is protected by a cloak of secrecy. The theory is that the cabinet must be seen to be united on everything. One of the more intriguing questions about cabinet secrecy is whether it will stand up in court. When the diaries of Mr Richard Crossman, a former British cabinet minister, were to be published in England, the attorney-general sought injunctions against the publishers to prevent publication. He failed. Lord Widgery, the chief justice, said the courts would restrain publication if it could be shown that the publication would be a breach of confidence; or that publication would be against the public interest because it would prejudice the doctrine of collective cabinet responsibility, and there was no compelling public interest why they should be published. The passage of time made a difference, however, the chief justice held. In that particular case a lapse of nearly ten years had occurred. In the circumstances it could not be demonstrated that the over-riding public interest in non-disclosure was continuing. Restraints on publication would be made only in the clearest cases.

In correspondence preceding the case, the secretary of the cabinet put the case for secrecy this way:

The conventions which in the public interest govern the publication of works by former Ministers have evolved over many years and been accepted by successive administrations. They flow from the two complementary principles of the collective responsibility of the Government as a whole and the personal responsibility of individual Ministers.

As regards the first of these, the cabinet meets in secret and the records of its proceedings are secret until of historical interest only ... Only in this way can completely frank discussion take place between Ministers in the Cabinet and in Cabinet Committees without the risk of extraneous pressure and controversy. It has also always been held vital for good government that other confidential communications between Ministers, or between Ministers and their senior civil servants, should be protected from untoward disclosure. This is not a matter which depends on the Official Secrets Act . . . It is based upon the inherent needs of government, and the mutual trust which needs to exist between Ministers and between Ministers and their senior advisers. It is an essential feature of the doctrine of collective responsibility which is at the centre of our system of government.

(Attorney-General v. Jonathan Cape, p.761)

Where no attempt is made to invoke the Official Secrets Act, the courts may be more liberal than the executive branch of government in allowing the free flow of government information. On the other hand, it is plain that the courts, as illustrated by the *Crossman* case, accept the need for confidentiality to surround the proceedings of cabinet for a substantial period. Whether collective responsibility is such an important feature of our government to warrant the protection afforded cabinet papers is open to debate. Certainly confidentiality at the time of decision seems necessary, although in many countries 'leaks' from such documents are published in the media. Two or three years after the decision should be long enough for the protection to last in many categories. The reasoning of the British cabinet office smacks of paternalism and at bottom depends on the view that the people should not know that the people who make decisions on their behalf may have different opinions from each other.

The courts also control a complicated branch of the law known as crown privilege. That arises where a citizen has sued the government (or perhaps some one else) and requires information from the government which will assist his case. At one time the courts would bow to any claim made by the government that the information sought should not be disclosed in the national interest. In recent years the courts have taken the view that they, not the minister, will make the final decision. And to that end a court will look at the information which is the subject of the dispute to see whether it can be disclosed. Again, in this area of the law, we find the courts saying that they will not order disclosure of cabinet documents until such time as they are of historical interest only. Neither will they allow disclosure of documents connected with policy-making and quite a wide range of other matters touching on foreign relations and law enforcement.

Some legislation and practices in New Zealand ensure that the public has access to some official information. The Public Bodies Meetings Act 1962 requires the meetings of a wide range of public bodies to be open to the public. The bodies include local authorities, university councils, school boards, catchment boards, and even the South Canterbury Wallaby Board. The power to exclude the public is given where it is considered that:

- publicity would be prejudicial to the public interest by reason of the confidential nature of the business to be transacted
- there are other special reasons arising from the nature of the business

- publicity would be likely to cause unnecessary personal embarrassment to or unnecessarily damage the personal reputation of any person
- a public body may treat the need to receive or consider recommendations or advice from sources other that from within the organization itself as a special reason why publication would be prejudicial to the public interest

The Public Bodies Meetings Act demands that where the public is excluded from any meeting the 'general subject of each matter to be considered while the public is excluded and the reason for the passing of that resolution' must be stated. (s.4) Any member of the public can attend a public body's office and inspect the minutes. It can be seen that the grounds for excluding the public are both wide and general. The public body which shies away from publicity is well able to shield itself. From time to time suggestions are made that local authorities all over New Zealand defy the law daily. Notwithstanding the infirmities of the legislation, the law is much stronger than the standing orders which regulate the conduct of parliament. Parliamentary select committees are closed to the public and to the media unless the house directs they should be open. Often it does not do so.

Demands for open government

Recently a chorus of criticism has been heard about the lengths to which government goes to preserve secrecy about public decisions. Mr Michael Minogue, National member of parliament for Hamilton West, deserves credit for having turned the issue into one of public concern. He has written:

What is required in New Zealand, as elsewhere, is a positive acknowledgment that the critical place of information in our political system requires the law, as established by the Official Secrets Act, to be changed. Such a change will so modify the political climate, and the attitudes that go with it, that reforms of Parliament which have been talked about by so many people for so long might then materialise. We know enough of what has happened in other places to be suitably alert and cautious when it comes to discussion of the real purposes reforms should be designed to achieve. The aim of freedom of information legislation is to enlarge the critical and investigatory role of Parliament, and of the press and the media generally. Its aim is to establish 'accountability' as a substantial basic check upon executive and administrative action.

(in *Politics in New Zealand*, p. 84)

In his 1976 report on the Security Intelligence Service the chief ombudsman, Sir Guy Powles, pointed out that excessive secrecy can weaken the controls which operate in a democratic society to regulate government agencies. 'There is nothing like having to justify one's opinions and emotional reactions to other people to ensure that one thinks these through as fully as possible.' (p. 74) In other words,

162

excessive secrecy is not only undemocratic, it is inefficient.

Sir Frank Holmes' Task Force on Economic and Social Planning observed at the end of 1976:

Clearly there is a strong case for lessening the extent of secrecy in government. There is a fine distinction between secrecy and poor co-ordination, and we encountered examples of the right hand being unaware of what the left hand was doing. Moreover, ministers themselves might find that departments hold information 'in the scrum' and become involved in elaborate tactical play over items of information that should be public property. The Official Secrets Act itself is thus tending to be turned against the democracy it is designed to protect. A review is long overdue.

(New Zealand at the Turning Point, pp. 380–81)

In 1977 Mr Richard Prebble, Labour member of parliament for Auckland Central, introduced as a private member's bill, the Freedom of Information Bill 1977. The preamble to the bill recited that 'the people of New Zealand have a political right to be informed by their Government concerning the public business so that the people may participate more fully in the democratic process' because open government is necessary for a strong democracy. The bill gave every person a right to official information, and that was a term which was broadly defined. Each government agency was to be under an obligation to maintain and make available for public inspection a register of the official information for which it was responsible. Where access was refused, the application could be taken to the Supreme Court. The bill applied to all government departments and a large number of quangos and local authorities.

The bill contained a large number of exceptions, situations in which access to information would be denied:

- cabinet documents and those of the executive council including the record of deliberations
- communications between ministers of the crown
- personal records, unless the person concerned consented
- documents touching upon the security of New Zealand
- information relating to intelligence systems, codes and communications relating to military operations
- trade secrets or financial information imparted in confidence
- medical records of a patient
- information the disclosure of which would have an adverse effect on the economic interests of New Zealand
- information which could assist someone under detention to escape
- documents relating to law enforcement and the giving of legal advice.

The bill did not meet with universal expressions of approval when it was debated in the House of Representatives. Mr Minogue, who had enjoyed something of a monopoly on the issue, described the approach as 'naive'. Both Mr Minogue and Ms Marilyn Waring were disposed to

163

criticize the bill for cutting out access from too wide a range of information, a point which had real substance considering the width of the exceptions. Mr B. E. Brill accused Mr Prebble of 'claim-jumping. He is riding on the speeches made by the member for Hamilton West, who has been studying the legislation in other countries for some months.' (*New Zealand Parliamentary Debates*, vol. 410, p. 516)

In 1978 the government responded to the pressure for freedom of information by setting up a committee to make recommendations on the subject. Chaired by Sir Alan Danks, the committee comprises government officials, with the exceptions of Sir Alan and Professor K. J. Keith of the Faculty of Law at Victoria University. One can be pardoned for wondering whether radical changes are likely to be recommended by such a group. The position of public servants is greatly strengthened by secrecy in government. It suits them as much as their political masters. On the other hand, it can be argued that if public servants recommend the changes, the public service will follow them when implemented.

A great deal more has occurred overseas in the field of access to official information than in New Zealand. The United States has had wide-ranging legislation on the books since 1967 and this legislation has recently been revised to make it more effective. In 1977 Congress passed the Government in the Sunshine Act which went further and required public agencies to hold meetings in which they deliberate in public. The legislation goes a great deal further than the provisions of public information, it requires access to the decision-making process. The policy of the Government in the Sunshine Act 1977 is:

It is hereby declared to be the policy of the United States that the public is entitled to the fullest practicable information regarding the decision making processes of the Federal Government. It is the purpose of the Act to provide the public with such information while protecting the rights of individuals and the ability of the Government to carry out its responsibilities. (s. 2)

Following such legislation in the United States, a large range of government documents has become available. These have been used, particularly by journalists, to probe various activities of government in the United States including the conduct of the Vietnam War, the Central Intelligence Agency and the use of tax records to harass dissident political groups. More information is now publicly available in Sweden. Proposals have been made in the United Kingdom. In Australia a government bill has been introduced. Concern about the issue has been sweeping the western world in the last five years or so.

A New Zealand solution

There are two routes towards reform. One is to pass legislation specifying the information to which the public may have access. The method by which the right shall be enforced must be spelt out, with a court being the ultimate arbiter. Under such a regime it would be costly to make information available on any widespread scale. And it would not be easy to work out in advance many of the problems which could arise.

The British Section of the International Commission of Jurists has recommended that the provision of a statutory right to information is not the appropriate route to take. Rather, these lawyers suggest, a Code of Practice should be established for all government departments. The code would require the disclosure of as much information as 'is reasonably and practicably possible relating to the actions and decisions of the government and other organs of public administration'. (A Report by Justice, para. 36) The purpose of the disclosure would be to enable the public to understand the reasons and the grounds for such actions and decisions. Departments would have a guide of documents or classes of documents subject to disclosure. Complaints that information had been withheld without justification would be made to the ombudsman. A key idea behind the scheme is that it would be capable of evolution in response to problems encountered.

The proposed Code of Practice contains exclusions for information:
- relating to law enforcement
- relating to defence, foreign relations or internal security
- which would be privileged against disclosure in litigation
- which has been entrusted in confidence to a government department
- the disclosure of which would infringe the privacy of the individual
- which if disclosed could reasonably expose the person disclosing it to significant risk of proceedings for defamation

The proposal has great strengths in the New Zealand context, although the exclusions seem more generous than necessary. It would avoid the need for legislation which would inevitably have to be amended, perhaps frequently. It would allow practice to evolve without suddenly throwing the administration of government into confusion or placing it in an adversarial relationship with members of the public. Yet it would provide for fundamental change in government's approach to the availability of information to the public. Such a proposal should be combined with the suggestion of Professor J. A. G. Griffith, discussed in chapter 6, which dealt with the provision of the fullest information available to the executive about a bill upon the occasion of its introduction to parliament. No change in the law is necessary to accomplish that.

Another change which could cut down the power of the executive would be to give parliamentary select committees much wider powers to elicit information from public servants and ministers. Ministers should have to appear before select committees and if they appear accompanied by their top public servants there should be no inhibitions about having questions answered. Real parliamentary scrutiny will never be effective unless there is a capacity to secure all relevant information and a willingness on both sides to be candid.

There are a number of areas where disclosure of information would be of practical importance to the citizen. The Department of Social Welfare operates through the use of manuals. These manuals tell staff how to handle various problems which arise in the processing of applications for benefit. They detail the manner in which certain discretions in the legislation are to be exercised. The effect of such a practice is that the department is administering a type of 'secret law', to which the people whom it affects have no access. The same sort of problem can be seen in a number of fields of government administration. Such manuals should be made public. There is no justification for keeping the rules secret. If they are fair and lawful they should be known; if they are not, they should be known so that they can be attacked. It should be government policy that all manuals relating to any matter in which a department deals with the public or a section of the public should be available for public inspection on request. Few policies could be as simple to implement and few would do more to remove suspicion from the minds of those who must deal with government.

14
Recommendations

Power and decisions

This book is about the exercise of power in the New Zealand government. Government makes decisions on behalf of all of us; those decisions affect us all. We all have an interest in seeing that those decisions are made as fairly as possible. The power exercised by government is divided among three elements:
- parliament
- the queen and the executive
- the judiciary

Too much of the power has become concentrated in the hands of the executive. Steps should be taken to distribute more power to the other branches of government, especially parliament. The recommendations made throughout aim at that goal; they must be seen as suggestions to change the balance of power within the whole system.

Restraints

The restraints upon the exercise of power by government in New Zealand are:
- the law and the courts
- public opinion, including the news media and elections
- parliament
- the ombudsmen
- the auditor-general
- pressure groups

Those checks and balances do not seem sufficient to ensure careful and measured decisions which satisfy the community's sense of justice. Changing the rules by which decisions are made could improve both the quality of decisions and the attitude with which people regard them.

The monarch

New Zealand should not become a republic. The monarchy itself cannot be said to be the source of any existing discontents concerning the functioning of government in New Zealand.

The governor-general

The governor-general can exercise power independently from the advice given by ministers only in a narrow range of exceptional situations. No major changes are required in the office of governor-general, although no-one should be appointed governor-general without broad political support. The 1917 Letters Patent and Royal Instructions are in dire need of revision.

Cabinet

Cabinet is the main location of power within the New Zealand government and it:
- acts as final decision-maker on most important matters
- approves the content of legislation
- decides on government spending
- co-ordinates the administration and gives the orders

What cabinet does is subject generally to the approval of all the government members of parliament who meet in a body called 'caucus'. Caucus exercises some check upon cabinet, but it is haphazard and in secret. The prime minister exercises considerable power and authority. A prime minister should never be minister of finance as well. Despite the substantial power exercised by cabinet and the prime minister, we would be better to locate new checking powers outside the executive rather than dismantle the existing executive.

The public service

Public servants carry out valuable and wide-ranging functions under our system, but they should be publicly answerable to a greater degree than they are. A new parliamentary select committee on government administration should be established. It should have power to summon before it public servants and the ministers in charge. Efforts must be made to clarify the goals public servants are to pursue. A concept of accountable management should be introduced. Steps should be taken to open positions in the public service to outsiders. The permanent career service must be nourished, but there should be greater flexibility in allowing people to move in and out.

Quangos

We have more than 1,200 quasi-autonomous national governmental organizations in New Zealand, known as quangos. They come in a bewildering variety of shapes and sizes. They provide thousands of positions for government appointment without open competition. Many quangos are not sufficiently accountable to the public for what they do. All quangos ought to be reviewed by a parliamentary select committee on government administration with the following questions in mind:
- why can an ordinary department not do the particular job?

- in the case of tribunals why can't the adjudication be carried out in the ordinary courts?
- in what ways is the quango accountable to parliament and the public?
- to what extent is the quango accountable to the minister?
- to what extent does the quango have clearly defined and coherent functions?
- to what extent does the quango overlap with other activities in government?
- in the case of each advisory body, does the record show that it has actually contributed anything of value?

Parliament

The key institution for changing the balance of power in our government is parliament. The functions of parliament are to:
- raise money and approve its expenditure
- pass bills into law
- act as a place for airing grievances
- act as a check on the executive
- serve as a forum for party political contest

More emphasis should be placed on the legislative and checking functions of parliament.

Reform of parliament

To enable parliament to scrutinize legislation better and act as a more efficient brake on the executive a number of steps should be taken.

1. Select committees should be strengthened. They should be able to initiate their own inquiries. Some of them should be chaired by members of the opposition. Minority reports should be permitted. The administrative facilities and staff available to committees should be increased. The staff should be expert and should be answerable only to parliament, not to the executive.

2. An increase to 120 members of parliament is necessary for the select committee system to function properly and to promote within parliament a feeling that it is more independent of the executive.

3. The speaker should be chosen on a free vote in parliament. Upon his election he should resign his seat and serve as speaker for a set period of five years with the possibility of re-election. In that way real independence in the chair would be assured and the conduct of parliament should improve.

4. The timetable of parliament should be altered to allow select committees more time to carry out their duties and to smooth legislative flow. Parliament should sit three days a week, three weeks a month, ten months a year.

5. All select committee hearings should be open to the news media with power to prohibit publication in the public interest by committee decision.

6. Parliament should be broadcast all the time it is sitting.

7. News programmes should be permitted to broadcast excerpts from debates as in the United Kingdom. Television transmissions should be tried, as in Canada.

8. Sittings of parliament beyond midnight should be absolutely prohibited.

9. Standing orders of parliament should be revised to prevent notices of motion being read out; to allow debate of petitions and provide for publication of the report of the government on what action has been taken on petitions; and to provide for limited time debates and so avoid tedious repetition.

10. Desks should be removed from the debating chamber.

11. The antique weapon of parliamentary privilege should be reformed so that it cannot be used for political purposes. The new independent speaker should chair the privileges committee, which should have two members from each side of the house.

12. Financial accountability and management in government should be improved by the implementation of the 1978 report of the auditor-general and the strengthening of the public expenditure committee of parliament.

Parliament and legislation

Better means must be used to secure public participation in the passing of legislation.

1. All bills, except money bills, should be referred to select committees. There should be no other exceptions, not even for small amending bills.

2. Select committees should sit all over New Zealand and times and places of hearing should be widely advertized.

3. Three months should elapse before any bill can be reported back from a select committee after it has been introduced.

4. A copy of every bill should be sent to every public library in New Zealand upon introduction.

5. When a bill is introduced it should be accompanied by a document that sets out the history of the bill and all other relevant information. The purpose would be to ensure that members of parliament are as well informed as the minister who introduced the bill.

How to avoid fast and incomprehensible law

New Zealand passes too many laws and it passes them too quickly.

1. We should stop and ask of each act of parliament and each regulation, 'Is this law really necessary?' We should not pass legislation for items which can be achieved without legislation. We should avoid using legislation to achieve ends it cannot be reasonably expected to accomplish and for political window-dressing. We should repeal old laws no longer needed.

170

2. A new timetable for parliament should allow the urgency provisions in standing orders to be done away with. We should be able to avoid rushed legislation which is insufficiently scrutinized and brings parliament into disrepute.

3. New legislation should be passed with the inclusion of specific expiry dates. No legislation should remain on the books without periodic review. The proposal would ensure that legislation is reviewed systematically, and that the tendency to pass amending acts would be reduced.

4. Every act of parliament passed should state when it comes into effect. And no act should come into effect before 1 April of the year after it is passed unless there are exceptional circumstances.

5. The annual omnibus measure, the Statutes Amendment Bill, which amends many acts every year, should be abolished.

6. We should double the number of parliamentary counsel and halve the number of laws they have to draft.

7. Every effort should be made to write laws in language people can understand.

8. The pattern of drafting in New Zealand should be changed so that principles are legislated – not details. Drafting should be more general and more concise.

9. The courts need to change their often literal approach to interpreting statutes.

10. New Zealand should develop systematic digests and indexes so that the law becomes easier to locate. Each year a new code of laws should be published which contains all the statutes in up to date form.

Regulations

1. New Zealand should find ways to avoid using regulations and rely on other methods of social control, such as codes of practice, wherever possible.

2. The use of regulations in important areas of public policy, especially the economy, should be cut down. If controls are necessary they should be implemented by act of parliament.

3. Consultations should be required as a matter of course before regulations are made. The Securities Act 1978 should be regarded as a model for consultation provisions.

4. Parliamentary review of regulations in New Zealand is little short of derisory. A special parliamentary select committee should be established to review the content of regulations: to see that they are within power, that they do not trespass unduly on personal rights and freedoms, that they do not make people's rights too dependent upon administrative decisions. The select committee should be empowered to disallow regulations.

5. Steps should be taken to codify and reprint all regulations in force in New Zealand.

6. Regulations should not come into force until after they have been published.

The courts and the ombudsmen

The courts exercise an important checking function upon the executive and legislative branches of government. There has been a tendency for the government to breach the provisions of the Bill of Rights of 1688, which is part of New Zealand law and in one case the courts declared government action illegal. Important constitutional cases are rare in our system because we have no written constitution. But the courts have shown increasingly their capacity to quash unfair administrative action by government and government officials. The expansion of these administrative law remedies should be encouraged by cutting away the technicality, reforming the law of standing and providing new remedies. The power of governments to reverse by legislation court decisions they do not like should be used sparingly; it is a power which can be used, and has been used, to reverse the effect of just decisions of courts without proper consideration.

The activities of the ombudsmen in investigating government decisions which affect individuals have acted as a check upon the bureaucracy. The ombudsmen have been a worthy addition to our government and have redressed the balance in favour of the citizen.

A written constitution and/or a bill of rights

The basic rules by which New Zealand is governed are not written down in any authoritative document. It would be possible to state the rules in a written constitution. A written constitution could contain provisions requiring special procedures to be followed for its amendment, making it more difficult to change than ordinary laws. The enactment of a bill of rights to guarantee fundamental freedoms could be added to a written constitution. A bill of rights of any substance would require that courts had the power to strike down acts of parliament and other governmental action if they were contrary to the provisions in the bill of rights. There are considerable problems involved in having a bill of rights with judicial review. It can be argued that organizations like the Human Rights Commission can do the same job just as well. The ultimate question is whether the limitations upon governmental power in New Zealand reach an acceptable balance without a bill of rights with judicial review. A number of recent examples persuade me that the existing restraints are not sufficient. A royal commission should be established to investigate whether New Zealand should adopt a written constitution and/or a bill of rights. The commission should recommend the form to be adopted in the event that its recommendations are in the affirmative.

A second house of parliament

New Zealand does not need a second house of parliament because all the advantages of a second chamber – delay in legislation, better scrutiny of it and review of government administration – can be carried out just as well by a reformed House of Representatives.

Electoral change

1. Important public questions should be submitted to referendum where 100,000 qualified electors petition parliament asking for a referendum.

2. General electorates for the New Zealand House of Representatives should be stabilized at eighty. Consideration should be given to drawing boundaries on the basis of numbers of qualified voters in an area, not total population.

3. The New Zealand first-past-the-post system of voting discriminates against third parties, who together obtained nearly 20 per cent of the vote in 1978. It encourages two party domination, an adversary style of politics and domination by the executive. To combat these features, forty additional members of parliament should be elected on a system of proportional representation. For this purpose New Zealand would be divided into three regions, and the forty members divided between them. Electors would have two votes, one for the single member electorate in which they live and the other for a regional party list. Seats in the multi-member constituencies would be allocated by the 'highest average' system, in which the seats are allocated one by one and each goes to that party which would have the highest average number of votes per seat if it received that seat.

Access to official information

Secrecy is an important source of executive power in New Zealand. At present the presumption is that all information held by government should be secret and that presumption is backed by draconian penal sanctions in the Official Secrets Act. That act needs to be revised. The New Zealand government should adopt a code of practice which will require the disclosure of as much information as is reasonably and practicably possible relating to the actions and decisions of the government and other organs of public administration. The purpose of disclosure would be to enable the public to understand the reasons and the grounds for such actions and decisions. Complaints that information had been wrongly withheld would be handled by the ombudsmen. The code of practice would contain exclusions for some categories of information which it would not be in the public interest to reveal. Manuals used by departments in their dealings with the public should be made available. Parliamentary select committees should exercise more widely powers to elicit information from public servants and ministers.

These recommendations are designed to make New Zealand government more democratic. They attempt to move the balance of power away from the executive towards parliament; new checks are offered to curb the abuse of power. The strategy for the recommended reforms is based on five principles which relate to one another:

- reform of parliament with the aim of making the executive more accountable to parliament
- a method of electing members of parliament which gives more representation to minority parties and of allowing for polls of the voters on specific issues of public concern
- less use of legislation but better scrutiny and more public participation in the making of it
- increased public access to official information
- ability of the courts to review government action by implementation of a written constitution and bill of rights to protect fundamental liberties

Bibliography

Chapter 1 : Government New Zealand style

Bagehot, W. *The English Constitution*, London, 1963
Barendt, E. 'Constitutional Reforms', in Lord Blake and John Patten (eds.), *The Conservative Opportunity*, London, 1976
Bickel, A. M. *The Morality of Consent*, New Haven, 1975
Birch, A. H. *Representative and Responsible Government*, London, 1977
Blackstone, W. *Commentaries on the Laws of England* (a reprint of 1st edn.), London, 1966, vol. 1
Brassington, A. C. 'The Constitution of New Zealand — Aspects of Change and Development', *New Zealand Law Journal*, (1963), 213
'Constitutional Cliff-Hanging', *New Zealand Law Journal*, (1971), 169
'It Could Happen Here . . .', *New Zealand Law Journal*, (1974), 553
Butt, R. *The Power of Parliament*, London, 1969
'Changing the System', *Economist*, 20 March 1976, p. 114
Clark, R. *The Development of the New Zealand Constitution*, Wellington, 1974
Cleveland, L. *The Anatomy of Influence*, Wellington, 1972
Government and Politics in New Zealand, Wellington, 1977
Cleveland, L. and Robinson, A. D. *Readings in New Zealand Government*, Wellington, 1972
'Consider the Constitution', *New Zealand Law Journal*, (1974), 373
Crick, B. 'Them and Us: Public Impotence and Government Power', *Public Law* (1968), 8
Crisp, L. F. *Australian National Government*, 4th edn., Melbourne, 1978
Crossman, R. H. S. *Socialism and the New Despotism*, London, 1956
Dicey, A. V. *The Law of the Constitution*, 10th edn., London, 1959
Friedrich, C. J. *Constitutional Government and Democracy*, Massachusetts, 1968
Griffith, J. A. G. 'The Place of Parliament in the Legislative Process', *Modern Law Review*, 14 (1951), Part 1: 279, Part 2: 425
Heuston, R. F. V. *Essays in Constitutional Law*, 2 edn., London, 1964
Jackson, K. *New Zealand: Politics of Change*, Wellington, 1973
Jennings, W. I. *The Law and the Constitution*, London, 1960
Johnson, N. *In Search of the Constitution*, Oxford, 1977
Keith, K. J. 'Constitutional Change' in I. Wards (ed.), *Thirteen Facets*, Wellington, 1978, p. 1
Levine, S. (ed.), *New Zealand Politics: A Reader*, Melbourne, 1975
Levine, S. *Politics in New Zealand*, Sydney, 1978
McIlwain, C. H. *Constitutionalism and the Changing World*, London, 1969
Marshall, G. *Constitutional Theory*, Oxford, 1971
Mitchell, A. V. *Government by Party*, Christchurch, 1966
Mitchell, A. *Politics and People in New Zealand*, Christchurch, 1969
Palmer, G. W. R. 'The Constitution and David Minogue', *New Zealand Law Journal*, (1976), 481
Powles, G. 'A Citizen's Rights Against the Modern State, and its Responsibilities to Him', *New Zealand Journal of Public Administration*, 26 (1964), 1

Powles, G. 'The Balance of Power', *New Zealand Listener*, 25 February 1978, p.10
'Reforming Parliament', *Economist*, 27 November 1976, p. 32
Roberts, J. L. 'H. J. Scott Memorial Lecture 1973 — Concerning Change', *New Zealand Journal of Public Administration*, 37 (1974), 1
Roberts, J. 'Society and its Politics' in I. Wards (ed.), *Thirteen Facets*, Wellington, 1978, p. 67
Robertson, J. F. 'Changes in the Machinery of Government and their Effects on Senior Officials', *New Zealand Journal of Public Administration*, vol. 40, No. 1 (1978), p. 31
Robson, J. L. *New Zealand: The Development of its Laws and Constitution*, London, 1967
Scott, K. J. *The New Zealand Constitution*, Oxford, 1962
'A Second-Rate Parliament for Ever', *Economist*, 29 May 1976, p. 14
Smith, B. *Policy Making in British Government: An Analysis of Power and Rationality*, London, 1976
de Smith, S. A. *Constitutional and Administrative Law*, 3rd edn., Harmondsworth, 1977
Stacey, F. *The Government of Modern Britain*, Oxford, 1969
Thomas, E. W. 'Parliamentary Control of the Administration of Central Government: Fact or Fiction?', *Otago Law Review*, 3 (1976), 437
Tribe, L. H. *American Constitutional Law*, Mineola, 1978
Victoria University of Wellington Law Faculty, *Materials on Constitutional Law*, 1978, vols. 1 and 2.
Vile, M. J. C. *Constitutionalism and the Separation of Powers*, Oxford, 1967
Wade, E. C. S. and Godfrey Phillips, G. *Constitutional and Administrative Law*, London, 1977
Yardley, D. C. M. 'Modern Constitutional Developments: Some Reflections', *Public Law*, (1975), 25
Entick v. *Carrington* (1765) 19 State Tr. 1029, [1558–1774] All England Reports 41, 11 Digest (Repl.) 437
Transport Ministry v. *Payn* [1977] 2 New Zealand Law Reports 50

Chapter 2 : The Queen and the Governor-General

Auckland District Law Society: Public Issues Committee, *The Holyoake Appointment*, Auckland, 1977
Bagehot, W. *The English Constitution*, London, 1963
Dutton, G. (ed.) *Republican Australia?*, Melbourne, 1977
Evans, H. *Case Against Robert Muldoon*, Christchurch, 1978
Evatt, H. V. *The King and his Dominion Governors*, London, 1967
Keith, K. J. 'What Need New Zealand Remember', unpublished, paper delivered at AULSA Conference, 1976
Marshall, J. 'The Power of Dissolution as Defined and Exercised in New Zealand', *Parliamentarian*, 58 (1977), 13
Oliver, W. H. 'A Partisan Governor-General', *New Zealand Comment*, vol. 1, No. 1 (1977), p. 3
Robson, J. L. *New Zealand: The Development of its Laws and Constitution*, London, 1967
Scott, K. J. *The New Zealand Constitution*, Oxford, 1962
Stevens, D. L. *The Crown, the Governor-General and the Constitution*, Wellington, 1974

Chapter 3 : Cabinet, caucus and the prime minister

Allen, E. A. 'The Role of the Whips and the Caucus in the New Zealand Parliament', *Parliamentarian*, 52 (1971), 35
Birch, A. H. *The British System of Government*, 3rd edn., London, 1973
Blondel, J. *Political Parties – A Genuine Case for Discontent?*, London, 1978
Brown, A. H. 'Prime Ministerial Power', *Public Law*, (1968), 28
Butler, D. 'Ministerial Responsibility in Australia and Britain', *Parliamentary Affairs*, (1973), 403
Craig, J. T. 'The Reluctant Executive', *Public Law*, (1961), 45

Emy, H. V. 'The Public Service and Political Control: The Problem of Accountability in a Westminster System with Special Reference to the Concept of Ministerial Responsibility', in vol. 1 of the appendices to the *Royal Commission on Australian Government Administration*, Canberra, 1976, p. 16

Hartley, T. C. and Griffith, J. A. G. *Government and Law*, London, 1975

Herman, V. and Alt, J. A. *Cabinet Studies – A Reader*, London, 1975

Holyoake, K. J. 'The Task of the Prime Minister', in L. Cleveland and A. D. Robinson (eds.), *Readings in New Zealand Government*, Wellington, 1972

Jennings, I. *Cabinet Government*, 3rd edn., London, 1969

Mackintosh, J. P. *The British Cabinet*, 3rd edn., London, 1977

May, T. 'Parliamentary Discipline in New Zealand since 1954', *Political Science*, 17 (1965), 37

Mulgan, R. G. 'The Need for More Graduate M.P.s: A Sceptical Note', *Political Science*, 29 (1977), 66

'The Concept of the Mandate in New Zealand Politics', *Political Science*, vol. 30, no. 2 (1978)

'Parties under Pressure', *Economist*, 257 (1975), 22

Roberts, N. 'New Models for New Zealand', *New Zealand International Review*, (1977), 14

Stankiewicz, W. J. *British Government in an Era of Reform*, London, 1976

Talboys, B. E. 'The Cabinet Committee System', *New Zealand Journal of Public Administration*, 33 (1970), 1

Wilson, H. *The Governance of Britain*, London, 1977

Royal Commission on Australian Government Administration, Canberra, 1976, Volume 1: Report; Volumes 1–4: Appendices

Security Intelligence Service – Report by Chief Ombudsman, Wellington, 1976

Chapter 4 : The state services and quango land

Benda, H. J. 'Bureaucrats and Politicians', *New Zealand Journal of Public Administration*, 13 (1956), 72

Cabinet Office, *Statutory and Allied Organisations*, Wellington, 1978

Chapman, R. A. (ed.) *The Role of Commissions in Policy Making*, London, 1973

Doig, A. 'Public Bodies and Ministerial Patronage', *Parliamentary Affairs*, (1978), 86

Emy, H. V. 'The Public Service and Political Control: The Problem of Accountability in a Westminster System with Special Reference to the Concept of Ministerial Responsibility', in vol. 1 of the appendices to the *Royal Commission on Australian Government Administration*, Canberra, 1976, p. 16

Graham, L. M. 'Do Politicians Rely on Administrators Sufficiently to Ease their Burden of Work?', *New Zealand Journal of Public Administration*, 27 (1965), 37

Hill, L. B. *The Model Ombudsman*, Princeton, 1976

Jennings, I. *Cabinet Government*, Cambridge, 1969

Roberts, J. L. 'Whatever Happened to your Obedient Servant?' *New Zealand Journal of Public Administration*, 35 (1973), 29

Robertson, J. F. 'Public Service Management in the 1970's', *New Zealand Journal of Public Administration*, 32 (1969), 23

'Changes in the Machinery of Government and their Effects on Senior Officials', *New Zealand Journal of Public Administration*, 40 (1978), 31

Scott, K. J. 'Advisory Committees in the New Zealand Public Service', *New Zealand Journal of Public Administration*, 4 (1942), 24

The New Zealand Constitution, Oxford, 1962

Stacey, F. *The Government of Modern Britain*, Oxford, 1969

Thynne, I. S. 'Permanent Heads and the Public', *New Zealand Journal of Public Administration*, 38 (1976), 1

Webley, I. A. 'State Intervention in the Economy: The Use of Public Corporations in New Zealand' in S. Levine (ed.), *Politics in New Zealand*, Sydney, 1978, p. 36

Wright, V. 'Muldoon's Fire Brigade', *New Zealand Listener*, 5 November 1977, p. 14

Report of the Committee on the Civil Service (Fulton Report), London, 1968, Cmnd. 3638

Report of the State Services Commission for the year ended 31 March 1978, Wellington, 1978

Royal Commission on Australian Government Administration, Canberra, 1976, Volume 1: Report; Volumes 1–4: Appendices

The State Services in New Zealand – Report of the Royal Commission of Inquiry, Wellington, 1962

Chapter 5 : Parliament

Algie, R. M. 'A Critical Examination of the Functioning of Parliament', *New Zealand Journal of Public Administration*, 8 (1946), 14

Alley, R. M. and Robinson, A. D. 'Electoral Aspects and Composition of the House: A Mechanism for Enlarging the House of Representatives', in Victoria University of Wellington Department of University Extension Seminar, 'Can Parliament Survive Without Reform? A Study of the Working of Parliamentary Democracy in New Zealand, 2 and 3 October, 1971

Butt, R. *The Power of Parliament*, London, 1969

Cleveland, L. *Government and Politics in New Zealand*, Wellington, 1977

Cleveland, L. and Robinson, A. D. *Readings in New Zealand Government*, Wellington, 1972

Cocks, B. 'Privilege and the Official Secrets Act', *Parliamentarian*, 51 (1970), 170

Griffith, J. A. G. *Parliamentary Scrutiny of Government Bills*, London, 1974

Jackson, K. *New Zealand: Politics of Change*, Wellington, 1973

Jayson, L. S. 'The Legislative Reference Service: Research Arm of the Congress', *Parliamentarian*, 50 (1969), 177

Keith, K. J. 'A Lawyer Looks at Parliament', in Sir John Marshall (ed.) *The Reform of Parliament*, Wellington, 1978, p. 26

Lidderdale, D. (ed.) *Erskine May's Treatise on the Law, Privileges, Proceedings and Usage of Parliament*, 19th edn., London, 1976

Littlejohn, C. P. *Parliamentary Privilege in New Zealand*, Wellington, 1969 (unpublished L.M. thesis)

'Privilege in the New Zealand Parliament', *Parliamentarian*, 53 (1972), 190

McGechan, A. 'The NZLS: Notable Zeal Limited Scope', *Papers of New Zealand Law Society Triennial Conference*, (1978), B5. 2

Mackintosh, J. P. *People and Parliament*, Westmead, 1978

McRobie, A. D. 'The New Zealand Public Expenditure Committee', *Political Science*, 26 (1974), 28

'Making Parliament Work', *Economist*, 5 August 1978, p. 15

Marshall, J. (ed.) *The Reform of Parliament*, Wellington, 1978

Minogue, M. J. 'Parliamentary Democracy Today', *New Zealand Law Journal*, (1976), 485

Mitchell, A. V. *Government by Party*, Christchurch, 1966

Muldoon, R. D. 'The Control of Public Expenditure in New Zealand', *Parliamentarian*, 55 (1974), 79

Nordmeyer, A. H. 'A Critical Examination of the Functioning of Parliament', *New Zealand Journal of Public Administration*, 8 (1946), 3

'Parliamentary Reform', *New Zealand Law Journal*, (1961), 209

'P.M. Announces Financial Streamlining', *Evening Post*, 2 December 1978, p. 8

Riddiford, D. J. 'The Three-Year Parliamentary Term in New Zealand', *Parliamentarian*, 49 (1968), 148

Rogaly, J. *Parliament for the People*, London, 1976

Rousell, E. A. 'Revision of New Zealand Standing Orders', *Parliamentarian*, 53 (1972), 369

Rowling, W. E. 'Address to Rotary Club of Masterton South', 18 April 1978

Rush, M. *Parliament and the Public*, London, 1976

Shand, D. A. 'Parliamentary Control of the Public Purse — How Real,' *New Zealand Journal of Public Administration*, 34 (1972), 59

Silkin, S. C. 'The Select Committee on Parliamentary Privilege in the U.K.', *Parliamentarian*, 51 (1970), 1

Thomas, E. W. 'Parliamentary Control of the Administration of Central Government: Fact or Fiction?', *Otago Law Review*, 3 (1976), 437

von Tunzelmann, A. 'Control of Expenditure and the New Zealand Public Expenditure Committee', *Parliamentarian*, 59 (1978), 221

'The Public Expenditure Committee and Parliamentary Control of Public Expenditure', *Victoria University of Wellington Law Review*, vol. 10, no. 1 (1978)

Victoria University of Wellington Law Faculty, *Materials on Constitutional Law*, Wellington, 1978, vols. 1 and 2

Webb, P. *Parliament and How It Makes Laws*, Wellington, 1977

Wheare, K. C. *Legislatures*, London, 1963

Woods, N. S. 'The Role of Pressure Groups in the Legislative Process', *Papers of New Zealand Law Society Triennial Conference*, (1978), B5.2

Standing Orders of the House of Representatives Relating to Public Business, Wellington, 1975

Second Report of the Controller and Auditor-General for the year ended 31 March 1976 — Trading Departments, Local and Public Authorities including Corporations, Marketing and Statutory Boards, Wellington, 1976

Report of the Controller and Auditor-General on Financial Management and Control in Administrative Government Departments, Wellington, 1978

Report of the Controller and Auditor-General for the year ended 31 March 1978 covering Trading and Administrative Departments, Local Authorities, Corporations, Marketing and Statutory Boards, Wellington, 1978

Public Expenditure Committee 1977, Wellington, 1977

Public Expenditure Committee 1977 — Interim Report, Wellington, 1977

House of Representatives, *Supplementary Order Paper*, 30 August 1978, pp. 571, 578, 579, 591

Chapter 6 : Select committees and legislation

Lord Chorley, 'Bringing the Legislative Process into Contempt', *Public Law*, (1968), 52

Drewry, G. 'Reform of the Legislative Process: Some Neglected Questions', *Parliamentary Affairs*, (1972), 286

Griffith, J. A. G. *Parliamentary Scrutiny of Government Bills*, London, 1974

Harvard Legislative Research Bureau, 'A Model Federal Sunset Act', *Harvard Journal on Legislation*, 14 (1977), 542

Herman, V. ' "Who Legislates in the Modern World?" ', *Parliamentarian*, 57 (1976), 93

Jackson, K. 'New Zealand Parliamentary Committees: Reality and Reform', *Parliamentarian*, 59 (1978), 94

Lee, M. 'The Human Rights Commission Bill — A Case Study in Legislative Influence' (Research Paper), Wellington, 1978

Licata, A. R. 'Zero-Base Sunset Review', *Harvard Journal on Legislation*, 14 (1977), 505

Morris, A. *The Growth of Parliamentary Scrutiny by Committee: A Symposium*, Oxford, 1970

'New Zealand: Notes on the Establishment of an Advisory Service for Select Committees,' *Parliamentarian*, 55 (1974), 208

Rush, M. 'The Development of the Committee System in the Canadian House of Commons', *Parliamentarian*, 55 (1974), 149

Stewart, J. B. 'Canadian Committee on Procedure', *Parliamentarian*, 49 (1968), 138
Turton, R. H. 'Reform of Parliamentary Procedure', *Parliamentarian*, 52 (1973), 69
   'Westminster: Further Proposed Procedural Reforms', *Parliamentarian*, 53 (1972), 160
Walkland, S. A. *The Legislative Process in Great Britain*, London, 1968
Wiley, F. 'Legislative Select Committees', *Political Science*, 21 (1969), 3

Standing Orders of the House of Representatives Relating to Public Business, Wellington, 1975
Report of the Department of Justice for the year ended 31 March 1978, Wellington, 1978

Chapter 7 : The fastest law in the west

Auckland District Law Society: Public Issues Committee, *Rush to Legislation*, Auckland, 1977
Barratt, R. 'Statute Law: A New System Needed', *Parliamentarian*, 56 (1975), 21
Bennion, F. A. R. 'The Renton Report', *New Law Journal*, 125 (1975), 660
Birch, B. 'The Law — Making It . . .', *New Zealand Listener*, 9 July 1977, p. 22
Black, T. ' "Sheep May Safely . . ." ', *New Zealand Law Journal*, (1977), 505
Brassington, A. C. 'Statute Law Deficiencies', *New Zealand Law Journal*, (1972), 97
The Capital Letter – A Weekly Review of Administration, Legislation and Law, Wellington, vol. 1, no. 1 1978
Chan, T. Y. 'Changes in Form of New Zealand Statutes', *Victoria University of Wellington Law Review*, 8 (1976), 318
'The Continuing Flood of Legislation', *Australian Law Journal*, 50 (1976), 108
'Correspondence — Incomprehensible Legislation', *New Zealand Law Journal*, (1975) 118
Crowe, R. 'Fruit Salad', *New Zealand Farmer*, 10 August 1978, p. 66
Dale, W. *Legislative Drafting: A New Approach*, London, 1977
Dhavan, R. ' "Legislative Simplicity and Interpretative Complexity" — A Comment on the Renton Report on "The Preparation of Legislation" ', *Anglo-American Law Review*, 5 (1976), 64
Dickerson, R. 'Legislative Drafting in London and in Washington', *Cambridge Law Journal*, 16 (1959), 49
   'The Diseases of Legislative Language', *Harvard Journal on Legislation* 1 (1964), 5
Drew, E. 'A Reporter at Large — A Tendency to Legislate', *New Yorker*, 26 June 1978
Findlay, K. 'The Hot Air Waves', *New Zealand Listener*, 4 June 1977, p. 13
Friedland, M. L. *Access to the Law*, Toronto, 1975
'Hasty Legislation: A Wrong System', *New Zealand Law Journal*, 8 (1932), 117
Hodder, J. 'Rest of the World Has Almost Caught Up', *National Business Review*, 28 June 1978, p. 14
Inter-Parliamentary Union (ed.), *Parliaments of the World* (prepared by V. Herman and F. Mendel), London, 1976
Jamieson, N. J. 'Towards a Systematic Statute Law', *Otago Law Review*, 3 (1976), 543
Kean, A. 'Drafting a Bill in Britain', *Harvard Journal on Legislation*, 5 (1968), 253
Keith, K. J. 'A Lawyer Looks at Parliament', in Sir John Marshall (ed.), *Reform of Parliament*, Wellington, 1978, p. 26
Kellock, T. O. 'Chaos in the Statute Book', *Parliamentarian* 54 (1973), 137
Lambert, B. 'The Law — Understanding It . . .', *New Zealand Listener*, 9 July 1977, p. 23
'The Late Mr H. D. C. Adams — Parliamentary Law Draftsman', *New Zealand Law Journal*, (1958), 234
'Lord Hailsham says there is too much Law', *The Times*, 1 February 1978, p. 7
Macken, R. F. 'The Session in Retrospect', *New Zealand Law Journal*, (1968), 25
   'Maintaining Respect of the Rule of Law', *Lawtalk*, 2 March 1978, p. 1
Manning, B. 'Hyperlexis: Our National Disease', *Northwestern University Law Review*, 71 (1977), 767
Marshall, J. (ed.) *The Reform of Parliament*, Wellington, 1978

180

Megarry, R. E. and Wade, H. W. R. *The Law of Real Property*, 3rd edn., London, 1966
New Zealand Labour Party Policy, Press Release by Rt. Hon. W. E. Rowling, 'The Reform of Parliament', 15 August 1978
Palmer, G. W. R. 'The Fastest Law-Makers in the West', *New Zealand Listener*, 28 May 1977, p. 13
Rowling, W. E. 'Address to Rotary Club of Invercargill East', 13 February 1978
Samuels, A. 'Improving the Quality of Legislation', *Anglo-American Law Review*, 3 (1974), 523
Scarman, L. *English Law – The New Dimension*, London, 1974
Lord Simon of Glaisdale and Webb, J.V.D. 'Consolidation and Statute Law Revision', *Public Law*, (1975), 285
Statute Law Society, *Statute Law Deficiencies*, London, 1970
  Statute Law: The Key to Clarity, London, 1972
  Statute Law: A Radical Simplification, London, 1974
Stewart, R. B. 'Foreword: Lawyers and the Legislative Process', *Harvard Journal on Legislation*, 10 (1973), 151
Ward, D. A. S. 'The Preparation of Acts of Parliament', *Otago Law Review*, 2 (1968), 294
  'Current Problems in the Legislative Process', *Otago Law Review*, 3 (1976), 529
  'The Law: Understanding the Draftsman's Dilemma', *New Zealand Listener*, 20 August 1977, p. 24.
Webb, P. *The J. C. Beaglehole Memorial Lecture, 1975 – Some Reflections on the Limitations and Capabilities of the Law*, Wellington, 1977
White, H. 'Incomprehensible Legislation', *New Zealand Law Journal*, (1974), 479
Whitelaw, W. H. 'Over-legislation', *Parliamentarian*, 59 (1978), 88
Woods, N. S. 'Why Laws Like This', *New Zealand Law Journal*, (1977), 352

Standing Orders of the House of Representatives relating to Public Business, Wellington, 1975
Acts Passed and Bills Not Passed: 1976, Wellington, 1977
House of Representatives, *Order Paper*, Wednesday, 4 October 1978
House of Representatives, *Order Paper*, Thursday, 5 October 1978
(1976) 408 *New Zealand Parliamentary Debates* 4366
(1977) 413 *New Zealand Parliamentary Debates* 2411
National Rehabilitation and Compensation Bill 1977 (Australia)
Statutes Amendment Bill 1978

Chapter 8 : More fast law – regulations

Algie, R. M. 'A System Open to Abuse', *New Zealand Law Journal*, 9 (1933), 93
Allen, C. K. *Law and Orders*, London, 1965
Cain, G. 'Regulation-Making Powers and Procedures of the Executive of New Zealand' (Research Paper prepared for the Public and Administrative Law Reform Committee), Auckland, 1973
'Delegated Legislation: A Retrospect', *New Zealand Law Journal, 20 (1944), 61*
Forbes, G. *'Delegated Legislative Powers'*, *New Zealand Law Journal*, 9 (1933), 92
Frame, A. and McLuskie, R. 'Review of Regulations and Standing Orders', *New Zealand Law Journal*, (1978), 423
Garner, J. F. 'Consultation in Subordinate Legislation', *Public Law*, (1964), 105
Hewitt, D. J. 'Delegated Legislative Power and the Problem of Control', *New Zealand Law Journal*, 27 (1941), 41
  'A Prayer for Freedom', *New Zealand Law Journal*, 25 (1949), 235
  The Control of Delegated Legislation, Wellington, 1953
Hood Phillips, O. *Constitutional and Administrative Law*, 4th edn., London, 1967
Keir, D. L. and Lawson, F. H. *Cases in Constitutional Law*, Oxford, 1967
Kersell, J. E. *Parliamentary Supervision of Delegated Legislation*, London, 1960

Lewis, R. 'How Mr Muldoon Waved a Big Stick Over the Unions', *The Times*, 14 April 1976, p. 18
McGechan, R. O. 'Time of Parliament and Delegated Legislation', *New Zealand Journal of Public Administration*, 4 (1942), 72
McKeag, W. 'The Evils of Legislation by Regulation', *New Zealand Law Journal*, 10 (1934), 291
Mallory, J. R. 'Parliamentary Scrutiny of Delegated Legislation in Canada: A Large Step Forward and a Small Step Back', *Public Law*, (1972), 30
The New Zealand Gazette — Extraordinary, Wellington, 29 June 1951
Pearce, D. C. *Delegated Legislation in Australia and New Zealand*, Sydney, 1977
'Proceedings of First Annual Legal Conference', *New Zealand Law Journal*, 4 (1928), 51
Robson, J. L. *New Zealand: The Development of its Laws and Constitution*, London, 1967
'Safeguarding Delegated Legislative Powers', *New Zealand Law Journal*, 8 (1932), 177
de Smith, S. A. *Constitutional and Administrative Law*, 3rd edn., Harmondsworth, 1977
Stephens, A. C. 'The Abuse of Delegated Legislation', *New Zealand Law Journal*, (1947), 80
'Subordinate Legislation', *New Zealand Law Journal*, 2 (1926), 487
'Tendency of Ministers to By-Pass Parliament Criticised by Committee', *The Times*, 9 February 1978, p. 3
Wade, E. C. S. and Godfrey Phillips, G. *Constitutional and Administrative Law*, 9th edn., London, 1977

Submissions by the Divers' Group to the Statutes Revision Committee on the subject of Regulations Prohibiting the Commercial Taking of Rock Lobsters by the Method of Diving (S.R. 1976/293)
'Report of the Delegated Legislation Committee 1962' (Algie Report), *New Zealand Appendix to the Journals of the House of Representatives*, Wellington, 1962, vol. 4
Committee on Safety and Health at Work, Report 1970–72 (Robens Report), Cmnd. 5034 (1972), para. 453
(1977) 416 *New Zealand Parliamentary Debates* 5354–5355
5 United States Code Annotated, s. 553

Chapter 9 : What the courts can do

Barton, G. P. 'Law and Orders: A Case Study', *Victoria University of Wellington Law Review*, 9 (1978), 393
Bickel, A. M. *The Least Dangerous Branch*, Indianapolis, 1962
Black, T. 'The Rule of Law in Action', *New Zealand Law Journal*, (1978), 17
Dally, L. 'The Ombudsman and Local Government', *New Zealand Law Journal*, (1977), 270
Davis, K. C. 'The Future of Judge-Made Public Law in England: A Problem of Practical Jurisprudence', *Columbia Law Review*, 61 (1961) 201
Dicey, A. V. *The Law of the Constitution*, 10th edn., London, 1959, p. 39
Griffith, J. A. G. *The Politics of the Judiciary*, Glasgow, 1977
Hamilton, A. *The Federalist*, London, 1888, no. 78
Henry, J. S. 'Privy Council – Bulwark or Anachronism', *Papers of New Zealand Law Society Triennial Conference*, (1978), B22.1
Hill, L. B. *The Model Ombudsman*, Princeton, 1976
Hood Phillips, O. *Constitutional and Administrative Law*, 4th edn., London, 1967
Keith, K. J. 'Administrative Law Reform 1953–1978', *Victoria University of Wellington Law Review*, 9 (1978), 427
Myers, M. 'The Law and the Administration', *New Zealand Journal of Public Administration*, 3 (1941), 38
Public and Administrative Law Reform Committee, *Report on Standing in Administrative Law*, Wellington, March 1978, p. 33

Public and Administrative Law Reform Committee, *Damages in Administrative Law – A Working Paper*, Wellington, August 1978

Robson, J. L. *New Zealand: The Development of its Laws and Constitutions*, London, 1967

de Smith, S. A. *Constitutional and Administrative Law*, 3rd edn., Harmondsworth, 1977

Veitch, E. 'Justice at the end of its Tether', *Public Law*, (1973), 45

Wade, E. C. S. and Godfrey Phillips, G. *Constitutional and Administrative Law*, 9th edn., London, 1977

Annual Reports of the Ombudsman, Wellington, 1962–8

Report of the Royal Commission on the Courts – 1978, Wellington, 1978

6 Halsbury's Statutes 490, 3rd edn.

Bank v. *Lower Hutt City Council* [1974] 1 New Zealand Law Reports 385

Clark v. *Wellington Rent Appeal Board and Smith; Clark* v. *Wellington Rent Appeal Board and Jennings* [1975] 2 New Zealand Law Reports 24

Fitzgerald v. *Muldoon* [1976] 2 New Zealand Law Reports 615

Furmage v. *Social Security Commission*, Wellington Supreme Court, 12 May 1978, M.500/77

Hamilton v. *Yates* [1930] New Zealand Law Reports 359; [1930] Gazette Law Reports 47

Reade v. *Smith* [1959] New Zealand Law Reports 996

Rowling v. *Takaro Properties Ltd* [1975] 2 New Zealand Law Reports 62

Strawbridge v. *Simeon and Others* [1959] New Zealand Law Reports 405

Van Gorkom v. *Attorney-General* [1977] 1 New Zealand Law Reports 535

Chapter 10 : A written constitution and/or a bill of rights

Atkins, L. and McBride, T. 'Liberty and the Law, 1976–1978', *New Zealand Listener*, 25 November 1978, p. 18

Bickel, A. M. *The Least Dangerous Branch*, Indianapolis, 1962

The Morality of Consent, New Haven, 1975

Braybrooke, E. K. 'A Written Constitution', *Political Science*, 3 (1951), 32

Braybrooke, E. K. 'A Written Constitution – A Reply', *Political Science*, 6 (1954), 41

Brown, N. L. 'A Bill of Rights for the United Kingdom?', *Parliamentarian*, 58 (1977), 79

'The Constitution of Fiji' in *The Laws of Fiji*, Suva, 1970, p. 362

Elkind, J. B. 'Giving Ourselves a Bill of Rights', *New Zealand Listener*, 25 November 1978, p. 52

Gunther, G. *Cases and Materials on Constitutional Law*, Mineola, 1975

Lord Hailsham, 'Is the British Constitution Wearing a Bit Thin?', *The Times*, 12 May 1975

'The Paradox of Oppressive yet Powerless Government', *The Times*, 16 May 1975

'Has the Time Now Come for a Bill of Rights?', *The Times*, 19 May 1975

'The Case for a New, Written Constitution', *The Times*, 20 May 1975

Hood Phillips, O. *Reform of the Constitution*, London, 1970

'Human Rights and Self-Determination' in Ian Brownlie (ed.), *Basic Documents in International Law*, Oxford, 1967, p. 132

'International Covenants on Human Rights' in Ian Brownlie (ed.) *Basic Documents in International Law*, Oxford, 1967, p. 138

Irvine, C. N. 'The New Zealand Bill of Rights', *New Zealand Law Journal*, (1963), 489

Jackson, R. *The Supreme Court in the American System of Government*, Cambridge, Mass., 1955

Lord Lloyd of Hampstead, 'Do We Need a Bill of Rights?', *Modern Law Review*, 39 (1976), 121

Palmer, G. W. R. 'A Bill of Rights for New Zealand', in K. J. Keith (ed.), *Essays on Human Rights*, Wellington, 1968, p. 106

Paterson, D. E. *First Draft, Constitution of New Zealand* (prepared for New Zealand section of the International Commission of Jurists), Wellington, 1977

Reid, T. 'A Bill of Rights', *New Zealand Listener*, 5 November 1977, p. 10

Scarman, L. *English Law – The New Dimension*, London, 1974
Scott, K. J. 'Civil Liberties and a Written Constitution', *Political Science*, 6 (1954), 29
Scott, W. J. 'What the Council for Civil Liberties Does', *Civil Liberty*, no. 4, June 1978, p. 4.
de Smith, S. A. *The New Commonwealth and its Constitutions*, London, 1964
Tribe, L. H. *American Constitutional Law*, Mineola, 1978
Wallington, P. and McBride, J. *Civil Liberties and a Bill of Rights*, London, 1976
'A Written Constitution and a Second Chamber', *New Zealand Law Journal*, (1960), 385
'A Written Constitution and a Second Chamber', *New Zealand Law Journal*, (1961), 145

Report of the Chief Ombudsman for the year ended 31 March 1976, Wellington, 1976
Report of Public Petitions M to Z Committee 1961, Wellington, 1962
Report of the Race Relations Conciliator for the year ended 31 March 1978, Wellington, 1978
Annual Report of the Wanganui Computer Centre Privacy Commissioner for the year ended 31 March 1977, Wellington, 1977
Report of Wanganui Computer Centre Privacy Commissioner, *Inquiry into Unauthorised Retrieval and Disclosure of Information by Police Constable – July 1977*, Wellington, 1978

Chapter 11 : A second house of parliament?

Algie, R. M. 'The Second Chamber in New Zealand', *Parliamentarian*, 42 (1961), 203
Benda, H. J. and Brookes, R. H. 'S.P.Q.R. – A Note on the Proposed Senate', *Political Science*, 4 (1952), 40
Clark, R. *The Development of the New Zealand Constitution*, Wellington, 1974
Jackson, W. K. *The New Zealand Legislative Council*, Dunedin, 1972
'The Failure and Abolition of the New Zealand Legislative Council', *Parliamentarian*, 54 (1973), 17
Joel, M. 'Plan for a Senate', *New Zealand Law Journal*, 28 (1952), 217
Marshall, J. (ed.) *The Reform of Parliament*, Wellington, 1978
Mentiplay, C. 'Promises, Promises', *New Zealand Law Journal*, (1974), 390
Riddiford, D. J. 'An Effective Second Chamber', *New Zealand Law Journal*, 26 (1950), 313, 329
'A Suitable Second Chamber for New Zealand', *New Zealand Law Journal*, 27 (1951), 102
'A Reformed Second Chamber', *Political Science*, 3 (1951), 23
Scott, K. J. *The New Zealand Constitution*, Oxford, 1962
Stewart, W. D. *Sir Francis Bell, His Life and Times*, Wellington, 1937
Wheare, K. C. *Legislatures*, London, 1963

Reports of the Constitutional Reform Committee – 1952, Wellington, 1952
Report of Public Petitions M to Z Committee 1961, Wellington, 1962
(1950) 289 *New Zealand Parliamentary Debates* 540

Chapter 12 : Electoral law

Alley, R. M., Robinson, A. D. and others, *Submissions on Electoral Reform*, Wellington, June 1974
Birch, A. H. *The British System of Government*, 3rd edn., London, 1973
Galbraith, J. K. *The Age of Uncertainty*, London, 1977
'How Elections Elect', *Economist*, 6 December 1975, p. 24
Report of the Hansard Society, *Commission on Electoral Reform, June 1976*, London, 1976
Levine, S. (ed.) *New Zealand Politics: A Reader*, Melbourne, 1975
'Electoral Rolls', *New Zealand Listener*, 18 November 1978, p. 10

Mackintosh, J. P. (ed.) *People and Parliament*, Westmead, 1978
'The Road to Electoral Reform', *Economist*, 31 May 1975, p. 8
'The Road to Electoral Reform', *Economist*, 2 August 1975, p. 13
Rogaly, J. *Parliament for the People*, London, 1976
Rush, M. *Parliament and the Public*, London, 1976
Scott, E. N. 'Electoral Law and Constitutional Change' Research Paper, Wellington, 1977

(1975) 397 *New Zealand Parliamentary Debates* 1067
(1975) 398 *New Zealand Parliamentary Debates* 2089
West's Annotated California Codes, *Constitution of the State of California*, Article 4, section 1

Chapter 13 : Access to official information

Auckland District Law Society: Public Issues Committee, *Freedom of Information*, Auckland, March 1978
Birtles, F. 'Big Brother Knows Best: The Franks Report on Section Two of the Official Secrets Act', *Public Law*, (1973), 100
Cabinet Office, *Protection of Classified State Papers or Information Held by Former Ministers of the Crown*, Wellington, May 1978
Crick, B. ' "Them and Us": Public Impotence and Government Power', *Public Law*, (1968), 8
Griffith, J. A. G. *Parliamentary Scrutiny of Government Bills*, London, 1974
Jacob, J. 'Some Reflections on Governmental Secrecy', *Public Law*, (1974), 25
'A Report by Justice', *Freedom of Information*, London, 1978
McMillan, J. *Recovering the Public's Right to Information*, unpublished, Paper presented to the AULSA Conference, 1976
    'Making Government Accountable – A Comparative Analysis of Freedom of Information Statutes', *New Zealand Law Journal*, (1977), 248, 275, 286
Minogue, M. J. 'Address to the Journalists' Union', Napier, 25 September 1976
    'The Law-Making Process and Individual Freedoms', *New Zealand Law Journal*, (1978), 215
    'Information and Power: Parliamentary Reform and the Right to Know', in S. Levine (ed.), *Politics in New Zealand*, Sydney, 1978, p. 78
Pearce, D. 'The Courts and Government Information', *Australian Law Journal*, 50 (1976), 513
Pope, J. 'Seeing Democracy Done', *New Zealand Law Journal*, (1971), 505
Sloat, R. W. 'Government in the Sunshine Act: A Danger of Overexposure', *Harvard Journal on Legislation*, 14 (1977), 620
Task Force on Economic and Social Planning, *New Zealand at the Turning Point*, Wellington, 1976
Wright, M. 'Ministers and Civil Servants: Relations and Responsibilities', *Parliamentary Affairs*, (1977), 293

Security Intelligence Service – Report by Chief Ombudsman, Wellington, 1976
(1977) 410 *New Zealand Parliamentary Debates* 498
(1977) 411 *New Zealand Parliamentary Debates* 784, 799
Attorney-General v. *Jonathan Cape* [1976] 1 The Law Reports – Queen's Bench Division 752

5 United States Code Annotated (West Supplement 1977), Government in the Sunshine Act 1977